For Jim -
Who came to Canada from Wishaw Scotland
June 1956 and created a wife 2 daughters, 1 son and 3 grandchildren
With love on our 48th Anniversary
Anne

GREAT SCOTS!

How the Scots Created Canada

By Matthew Shaw

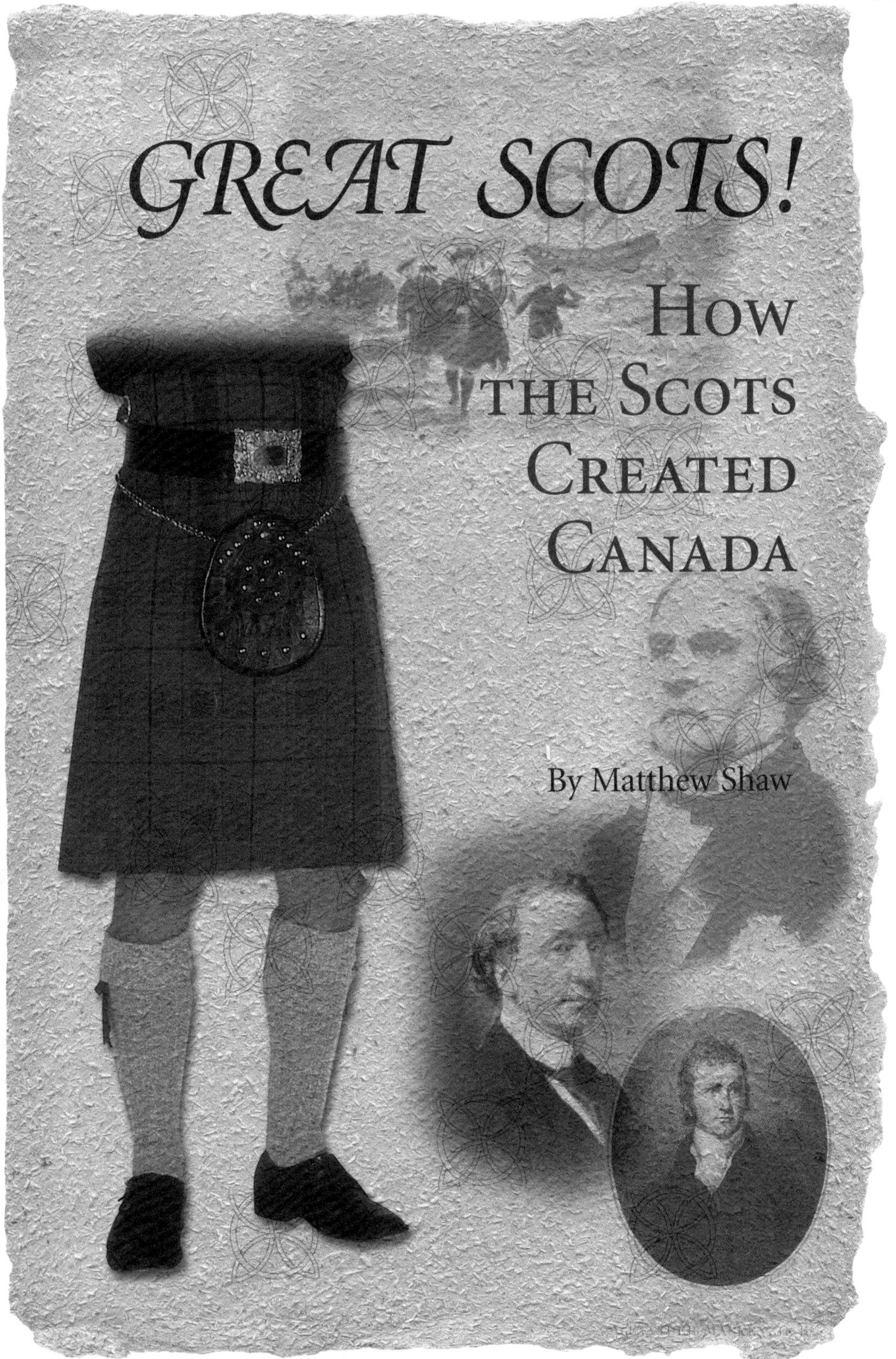

MACDONALD OF SLEAT TARTAN, COURTESY OF ALAN AND JAMIE HOWISON / SPORRAN, KILT HOSE, SHOES AND BELT COURTESY OF THE SCOTTISH CROFT, SYDNEY, BC.

Credits

Editor
Barbara Huck

Editorial assistance
James W. Burns, O.C., Hon. Duff Roblin, P.C., C.C., O.M., LLD,
Hon. D.D. Everett, Marsha Skuce, Peter St. John, Debbie Riley, Louise Duchastel-Auriol

Design
Dawn Huck

Photography
Jack Most

Photographic assistance
Nancy Most, Sheri Cormie, Jane Huck

Photographic models
Matthew Cormie, Loren Macklin

Prepress
Avenue 4, Winnipeg, Canada

Printing
Friesens, Altona, Canada

Cover image
Parliament Hill cam image, courtesy of the Government of Canada.
Painting of 48th Battalion, Highlanders, Toronto 1899 by Arthur H. Hider, National Archives of Canada C-096906

Back cover image
The ruins of William Lyon Mackenzie's printing office in Queenston, Ontario,
by T.M. Wilkinson, National Archives of Canada, C-029330

National Library of Canada Cataloguing in Publication

Shaw, Matthew, 1964-
Great Scots! : how the Scots created Canada / by Matthew Shaw.

Includes bibliographical references.
ISBN 1-896150-44-6 (bound).--ISBN 1-896150-01-2 (pbk.)

1. Scottish Canadians--History. 2. Scots--Canada--History. I. Title.

FC106.S3S52 2003 971'.0049163 C2003-906409-3

How
the Scots
Created Canada

GREAT SCOTS!

By Matthew Shaw

Heartland Associates, Inc.
Winnipeg, Canada

Printed in Manitoba, Canada

Acknowledgements

So many people contributed to the creation of this book that it is hard to know where to begin. First and foremost, I wish to express my deep gratitude to Barbara Huck, whose initiative, encouragement, and guidance played an incalculable role in creating this book. Thank you, Barbara, for your unwavering faith in me. What an invaluable mentor you have become. I would also like to express my appreciation to Peter St. John, whose feedback and remarkable humanity constantly helped to keep me focussed.

My heartfelt thanks goes to Jim Burns, whose character closely resembles many of the intrepid Scots described in this book. Jim, thank you for your vision, generosity, and amazing ability to make things happen. I am also grateful to the Honourable Duff Roblin, who not only read the first draft, but made judicious suggestions and agreed to write the foreword. Marsha Skuce also went through the initial draft and I am indebted to her for her thoughtful comments.

The photographs that open every chapter were an attempt to display at least a few of the many tartans found in Canada today. Gathering a dozen kilts, several sporrans and dirks, and appropriate kilt hose and brogues in one place to be photographed, with appropriate props, took the assistance and cooperation of people from all corners of the country. They included Councillor John Angus, Lorne Campbell QC, Alan and Jamie Howison, Duncan Jessiman, Colonel Doug Ludlow, Harry Mardon, Dwayne MacAulay, Dr. Don McInnes, Jack MacIver, Ray Turnbull and Bob Vandewater, all of Winnipeg; and Blair MacAulay of Oakville, Ontario; Alex and Scott Robertson of Robertson's Trading Post in Lac La Ronge, Saskatchewan, and Ken and Paula Jones and Annette and Jim Moman of Victoria.

Joan and Tom Ferguson, the owners of the Scottish Croft in Sydney, BC. lent us Highland regalia, while manager Gary Miller of the Victoria Curling Club and Lynne Griffiths Studios of Highland Dance in Victoria, as well as the Queen's Own Cameron Highlanders in Winnipeg assisted with other specific items. We are very grateful to all of them.

Matthew Cormie of Victoria modelled the kilts, while Loren Macklin, one of Canada's premier Highland dancers, posed for the final section. Sheri Cormie and Nancy Most in Victoria, Annette Massey and Lynne Saurette in Winnipeg collected and organized the many props.

As always, the staff at the National Archives and the National Library in Ottawa were of great assistance, as was Yolaine Toussaint, archivist with the BMO Financial Group in Montréal, who allowed us to use a number of paintings and images in the bank's collection, answered questions and provided information.

Finally, thanks to my wife, Joanne Shaw, and my little son, Jon, who saw very little of me during the months it took to write this book. I marvel at your unflagging patience and confidence.

Table of Contents

Foreword

There is an opinion, generally received among us, that Canadians are not inclined to be mindful of the significance of their history. Perhaps our modest national dedication to "peace, order and good government" sets limits on our patriotism. We tend to think of our past, rather smugly and narrowly perhaps, as a smooth and bland progression from the arrival of Europeans to today's role as helpful facilitator at the United Nations. Superficially, we perceive our story as a steady, non-violent and rather unexciting record of nation-building, with none of the bravura and bravado claimed by the United States or indeed Mexico.

Well, as *Great Scots!* eloquently explains, it was not quite like that on the ground. This closer look at ourselves makes it clear that we have a lot more to answer for – not only bold initiatives, adventure and risk-taking, but also violence and failure - indeed more challenges than we are usually credited with or accustomed to claiming. To right the balance, this book speaks to a realistic, stirring, even romantic vision of Canada's story as seen through Scottish eyes.

Of course the Scots were not alone. They are only part of the Canadian story and must take their place among other crucial strands of the braid, including the Native Canadians, French-speaking Canadians and even United Empire Loyalists whom the Scots met on their arrival here, as well as other settlers from every part of Europe and beyond, who have arrived in the past century or more. All can claim a contribution to the Canada of today. Nevertheless, the contribution of the Scots is remarkable in so many fields and to so great effect that it is worthy of this book.

The story begins with the fur trade, and the extraordinary saga of Scottish penetration of the west and the north. Following routes mapped by the French, and accompanied by Aboriginal guides, Scots staked Canada's claim to half a continent. The proceeds of the fur trade, combined with their business acumen, allowed them to construct a financial and commercial empire in Montréal that culminated with the building of the CPR. This prodigious achievement provided the physical sinew that tied the nation together and validated Canada's thrust to the Pacific Ocean. Meanwhile, Scottish entrepreneurs made significant contributions to education and the growth of Canada's civic society.

But it was in politics, and particularly in the act of Confederation that the Scottish genius, allied to the indispensible contribution of their French-Canadian colleagues, shone the brightest. Indeed, Canada's existence as an independent state in North America, a nation apart from the American super power, is a balancing act that owes much to a Scottish sense of the possible, the Scottish style of management and their own long history of living in the lee of a great power.

Yet this is not a paean of praise to the Scots. The names and personalities that adorn this book include representatives of every character, admirable and otherwise. And we are not called upon to approve the actions of everyone, but it is all but impossible to ignore the fact that the combination of their courage, enterprise, endurance, practicality and judgement created a formidable inheritance that we as Canadians would do well to celebrate. We have entered into their labours and we can be satisfied.

I close this with a word of appreciation for a friend and fellow Manitoban, James W. Burns – yet another remarkable Scot – who is the *deus ex machina* of this work. And I add a small disclaimer: as I am only one-fourth Scots – Andrew Murdoch, my mother's father, was born in Aberdeenshire – the other three-fourths approached this book with attempted impartiality.

The Honourable Duff Roblin, P.C., C.C., O.M., LLD
Premier of Manitoba 1958–1967
Senate of Canada 1978–1986

The Scots created Canada?

At first glance, the title of this book might seem exaggerated, even outlandish. After all, didn't other ethnic groups contribute enormously to building Canada? The answer, of course, is yes. No one can deny that First Nations, the French and the English had a huge hand in nation building. Moreover, Ukrainians, Chinese, Italians and Germans, as well as countless other national groups also made significant contributions. Why, then, focus on the history of the Scots in Canada to explain Canadian values, culture, and identity? Good question.

From the very beginnings of immigration into what we now call "Canada", the Scots have differed from other groups in a number of important ways. First, Scottish immigrants spread themselves relatively evenly throughout the upper half of North America, unlike other immigrant groups, which often tended to gather in limited geographic pockets. Second, the Scots kept coming and coming … and coming. Unlike, say, the Irish, who arrived in British North America primarily between 1820 and 1870, Scots have poured into the region, in wave after wave, since 1702. Thus, for three centuries, what we now know as Canada has received a constant infusion of ideas and attitudes from Scotland. Finally, individual Scots, far more than those from any other immigrant group, have aggressively initiated growth and development and placed themselves in positions of power, controlling and influencing key institutions at critical points in the development of the Canadian Nation. The ubiquity, dominance and range of their accomplishments are truly astonishing.

Of course, Scottish émigrés were not destined only for the northern colonies of North America. During the eighteenth and nineteenth centuries, the British Empire covered as much as one-fifth of the Earth's surface. Opportunities for enterprising Scots presented themselves throughout the far-flung Empire – in India, Australia, New Zealand, South Africa and the thirteen American colonies. Even after the American Revolution, Scots continued to flow into the United States. And in these countries, as in Canada, Scots met with a remarkable degree of success. This phenomenon prompted British Prime Minister Benjamin Disraeli, perhaps the staunchest proponent of Empire, to comment, "It has been my lot to have found myself in many distant lands. I have never been in one without finding a Scotchman, and I never found a Scotchman who was not at the head of the poll."

In terms of actual numbers, Scottish emigration was never large compared to that of other nations. While no conclusive records survive, most historians estimate that no more than three million ultimately left Scotland's austere shores. Of those, only a small percentage made their way to the northern half of North America; yet it was here that they eventually exercised, arguably, their greatest influence on the development of any nation with the exception of Scotland itself. This may be due to the fact that British North America was extremely sparsely populated, and Scottish immigration thus had a disproportionately large impact. Shortly after Confederation, Canada's first census recorded that those with Scottish roots made up 15.7 per cent of the population. Surprisingly perhaps, this percentage remains virtually unchanged today.

Moreover, because the Scots were part of the United Kingdom, they had a head start in establishing themselves in British North America long before other non-British immigrant groups began to arrive in large numbers. And once here, the Scots, no strangers to a challenging, often miserably cold environment, proved to have an almost instinctive understanding of and affinity for the imposing geography and severe climate of their new land. In short, they thrived.

Before we begin to explore what impelled the Scots to leave their homeland and make their way to "Canada", it is necessary to know a little about Scotland itself. First of all, Scotland is small (only two-thirds the size of New Brunswick) and relatively sparsely populated. In 1800, there were only 1.6 million Scots in Scotland; in 1900, there were 4.5 million and even today there are only about five million. To the north of the Scottish mainland lies Orkney, an archipelago of some seventy fertile, remarkably balmy (given their latitude) but undeniably windswept islands. In 1702 the Hudson's Bay Company, stopping for fresh water en route to Hudson Bay, discovered Orkneymen, a rugged, self-reliant breed of men who were completely at home at sea. From that time forward, Orcadians – as they are properly called – played a vital part in the Canadian fur trade. But these were Scots of a different breed; they are not Celts like their mainland cousins, but rather are descended from the Norse, who supplanted the earlier Picts in Orkney during the ninth century. This distinctive lineage might explain their stoically independent nature, very different from the other proud, often fiery mainland Scots.

Yet Scotland itself has produced at least two cultures, defined largely, it seems, by geography. The Scottish mainland consists of the Highlands, a beautiful, moody region of rocky hills and mountains that extends from the north and west coasts down through the centre, and the Lowlands, a relatively fertile plain that covers the east side, where it meets another plain that encompasses roughly the southern third of the country.

In the mid-eighteenth century, Scottish Highlanders lived mainly pastoral lives as herdsmen, tending small flocks of sheep and herds of cattle. Though they attempted to farm, their results were, more often than not, disappointing, as the rocky soil and brutal climate often produced stunted crops incapable of feeding the people. Because Highland males considered themselves warriors, it was the women who did the majority of the work while the men and boys practised martial activities, such as swinging their broadswords at one another. The predominant form of social organization was the clan, a loose, interdependent alliance of relatives, often distant ones, who lived on plots of land controlled by a chieftain. The clan chieftain was all-powerful, a kilted version of the Godfather. He expected loyalty, particularly when he went to battle with a rival clan; in return, he settled disputes amongst clan members, doled out property rights, and generally looked after the common good of his people.

Life was difficult for the average Highlander. Samuel Johnson, one of the most accomplished writers and scholars of the eighteenth century, commented that Highlanders were a people, "whose whole time is a series of distress; where every morning is labouring with expedients for the evening; and where all mental pain or pleasure arose from the dread of winter, the expectation of spring, the caprices of their chiefs, and the motions of the neighbouring clans."

The mountainous Highland region was a land unto itself, where few non-Highlanders dared to venture. There were virtually no roads, and the only laws stemmed from codes of honour and pacts between various clans. Vicious Highland blood feuds were legendary and most Lowlanders, as well as the English, considered the Highlands to be a dark, primitive, lawless land full of aggressive barbarians, a sort of Wild West of the United Kingdom. For centuries, therefore, Highland culture was left to evolve on its own.

Highlanders also differed from Lowlanders in other ways. They were largely illiterate, while Lowlanders, in general, were amongst the best-educated population in the world. Highlanders spoke Gaelic, while Lowlanders spoke "Scots", their own variety of Anglo-Norman, though during the seventeenth and eighteenth centuries they were becoming more Anglicized all the time. Finally, Highlanders were primarily Catholic, as the Reformation had been unable to penetrate much of the isolated Highlands. Lowlanders, by contrast, were generally Protestants of the Presbyterian faith.

In essence, the Lowlands, in many important ways, resembled the agrarian and commercial society of England and Europe, with bustling cities like Glasgow and Edinburgh that served as financial and intellectual centres. The poverty-stricken Highlanders, in contrast, were stuck in a mean cycle of bare subsistence, hardship and despair. Yet despite the cultural divergence between the Lowlanders and their Highland cousins, Scots of both backgrounds have always been bound together by a deep, inexplicable understanding of one another. Robert Louis Stevenson commented on this phenomenon: "The fact remains: in spite of the differences of blood and language the Lowlander feels himself the sentimental countryman of the Highlander. When they meet abroad, they fall upon each other's neck in spirit; even at home there is a kind of clannish intimacy in their talk." This observation is certainly true of the Scots who made their way to British North America. In the egalitarianism of the new land, Scots of both backgrounds generally recognized their shared "Scottishness" and cared little for the old cultural distinctions that defined them back home.

The events of 1745 marked a major turning point for the Highlanders and for Scotland in general. By '45, the Highland clans were hungry, having had to endure several poor harvests in a row. They were also agitated that their ancient way of life was beginning to be threatened, as the Lowlands, like the rest of Britain, was rapidly transforming itself into a powerful commercial society. The chieftains also knew that the British saw Highlanders as an unpredictable, potentially subversive and dangerous warrior culture and had plans to undermine the chieftains' authority. Unexpectedly, Charles Edward Stuart, the Catholic grandson of the deposed British monarch, James II, showed up in the Highlands from exile in Italy with an audacious plan. He appealed to the Highland chieftains to join him in a military march on the Lowlands and then on to London to restore the glory of the Stuart Dynasty and the Catholic faith in Britain. The reasons the chieftains actually joined "Bonnie Prince Charlie" are complex. Most cared little about him or his cause. Most historians agree that, in effect, the chieftains decided that this was an opportunity to make a desperate last stand for their doomed way of life.

For several days, the clans gathered and prepared themselves for battle. Word soon reached Edinburgh that they were on the march, and the city was thrown into a panic. The ferocious-looking Highlanders, decked out in military kilts and carrying heavy broadswords and axes intimidated Edinburgh into a quiet surrender. The clans then turned southward and twice came up against British armies. Each time, when the Highlanders charged, bellowing like wild men, the terrified British armies beat a speedy retreat. Samuel Johnson wrote of the English Redcoats, "Men accustomed only to exchange bullets at a distance are discouraged and amazed when they find themselves encountered hand to hand, and catch the gleam of steel flashing in their faces."

Buoyed by their successes and feeling that they had made their point, the independent-minded Highlanders stopped a hundred miles from London and decided to head back north, much to the dismay of the bonnie prince. Deliberating on what to do next, the Highlanders decided to take Glasgow, which fell with almost no resistance. In the meantime, the English, mortified at the thought that a barbarian army from the North had almost penetrated the very heart of England, recalled a crack professional army from war in Europe to engage and destroy the Highlanders. The two armies eventually met at Culloden, not far from Inverness, in the spring of 1746.

The Highlanders charged ferociously, as they had done in previous engagements, but this time the lines of battle-hardened Redcoats held. What followed were furious volleys of grapeshot and musketry, shrouded in thick blankets of gun smoke. Even when some of the clansmen did manage to reach opposing lines, they met with the points of bayonets wielded by skilled soldiers. When the Highlanders could no longer stand up to the carnage, they retreated. The Redcoats pursued, under strict orders to kill every Highlander they saw, without pity. Thousands were mercilessly executed, and many more were to follow.

During the winter of 1746–47, in a wicked crusade of retribution, the English purged the Highlands, burning houses and executing and imprisoning anyone whom they suspected of sympathizing with the Highlanders' cause. Being a prisoner of the English was a virtual death sentence. Overall, it was a monstrous campaign of terror.

An astounding irony of Canadian history stems from the fact that one of the English officers fighting at Culloden was Major James Wolfe. A dozen years later, General Wolfe, with Highland soldiers under his command, many of whom had fought against him at Culloden, would defeat the French on the Plains of Abraham. To Wolfe's credit, he refused to take part in the atrocities against the Highlanders following the battle at Culloden and even offered to resign his commission in protest.

After Culloden, Highland culture was forever changed. The British began to build roads into the previously impenetrable Highlands, and a money-based economy soon followed. Highlanders were forbidden to own weapons and even to wear kilts, laws were passed that essentially stripped away the power of the chieftains, and over the next several decades, schools begin to spring up. These changes took time, however, and for decades, there was little relief from grinding poverty in the Highlands.

One of the saddest chapters of Scottish history is the "Highland Clearances". For decades after Culloden, landlords, many of whom lived no-where near the Highlands, bought up Highland agricultural land. It soon became clear that sheep farming was far more profitable than leasing the land to Highland peasants, so over the next century, the landlords forcibly evicted many thousands of Highland families who had been on their modest plots of land for countless generations. Sometimes, when families would refuse to leave, strong-arm gangs, employed by the landlords, would show up in the middle of the night with torches to burn down the peasants' homes.

It is important to understand Culloden and the century that followed, for this period sheds light on some of the cultural dynamics at work in the Scotland of that era. It also explains, in large part, the catalyst that drove so many Highlanders to leave their homeland to seek a better life elsewhere. Due to their skill as warriors, many joined the King's army and fought all over the world. Many sought arduous work in the newly developing industries proliferating throughout the United Kingdom, and many thousands spread out, in an immense diaspora, to colonies such as British North America. Between 1745 and 1815, approximately 15,000 Highlanders emigrated directly from Scotland to territories that now belong to Canada. During the same period, several thousand Loyalist Scots, again primarily Highlanders, fled the repressive atmosphere of the post-Revolution United States and joined their countrymen in the North. The impact of these Highlanders in the sparsely populated British North America left a lasting imprint on its developing culture.

GEORGE SIMPSON, SEEN ON A TOUR OF INSPECTION, WAS ONE OF MANY SCOTS WHO LAID THE FOUNDATIONS OF CANADA DURING THE FUR TRADE ERA.

While the commercial classes prospered in Scottish cities during the latter half of the eighteenth century, the wretchedness of rural poverty remained unchanged. Throughout the Lowlands, agricultural labourers had lived lives of unremitting misery, generation after generation, but there seemed to be few options. When the Industrial Revolution spread from England to the Lowlands, however, powerful economic forces were unleashed, and things began to change. New farming techniques were being developed, and indeed, farming itself began to be industrialized. New tools and technologies, such as the iron mouldboard plough, drastically reduced the need for farm labourers. Moreover, the Napoleonic Wars in Europe had resulted in a major recession in Britain, and this meant falling wages and agricultural commodity prices. By the turn of the century, thousands of farm workers had been displaced and forced to find work in the gritty industrial mills that began to belch choking black smoke throughout the countryside. While many were able to find employment, many others were not, and the parishes of Scotland were inundated with the poor on the edge of starvation.

In 1815, the ruling classes of Britain came to the conclusion that exporting the poor, and at the same time filling empty colonies, made good economic and political sense. The idea of a swelling, disgruntled, indigent urban rabble so close to home was distasteful to many members of the British aristocracy. Perhaps thoughts of the French Revolution were on their minds. In any case, the government enthusiastically passed laws to help facilitate emigration. From 1815 to Canadian Confederation in 1867, approximately 170,000 Scots, this time the majority of them Presbyterian Lowlanders, streamed into British North America. It was not only the poor, however, who chose to emigrate. Shifting prospects at home and the promise of new opportunities in a new country also prompted a small percentage from the professional and business class to leave Scotland. After Confederation, another three quarters of a million Scots chose Canada as their home, albeit in ever declining numbers as the twentieth century wore on. Today, of course, Scotland is a relatively prosperous, semi-autonomous region of the United Kingdom, which is experiencing something of an economic and cultural renaissance. Unlike the Scotland of the previous 250 years, Scotland today imports more people and talent than it exports.

While the forces responsible for Scottish emigration to Canada are fascinating, the truly astonishing part of the story is what happened after the Scots arrived: In very short order, they literally took over the country, dominating all institutions in the budding nation to such an extent as to defy credulity. The Scots became so prominent so quickly and continued to exert such power throughout the development of Canada that the whole phenomenon is certainly one of history's great anomalies, one that merits considerable attention. Yet, ironically, most Canadians know very little about how the Scots controlled and moulded the nation, and in fact very few historians have systematically attempted to understand the inordinate influence of the Scots as well as their potent impact on our culture. Thus, how the Scots created Canada remains, to a large extent, an untold story.

There is no single factor that easily explains the Scots' exceptional success in British North America; rather it was a combination of many things. The most obvious is the fact that Scotland, like Canada, is a northern nation where the brutal climate must always be anticipated and revered. For their entire history, Scots have coexisted with the icy winds that whip their country from the Atlantic and the North Sea. Trudging through snowy hills clad only in a tartan and kilt was second nature to a Highlander. A common part of an Orcadian's daily life was wading into ice-cold seas to guide his boat while rain soaked his clothing and cold gales chilled his bones. A Lowlander often worked the land in a frigid drizzle all day and then retreated to his chilly, dank hut for a few hours of repose, only to repeat the routine the next day. Unlike some immigrant groups who were intimidated by the unforgiving Canadian climate, the Scots and Orcadians were as perfectly adapted as anyone could be. They were no strangers to physical hardship and were extremely hardy and tough. Thus, their own geography had given them a distinct advantage in their new land.

In addition to being tough, the Scots proved to be extremely adaptable. Historian W. Stanford Reid comments that this ability has made them, "some of the best settlers history has known. Like the Jews, they have been able to move into new situations, face new hazards and difficulties and by a power of adaptation overcome, while at the same time maintaining their identity." This trait probably originates from the Scottish intellectual tradition that holds that human nature is universal. Scottish schools and churches generally taught that despite cultural differences, all human beings were the same in every way that mattered. In other words, nurture was far more important than nature. This core belief manifested itself in the fundamental respect the Scots showed towards people of other cultures and races. The French and Native North Americans, for example, often preferred to deal with Scots rather than the English. Moreover, the Scots had an uncanny facility with languages, able to pick up French and Native languages, while the English generally chose to speak only English. Indeed, on arrival in North America, many Scots already knew Gaelic, Scots and English. Acquiring new languages had been part of their lives for generations. Overall, the unique Scottish power of adaptability played no small part in their success.

Education also afforded the Scots a huge advantage over other immigrant groups. By the seventeenth century, most Lowland parishes had excellent schools, where even the poorest Scot could learn to read and write. Some historians call this unique tradition, the concept of the "democratic intellect", Scotland's greatest contribution to western civilization. While the Highlands lagged far behind, the Lowlands had the best-educated population in the world. In 1750, for example, the male literacy rate in the Lowlands was as high as seventy-five per cent, compared to only fifty-three per cent in England. Historian Arthur Herman writes that because of Scotland's egalitarian system of education, "no other society was as broadly prepared for 'takeoff' into the modern age as was eighteenth-century Scotland." And take off the Scots did, particularly after they reached Canada. No longer constrained by a rigid class system, well-educated Scots quickly assumed leadership roles in their new country. In a developing British North America, where the population was largely illiterate, the Scots were ideally trained to take over key clerical, administrative and business positions.

The Scots also flourished in Canada due to the pent-up history of their proud, independent nature. For centuries, Scotland had been dominated by England, the cultural, economic, political and military juggernaut to the south. Although Scots adapted over centuries to this unequal relationship and managed to preserve their distinctiveness, England essentially called the shots and the Scots had to like it or lump it. In British North America, all this changed. Scots, for the first time in their lives, found themselves in control, and found they liked it. Even though life in their new country was in many ways extremely difficult, compared to back home it was downright pleasant. Land was readily available – free from the oppression of landlords – taxes were low, military service was not required, class distinctions were a thing of the past, religious freedom was a reality, and political life was open and relatively democratic. Finally, after centuries, the Scots' innate sense of pride and independence could be fully expressed, and they were quick to make the most of their new freedoms.

The various factors, as described above, combined to make the Scots in Canada a dynamic and inexorable force. It's no surprise, perhaps, that Scots controlled the fur trade, Canada's first large-scale commercial enterprise, which set the stage for modern commercial society. Scottish adventurers mapped out the country and laid the foundation for future settlement. Scottish politicians, including Canada's first two prime ministers, eight out of ten fathers of Confederation, and many provincial premiers, steered Canada's early growth and development and bent the country to their will. Scots dominated commerce, including heavy industry, banking and merchandizing. In fact, three quarters of commercial capital in the nineteenth century was firmly controlled by Scottish magnates. Scottish teachers and academics established educational institutions, including Canada's first universities, along Scottish lines and led Canada's education revolution. In fields such as the arts, the military, science, the labour movement, and the media, Scottish hegemony and influence are no less impressive. When we actually examine the vast range of Scottish achievements in Canada, the title of this book may not seem so outlandish after all. In a very real sense, the Scots did have a disproportionately large hand in creating our country. Their ubiquity in every field of endeavour, the surprising extent of their power and influence, and their lasting impact on Canadian society and culture are truly one of the great and largely unexplored chapters in the story of Canada.

Blueprint for a Nation

It is impossible to overstate the fur trade's impact on Canada's development. In pursuit of furs, traders moved farther and farther into the daunting, uncharted Northwest, as the best pelts naturally came from colder climates. In so doing, they opened Canada to Europeans and inadvertently laid down the blueprint for a nation.

FRASER TARTAN COURTESY OF ROBERT VANDEWATER / SPORRAN COURTESY OF ALAN AND JAMIE HOWISON / KILT HOSE, SGIAN DHUB, SHOES AND BELT, COURTESY OF THE SCOTTISH CROFT, SYDNEY, BC. / SNOW SHOES COURTESY OF THE MOST FAMILY

While charting and governing their territories, fur traders kept much of Canada from being overtaken by Americans, who constantly tried to press north. After 1870, when the fur trade's best days were over and the Hudson's Bay Company sold its vast territories to Canada, settlers wasted no time in filling the enormous swath of arable land within its boundaries.

It is no exaggeration to claim, therefore, that fur traders literally determined the size and shape of Canada and had a huge hand in moulding its character. Historian John Foster writes, "For nearly all regions of Canada, recorded history begins with the fur trade. Its history is a kaleidoscope of experiences, ranging from the demi-heroic achievements of individuals to the machinations of empires headquartered in distant homelands." And it's fascinating to consider that empires and nations can be built on the back of an innocuous rodent.

It's also fascinating to consider the role of Scots in the fur trade. Though one must never underestimate the vital role the French played, particularly in the seventeenth and early eighteenth centuries, from 1760 on it was the Scots, to a large extent, who ran the fur trade. In the upper half of North America, the expanding trade offered greater opportunities than other commercial enterprises of the day. Hardy, pragmatic, ambitious Scots quickly exploited such opportunities. All stripes – Orcadian, Highlander and Lowlander – soon found they possessed unique talents as well as attitudes – including self-sufficiency, common sense, perseverance and a talent for languages – that suited them extremely well to the fur trade. After the Scots had ensconced themselves in leadership positions, their clannish nature kicked in, and they tended to recruit primarily other able Scots. Thus, their dominance perpetuated itself and endured unabated for more than a century, until the fur trade eventually ran its course.

When attempting to address the extent to which Scots controlled the fur trade, one is likely to be overwhelmed. Even Peter C. Newman, author of the fur trade tome, *Empire of the Bay*, dared not attempt to tackle the sheer number of great Scots who made vital contributions. Newman writes:

> Nearly all of the great names in the [Hudson's Bay Company's] annals grew up in Scotland; not just Sir George Simpson, Donald Smith, and Sir James Douglas, the trio who dominated the Company's nineteenth-century history, but others: Chief Factor Robert Campbell, who spent eleven years fur trading and map making ... [in the] Yukon; Chief Factor Alexander Hunter Murray, who plunked down Fort Yukon in Russian Territory and told Imperial Russia to like it; John Maclean from the Island of Mull, who unlocked the savage country of Ungava; Thomas Simpson, descendent of Duncan Forbes of Culloden, who mapped some of the most forbidding parts of the Arctic coast; James Leith of Aberdeenshire, who left half his estate for the propagation of the Protestant faith ... ; John Stuart of Strathspey, who first penetrated the region that became northern British Columbia; and many, many more.

Newman left his list at that, and due to the sheer number of important Scots in the fur trade, and considering the purpose of this book – to offer a general survey of Scottish achievement and influence in Canada – we will add only a few, examining the contributions of only the most remarkable Scots in the field.

Of course, the motives of fur traders had nothing to do with lofty notions such as nation building. The trade was strictly a commercial enterprise, where the right kind of man could earn a good living. During much of the seventeenth, eighteenth and nineteenth centuries, three factors combined to set the stage for one of the most unlikely ventures in history. First, there was an almost inexhaustible demand in Europe for beaver pelts, from which to make high quality hats for gentlemen and those who aspired to be gentlemen. Second, traders had access to a vast, seemingly endless continent, where every waterway appeared to ripple with beavers. Third, a large indigenous North American labour force coveted European goods and was prepared to hunt or trap beaver and other furs in order to obtain them. In fact, initially at least, Native North Americans did very well in the fur trade. In 1634, a Native trapper joked to Jesuit Father Paul Le Jeune, "The beaver does everything perfectly well; it makes kettles, hatchets, swords, knives, bread; in short, it makes everything." Flashing a beautiful knife, he chuckled, "The English have no sense; they give us twenty knives like this for one beaver skin." Such are the historical and economic forces that give birth to empires.

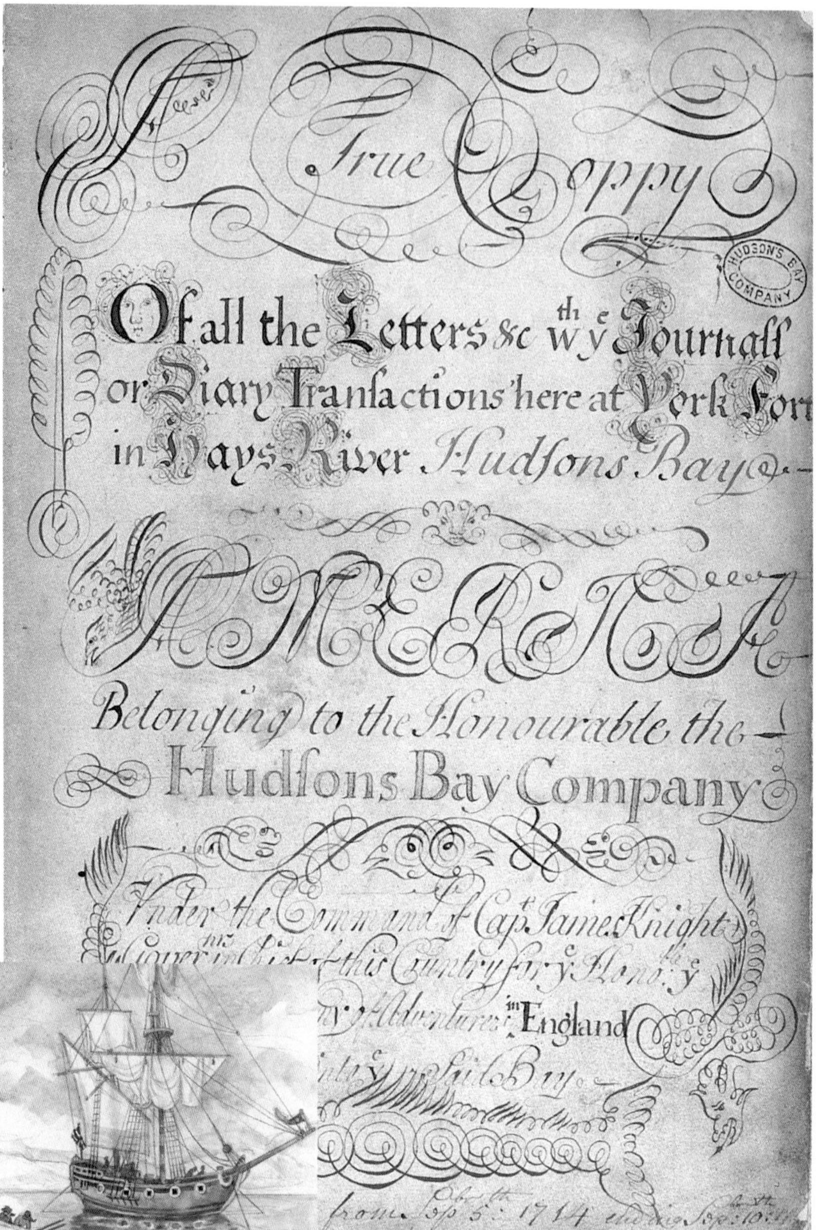
A True Coppy
Of all the Letters &c wth ye Journall
or Diary Transactions here at York Fort
in Hays River. Hudsons Bay
AMERICA
Belonging to the Honourable the
Hudsons Bay Company
Under the Command of Capt. James Knight
Governr in Chief of this Country for ye Honble ye
...ny of Adventurers in England
...into ye said Bay
from Sept 5: 1714 ending Sept 10: 17...

HUDSON'S BAY COMPANY ARCHIVES / PROVINCIAL ARCHIVES OF MANITOBA / B.239 / a / 1 title pag

BARBARA ENDRES

THE LOCAL CREE WERE ASTOUNDED WHEN THOSE ABOARD THE *NONSUCH*, LEFT, WINTERED ON THE WINDSWEPT SHORE OF JAMES BAY. THE ENGLISH SOON FOUND HUDSON BAY WINTERS TOO HARSH AS WELL; BY 1714, YORK FORT AND OTHER POSTS WERE STAFFED BY TOUGH, UNCOMPLAINING ORKNEYMEN.

In the early seventeenth century, the fur trade was conducted primarily by small enterprises and independent *coureurs de bois* in New France, until two French-Canadian traders, young Pierre-Esprit Radisson and his brother-in-law Médard Chouart des Groseilliers, conceived of an audacious plan: to sail a ship over the north coast of Québec and into Hudson Bay, winter there, trade directly with the Cree, and sail back to London come springtime. The pair had already been charged with trading without a licence in Québec, so in 1662, they took their idea south to Boston to solicit English help. However, an attempt the following year had to be aborted at the mouth of Hudson Strait. Frustrated, the pair sailed to London. Here, perhaps surprisingly, since previous English expeditions into Hudson Bay had ended in disaster, the brothers-in-law found an interested audience. A successful trading venture to James Bay in 1668 led to the founding of the Hudson's Bay Company in 1670, with a trade monopoly in all the lands that drained into Hudson Bay – though no one at the time had any idea of the extent of how large that territory might be. It turned out to be enormous – about fifteen times the size of Great Britain – and encompassed nearly half of what would eventually be Canada, as well as a large portion of today's North Dakota and Minnesota.

For the next four decades, the French and English fought for control of the fur trade, and battles of various sorts caused the trading posts on Hudson Bay, erected tenuously on the shores of that frozen, intimidating inland sea, to change hands many times, until the French finally abandoned their claims in 1713. During this period, the company had severe problems staffing its trading posts. Life on the bay was, to put it mildly, hard, and many of the company's English employees, most of whom had been recruited from urban slums, did not take well to the freezing, monotonous, isolated life of a bay man. If it was to survive and prosper, the company needed a more diligent, obedient, reliable work force.

At the beginning of the eighteenth century, the HBC found the solution to its staffing problems when it began to recruit Orcadians, or "Orkneymen" as the company called them, from the Orkney harbour town of Stromness. At first, recruiting the lads from Stromness was essentially unplanned. The picturesque town on the slope above Scapa Flow – not incidentally one of the great harbours of the world – was simply the last stop where ships could take on fresh water and provisions before making the gruelling Atlantic crossing to Hudson Bay. In 1702, one of the early ship captains, short of crew, decided to hire a few locals. So able were these Orcadians that the company was soon recruiting an average of seventy per year so that by 1799, of the 530 men on the company's overseas payroll, 416 were Orcadians – roughly four of every five.

The Orkneymen were inscrutable, stoic employees – the Hudson's Bay Company called them "servants" – who quickly became known for their compliant nature, their endurance and their willingness to accept physical hardship. Most had been brought up fishing, kelping and farming, and thus could cannily handle a boat as well as work tirelessly on land. Unlike their English or Mainland Scottish counterparts, they were seldom given to excess. They had little penchant for drinking, were not prone to arguing with co-workers, and while many eventually married Native women and made new lives in North America, they were less likely to seek out recreational liaisons with the Cree and Dene women they encountered on the bay. In short, they did what they were contracted to do, did it well, and when off duty, generally stuck to themselves.

Their motives, at least in the early years, were clear. Prospects at home were next to nil, but by signing on for a five-year or ten-year term with the company, a young man could return home with enough money to buy a small farm, marry, and pursue an independent life, much to the envy of other islanders. This is exactly what most did, and while a few stayed on in the savage new country and took Native wives, for most of the first century, a majority returned home. The Hudson's Bay Company was simply the most promising avenue to future security.

In an organization run mainly by Englishmen, the Orcadians – though on the whole relatively well educated and hard-working – generally found the upper echelons of the company closed to them. Thus, they often appeared cool and aloof. With only a few exceptions, they simply followed their own independent agendas and felt comfortable "knowing their place" in the company's great, convoluted pecking order.

When considering the fur trade as a whole, it is easy to concentrate on icons, such as the dashing Highlanders whose later exploits provide the fur trade with much of its romanticism. History depends on documents, such as journals and company records, but as is often the case with people of the working class, the Orcadians left few documents. Thus, their historical imprint is not deep. Instead, they did the actual work of the fur trade: backbreaking paddling, toting fur bundles, monotonous accounting, erecting buildings, and executing the prosaic chores that made the company's fur trade possible. Sir John Franklin, who commanded a group of Orcadians on a northern journey, offered this assessment: "It is not easy for any but an eyewitness to form an adequate idea of the exertions of the Orkney boatmen. The necessity they are under of frequently jumping into the water to lift the boats over the rocks compel them the whole day to remain in wet clothes, at a season when the temperature is far below the freezing point. The immense loads they carry over the portages is not more a matter of surprise than the alacrity with which they perform these various duties."

The fur trade owes a great deal to the Orcadians, though history has not yet given them their due. Perhaps the best tribute to date is historian Bernard De Voto's famous and enduring phrase that Orcadians in the trade "pulled the wilderness round them like a cloak, and wore its beauty like a crest."

For much of the eighteenth century, protected by its monopolistic charter, the Hudson's Bay Company continued its conservative corporate slumber on the edge of Hudson Bay, collecting furs from Cree and Nakota trappers and traders willing to make the long journey north, and not taking risks of any kind that might expand the company's future earnings. To the south, however, things were very different. In spite of the Hudson's Bay Company's dominance in and around the bay, the French continued to control most of the trade in North America, ultimately building a vast network of trading posts along inland waterways and claiming much of the Canadian interior, all the way to the Rocky Mountains, for New France. But times were changing. When General Wolfe and his division of Highland soldiers – some of whom had fought against Wolfe at Culloden less than a decade and a half before – defeated the French on the Plains of Abraham in 1759, new dynamics were unleashed. British North America was born, and working from a base in Montréal, Scots began to take over the trade.

It is important to acknowledge just how critical was the role the French had played in establishing the fur trade. In spite of the Hudson's Bay Company's dominance in and around the bay, the French continued to control most of the trade in North America, ultimately building a vast network of trading posts along inland waterways amd claiming much of the Canadian interior, all the way to the Rocky Mountains, for New France. After the colony fell to Great Britain, British traders from all over the empire moved in to capitalize on the impressive trading infrastructure built by the French. In essence, the fur trade after 1759 could never have flourished the way it did without the preceding two centuries of French exploration and initiative.

Many of the newcomers were Scottish Highlanders, who as indicated above, had been defeated less than fifteen years before in "the '45", the deadly battle of 1745 that ended Bonnie Prince Charlie's all-but-successful attempt at overthrowing the English crown. The British victory on the Plains of Abraham also coincided with the early years of the Highland Clearances, when hardy, capable Highlanders, displaced from their ancient way of life, were beginning to fan out to search the world for prospects. Many ultimately found their destiny in the Montréal fur trade.

Very soon, the Hudson's Bay Company was feeling the effects of these changes in the south. By the mid-1760s, the company began to be alarmed by the declining number and poor quality of furs that were arriving at its northern warehouses. Using trade routes developed by the French, and working with experienced *coureurs de bois*, the new Montréal traders had begun to winter in the interior, establishing close relationships with Anishinabe, Nakota and Cree trappers, and intercepting most of the high-quality pelts that otherwise would have gone north. At first the bay men dismissed the Montréal traders as nothing more than "pedlars", but within a few years it became clear that the pedlars were onto something big. They were exploiting rich new territories while the Hudson's Bay Company sat idly by and watched its trade erode.

Meanwhile, in Montréal, individual traders who had initially made money soon began to undercut one another to the point that fur trading became unprofitable. This cutthroat and often violent competition continued unabated for several years, until a leader emerged who was able to cobble together a cartel of sorts.

Simon McTavish, a Highlander, had initially emigrated to New York at thirteen to apprentice in the fur trade. By twenty-five and already very successful, he moved to Montréal in search of greater opportunity. After several years in the brutally competitive Montreal trade, he realized that someone had to seize the initiative or all players would be forced to abandon the trade altogether. In 1783, he convinced several independent traders to cooperate under a single banner, and the North West Company was born. Of the original partners, McTavish and three others were Scots, two were English, and an American, a Frenchman, and an Irishman comprised the rest. It wasn't long, however, before McTavish dominated the company, acting as its visionary CEO and developing a corporate strategy that became one of the most intrepid and daring experiments in the history of capitalism. Within several years, he controlled a majority of the shares and directed the company, unopposed, with bold energy, foresight and sometimes ruthlessness.

SIMON MCTAVISH IN HIS PRIME

C.W. JEFFREYS/ NATIONAL ARCHIVES OF CANADA / C-069913

Under McTavish, the North West Company's roster of Scots was no less impressive than the Hudson's Bay Company's. Author Peter C. Newman writes, "At one time or another, there were on the NWC rolls seven Simon Frasers, four Findlays, five Camerons, six McTavishes, seven McLeods, eight McGillivrays, fourteen each of Grants and Mackenzies and so many McDonalds that they had to differentiate themselves by including home towns in their surnames, as in John McDonald of Garth." Indeed, the company seemed to possess a great camaraderie and synergy, probably due to the fact that most of the partners not only belonged to the same nationality, but in many cases to the same clan, and often even to the same family.

Simon McTavish chose men he knew he could count on. In her book, *The North West Company*, Florida Town writes, "McTavish and his relatives permeated the fur trade. As the company grew, so did the list of McTavish's relatives. In addition to John George McTavish and Angus Shaw, the trade included John McDonald of Garth, who married one of McTavish's nieces; Roderick McKenzie, who married McTavish's sister-in-law; Simon Fraser and John Fraser, both cousins; his great-nephews Simon and Joseph McGillivray; Alexander Fraser, a distant cousin; Judge Reid, who married yet another of McTavish's nieces; James McTavish, a relative of unknown closeness; and Donald McTavish, another cousin. There were also uncounted numbers of clansmen for whom McTavish found jobs in the trade."

Although McTavish's hiring practices at first appear to be flagrant nepotism, this is only partly true. The North West Company was actually a great meritocracy; only those who deserved to rise in the ranks did so. Getting hired was only the first step. The trade at this point was increasingly complex and geographically extended; therefore, efficient, decisive, educated managers were required more than ever. Scots in general filled the bill better than anyone else.

Despite his toughness in business, Simon McTavish was apparently a likeable and charming fellow. As the city's richest merchant and a bachelor until he was well into his forties, he became the toast of Montréal society. During the thirty years he controlled his business empire, he never lost his enthusiasm for the cocktail circuit, gala balls and dinner parties. He enjoyed his personae as *bon vivant* and man-about-town and with alacrity indulged his penchant for "good wine, good oysters, and pretty girls". He finally married, and as a gift to his wife and a monument to his success, he built himself a truly colossal mansion that was the talk of the town. This helped solidify his reputation for haughtiness and earned him the mocking nickname, "the marquis".

Yet in business, McTavish possessed an unfaltering, steely discipline. He regularly intimidated, undercut and crowded out independent fur companies and negotiated treaties with Americans that prevented them from expanding into his sphere of influence. As chieftain of his empire, he spent his days stamping out a never-ending series of crises with amazing determination and efficiency.

The North West Company's basic strategy was to take the trade to its Native partners, rather than waiting for Native trappers and traders to come to them. This required enormous manpower to move goods by canoe west from Montréal, through the Great Lakes, north on Lake Winnipeg, and ultimately to the Lake Athabasca and Peace River regions. To the farthest reaches of the empire, it was a journey of several thousand miles by fragile birchbark canoe. The scheme depended on the muscle power of extraordinarily tough *voyageurs*, mostly young, illiterate French Canadians who sought independent lives away from the monotony of the family farm. The company developed a huge network of forts and distribution warehouses along the route, where traders wintered and bartered with various Native nations. When springtime arrived, the arduous process of transporting thousands of bundles of pelts to Montréal began. As far-fetched as the North West Company's strategy seemed, it worked and was immensely profitable. By 1800, McTavish controlled seventy-eight percent of the fur trade, and the company's partners were becoming increasingly wealthy.

All this did not go unnoticed by the Hudson's Bay Company. As dividend payments dried up and share prices plummeted, the managing directors in London realized something had to be done. Beginning in 1774, they made faltering steps to emulate the success of the Nor'Westers by breaking with their passive tradition on the edge of Hudson Bay and establishing their first real headquarters inland. The post, on an island in the Saskatchewan River Delta in what is now north-eastern Saskatchewan, was called Cumberland House. Constructed by a crew under the leadership of young Samuel Hearne, it was soon managed by a veteran of the trade, William Tomison.

When writing about Canada's fur trade, most historians tend to focus on the exploits of traders who charted the unknown expanses at the extremities of the continent. The reality, however, was a good deal more complex. In fact, just as much exploration was continuously taking place inland.

Tomison was among the most respected of the interior traders, and after 1786, he became the HBC's first "Governor, Inland". While most of those who occupied the upper echelons of the company were English, Tomison was an Orkneyman, and that, as they say, made all the difference. While always keeping an eye firmly fixed on the bottom line, Tomison nonetheless displayed an empathy for the lower ranks of the company, as well as for the Native trappers that were its lifeblood, that is impossible to imagine in his English colleagues. He believed in basic human equality when the prevailing order was Eurocentric and hierarchical; he was self-effacing when self-aggrandisement was better understood and though he wrote volumes of letters and reports (and wrote well, though he always regretted his lack of formal education), he left no autobiography, no list of his many accomplishments.

William Tomison was born on South Ronaldsay, the southernmost island of Orkney, about 1739. He signed on with the HBC in 1760 and spent fifty-one years in Canada. Initially posted on Hudson Bay, he quickly learned Cree and was one of a handful of men the HBC sent inland in the late 1760s and early 1770s to attempt to attract trade to the bayside posts (and away from the growing influence of the Montréal-based Nor'Westers).

His first senior posting came at Cumberland House in 1776 and for nearly twenty-five years, though he travelled prodigiously in all seasons of the year,

Cumberland remained at the heart of his vision for the HBC. But the first years were a trial. In 1781, smallpox swept across the western plains and parklands, killing thousands. The Cree around Cumberland, weakened by famine, were particularly hard hit and turned to the post for help. Tomison put his men on half-rations to feed the growing crowd and worked day and night to try to stem the tide of death. Yet typically, he did not neglect the business of the post. He sent his unwilling men out to Native camps where every man, woman and child had died, to salvage the furs they had left behind. Death and business – for William Tomison they were two separate matters.

In the same way, he could be generous and frugal, often at the same time. Some, including young David Thompson (about whom more later), found the habit of thrift annoying. Thompson suffered a badly broken leg as a teenager, resulting in months of enforced inactivity. Tomison fussed over him, caring for him like a son, then gave him the opportunity to learn the art of surveying that would ultimately make him famous, from the company's first trained surveyor, Philip Turnor. Yet decades later, when Thompson wrote his memoir, it was Tomison's annoying habit of retrieving every tiny bead or nail that fell onto the trading post floor that was remembered.

Tomison has also been criticized by historians for his focus on the Saskatchewan River when others had their sights on the Athabasca – the Eldorado of the North. Yet, having travelled thousands of kilometres annually for decades, he knew better than most of his English colleagues how the company's workforce was already stretched past its limit, particularly after the heavy, unwieldy York boats were put into service in the 1790s. While other senior officers sat by the bay, Tomison took a full share of the load as he travelled inland with the brigades every year.

It was better, he felt, to establish posts that were supportable and create trade networks from each of them. Between 1778 and 1795 he did just that, founding a string of fur trade posts all the way out to the Rockies, including Edmonton House.

Throughout his long career, he also waged regular battles with his colleagues and even with the committee in London for better treatment of his employees and against liquor as a trade item. But perhaps his biggest priority was education. Like many others in senior positions with the company, he was a wealthy man by the time he retired. But unlike most, who retired to Montréal or London, built themselves grand homes and lived like gentlemen, Tomison went home to Orkney and endowed a school, Tomison Academy, that served South Ronaldsay for 150 years.

He embodied, in short, what we now consider to be the best of modern Canadian values – egalitarianism, a social conscience, and a belief in moderation and the worth of public education.

By the late eighteenth century, Europeans were becoming more aware of the west coast of North America. While it was reasonably clear that no continuously navigable waterway existed from the east to the west coasts, finding and establishing an overland route to the Pacific Ocean became the Holy Grail of the fur trade. Captain James Cook, who was incidentally the son of Scottish farmers, had recently mapped part of the west coast of British North America, but the vast region between the fur trade territories and the Pacific Ocean remained largely unknown.

In 1789, North West Company partner Alexander Mackenzie, a proud and somewhat arrogant young Scot, originally from the Isle of Lewis, volunteered to find an overland route to the Pacific. On June 3rd, he set off from Fort Chipewyan on the shores of Lake Athabasca with five *voyageurs* and a small group of Native guides. After several gruelling weeks of paddling in cold rain, portaging through swampy muskeg, and steering their flimsy canoes through jagged ice sheets in Great Slave Lake, the party began to descend what would later be named the Mackenzie River. Ten days later, Mackenzie began to realize that since the river had suddenly bent north, his dream of finding a route to the Pacific was probably doomed. Nevertheless, with obstinate determination, he persevered, ignoring not only the great peril to himself but to his companions as well. In his journal, Mackenzie wrote, "It was evident that these waters emptied themselves into the Hyperborean Sea; and though it was probable that we could not return to Athabasca in the course of the season, I was determined to penetrate to the discharge of them."

This is an interesting comment, as attempting to winter so far north would have been a virtual death sentence for the puny expedition. The note is testament to Mackenzie's single-minded tenacity, as well as his egocentricity. Luckily, after several days, myriad hardships and continuous mutinous rumblings from his companions, the company paddled into the Beaufort Sea, a desolate inlet of the Arctic Ocean. Mackenzie's goal attained, he turned back to Fort Chipewyan just before the killing arctic temperatures set in. He referred thereafter to the route as his "River of Disappointment".

Mackenzie's journey and the information that ensued were of little commercial value to his company, and aside from the occasional slap on the back from fellow wintering partners – those partners in the company who lived in the far reaches of the North West year round – his achievement was largely ignored. Not surprisingly, however, the obdurate young Scot was already making plans for a second attempt at finding a route to the Pacific. During his first expedition, he had learned a few things; the most important was that he lacked critical navigational skills. He decided to spend the winter in England studying astronomical, navigational, and surveying skills; by May 1793, he was equipped and prepared to make history.

Mackenzie's motives for undertaking such treacherous expeditions were very largely for financial gain and personal glory. He had a vision of finding a route to the sea and linking the fur trade with commerce in the Orient. He knew that a Pacific port would give his company direct shipping access to the industrial might of Great Britain. In fact, so large-scale and, one might argue, so prescient were his ambitions of fashioning a commercial empire that he advocated the merging of the North West Company with the Hudson's Bay Company and the monopolistic, imperial East India Company operating in India. This would allow British commerce to proliferate, unrivalled, throughout the world. In short, Mackenzie was a bold opportunist who, to the end of his life, sought the recognition he felt was his destiny.

During his voyages, Mackenzie was always aloof and imperious towards his companions. He had little interest in his Native guides or their culture and treated them condescendingly; in his view they were simply servants whose help he needed to get what he wanted. And despite traversing some of the most spectacular landscapes in the world, Mackenzie was seldom awed or inclined towards philosophical reflection. His journals are generally straightforward accounts that reveal his nature as a focused businessman with specific targets in mind.

On May 9, 1793, Mackenzie, a company clerk, six *voyageurs* and two Native interpreters set out in a large canoe up the Peace River. Within a week, they had reached the hazardous canyons carved out of the daunting Rocky Mountains by the ancient, rushing

THOMAS LAWRENCE / NATIONAL ARCHIVES OF CANADA / C-001348

NATIONAL ARCHIVES OF CANADA / C-021296

INSET: ALEXANDER MACKENZIE IN 1801; ABOVE: THE WIDE PEACE RIVER VALLEY IN WHAT IS NOW NORTHWESTERN ALBERTA

Peace. Day after day, Mackenzie and his party toiled toward west and south toward the Continental Divide. By late afternoon, the party was often so exhausted that it collapsed and slept until the following morning, sometimes enduring near-freezing temperatures.

The party followed the Parsnip River south, its rations dwindling dangerously. With the help of some Sekani guides encountered along the way, the travellers surmounted the pass and began their descent towards the ocean. After obstacles such as escaping the wrath of a party of hostile Carrier or Dakelh, capsizing and smashing their canoe almost beyond repair, and losing most of their gear in a particularly wild torrent, the expedition made it to the upper reaches of the Fraser River. Grateful, they began to follow it, but when the river suddenly turned south, Mackenzie opted to go west overland. As on his previous journey, his companions became dispirited and were often on the verge of revolt, and he had constantly to cajole and placate them with rum rations to keep them going. He later boasted in his journal, "I determined to proceed with resolution, and set future events at defiance."

A group of Nuxalk people, who were travelling an ancient trading route to the coast, guided Mackenzie and his party west. After another month of overland trudging, they finally reached Dean Channel, a small Pacific inlet. There they were met by Heiltsuk or Bella Bella people, who believed the strangers might be spirits, likely to destroy their stocks of salmon. One of Heiltsuk made terrifying threats, and was, Mackenzie wrote, "so violent that he foamed at the mouth … My people were panic-struck, and some of them asked if it was my determination to remain there and be sacrificed."

Seeing the futility of reaching the Pacific itself, Mackenzie contented himself with writing on a rock the following inscription – a pictograph of sorts – in grease and vermilion: ALEX MACKENZIE FROM CANADA BY LAND 22ND JULY 1793.

Despite having followed routes travelled by Native North Americans for millennia, from a Euro-Canadian perspective Mackenzie's achievement was enormous. His voyage had put the British in a strong position to make legitimate land claims on the west coast, much to the disgruntlement of the American government. A subsequent book based on his exploits propelled Mackenzie to hero status, not only in British North America but throughout the world. Even Napoleon Bonaparte became an admirer.

Mackenzie's imprint on history does not end with his daring voyages. Bolstered by his new notoriety, he began to seek more power in the North West Company, something that irked Simon McTavish, the company's long uncontested chieftain. Soon, a group of younger wintering partners, almost entirely Scots who felt they were not being advanced quickly enough, sought Mackenzie's advice. They began to criticize the "marquis", as well as his nepotistic hiring practises, and with Mackenzie's counsel and moral support, though without his active participation, many broke away and formed the competing XY Company. Not surprisingly, this made McTavish furious, and a bitter open feud developed between him and Mackenzie. Meanwhile, although the XY Company initially cut into the North West Company's profits, the threat was manageable until two years later in 1800 when Mackenzie added his experience and weighty prestige to the upstart company, renaming it Alexander Mackenzie and Company.

For the next four years, the companies threw themselves into a competitive grudge match, not unlike the clan struggles of old. Mackenzie's company steadily gained on its older rival and the stress caused by the NWC's losses, as well as his intense hatred of Mackenzie, probably contributed to McTavish's early death in 1804, at the age of just fifty-four. It certainly made his last years the most acrimonious of his life and many thought the clashing pride of the two obstinate Scots was terrible to behold.

After McTavish's death, William McGillivray, McTavish's highly intelligent nephew took over the wounded North West Company. Now the way was clear to negotiate a truce, which McGillivray and Mackenzie did within four months, with Mackenzie's company being absorbed. Under the new arrangement, Mackenzie soon lost his hefty influence in the trade, so he left the company to pursue a half-hearted political career as a parliamentarian in Lower Canada. So bored by politics that he seldom bothered to show up to the chamber, he soon quit. By 1805, he had turned his back on Canada altogether and retired to Scotland. There, at the age of forty-eight, he married a fourteen-year-old girl from his own clan and settled into a desultory life until he, too, died early at fifty-six. Though his grand visions of creating an international commercial empire were unrealized, Mackenzie managed, through dogged determination and resolute discipline, to leave an enduring stamp on Canada.

WILLIAM MCGILLIVRAY

For ten years after Mackenzie's bold passage to the sea, there were no further expeditions beyond the Rockies. The North West Company continued to exploit the vast territories to the east of the mountains, but a commercially viable route west seemed a lost cause. William McGillivray, however, was soon putting his own stamp on the company.

Unlike his uncle, McGillivray had spent many long winters inland, gaining an intimate knowledge of the complexities of the trade. Born, raised and educated in Scotland, he had come to Canada as a young man at the bidding of his uncle and had risen meteorically through the company ranks. His younger brothers, Duncan and Simon, had also become influential partners. But he was of a very different temperament than his uncle and by the time he supplanted McTavish in 1804, William McGillivray already had a reputation in the company for fairness and pragmatism.

During his tenure, the North West Company faced many problems. In 1803, the United States had expanded its holdings by buying from the French all the lands that drained into the Mississippi. This effectively denied the North West Company access to much of the rich territory south and west of the Great Lakes. Furthermore, as territories were trapped out, the company was forced to travel farther and farther from its shipping headquarters in Montréal, putting it in a vulnerable, overextended position. Unlike the Hudson's Bay Company, the Nor'Westers did not possess a shipping port in the middle of the continent, nor did they have a legal monopoly on their territory. Indeed, upstart companies were always attempting to trap and trade on land the NWC considered its own and it had often felt forced to resort to physical intimidation and even force to guard its holdings. William McGillivray realized that the vast continental transportation network was simply not viable. The only way to keep the precarious enterprise from imploding, he believed, was to open up a viable trade route to the west and establish a Pacific port.

And the man for the job of establishing a string of trading posts over the mountains and finding a navigable route to the Pacific, he felt, was Simon Fraser. While Alexander Mackenzie had chosen to abandon the large southerly-flowing river beyond the continental divide, Simon Fraser would follow it all the way to the sea. This, it was hoped, would lead to the mouth of the "Columbia River", which various captains sailing the Pacific Coast had spotted from their ships.

Simon Fraser was born in Vermont in 1776, the year of American Independence, though for the Frasers, it meant something else entirely. His clan, the Frasers, had been one of the best known in Scotland, but after Culloden, the English had spitefully burned down his grandfather's house, as they did so many others, and the family was dispossessed. Simon's parents followed a flood of emigrants to the American colonies, arriving in 1773. There, they worked hard to establish a prosperous farm, but, when forced to choose between British and American, like many others his father chose to fight for the former. Captured by revolutionaries, he was imprisoned and died of brutal treatment. His mother and her children made their way to Canada in 1784, among many thousands of British Loyalists to arrive during that period.

Life was difficult for the family, and Simon had only two years of schooling before he had to make his own way, apprenticing in the fur trade as a teenager.

To his credit, he became a full partner in the North West Company when he was only twenty-five, no small accomplishment.

Between 1805 and 1807, during the first three seasons of his western mission for the NWC, Fraser established several trading posts in the intermontane region between the Rockies and the Fraser River. Recalling his mother's tales of Scotland, "a land of brown heath and shaggy wood", he named the region New Caledonia. In the spring of 1808, Fraser was ready to descend the "Great River" and thus enhance his company's future prospects.

The Fraser is a monstrous river of 1,368 kilometres, into which run countless smaller tributaries. It can be calm at times, but unexpected, raging white water often blasts through narrow canyons with treacherous force. Of course, Fraser knew none of this when he set out, along with two traders, nineteen *voyageurs*, and two Carrier guides; they soon passed the point where Mackenzie had turned west to travel overland.

The party met many Native North Americans along the way and although they were initially helpful and accommodating, Fraser nevertheless assumed an arrogant, patronizing attitude. In his journal he wrote, "However kind savages may appear, I know that it is not in their nature to be sincere in their professions to strangers. The respect and attention, which we generally experience, proceed, perhaps, from an idea that we are superior beings, who are not to be overcome; at any rate, it is certain the less familiar we are with one another the better for us."

Canyon after hellish canyon menaced the expedition. The men forced

NATIONAL LIBRARY OF CANADA / 22645

SIMON FRASER AND HIS PARTY SHOOTING THE RAPIDS OF THE RIVER THAT NOW BEARS HIS NAME themselves with great trepidation to scale rock walls, again and again groping for precarious hand and footholds. They tied themselves together with rope and prayed for salvation. The exploding rapids and jagged rocks below lay waiting, ready to rip the party to shreds at the first false step. A month of unspeakable hardship and harrowing close calls followed in rapid succession. Showing a slight crack of desperation in his usually composed nature, Fraser wrote in his journal, "I have been for long periods among the Rocky Mountains but have never seen anything like this country … I cannot find words to describe our situation at times. We had to pass where no human being should venture …"

Relief seemed to come when the party finally reached the wide, fertile river delta, which emptied into the ocean. Here, however, Musqueam warriors – obviously not intimidated by their white-skinned visitors – surrounded the party, and Fraser realized that attempting to proceed was hopeless. He took a quick latitude reading, which confirmed his fear that he was far north of the mouth of the Columbia, and headed back up the hazardous river. The return trip was even more harrowing, as the party was attacked on several occasions with arrows and rocks. Against all odds, the expedition returned to Fort George, on the site of today's Prince George, exhausted and traumatized.

While Fraser's discovery had no commercial value, it was very important in the race to claim the West. Like Mackenzie, Fraser had established a well-known British stake on the vast western territory, which helped keep the Americans at bay. It also opened the western fur trade, which in turn ultimately paved the way for settlement.

Another of Simon Fraser's little known contributions to history, a small gesture with huge ramifications, was that he convinced David Thompson, the Welsh geographer, surveyor and mapmaker, to defect from the Hudson's Bay Company and join the Nor'Westers. Thompson eventually charted much of British Columbia's interior, established many trading posts, and made his way to the mouth of the Columbia River, claiming everything along the way for the North West Company and Great Britain. Unfortunately, he arrived at the Pacific several months after American fur traders had made claims of their own, with their flag planted and flapping in the wind.

During the fur trade's first two centuries, a phenomenon took place that would have profound long-term consequences. From the outset, Europeans sought close contact with First Nations peoples, initially to establish a market relationship based on mutual self-interest. Later, both the bay men and Nor'Westers lived for months and often years on end in the continental interior, beyond the reach of the clergy and far removed from white women. As the two disparate peoples became familiar to one another, the inevitable happened. Open-air romances between European or Canadian traders and Native women became extremely common, as did the practice of taking a "country wife". Across much of the continent, a new set of customs evolved, based on necessity and the logic of circumstance. Traders would often take a bride, usually secured by giving the girl's father a gift, often a gun or a jug of rum, and live with her during his contracted time with the company. Although the Hudson's Bay Company initially frowned on this practice, its prohibition was in fact more illusion than reality, for even company officers almost invariably took country wives.

On the other hand, the North West Company actively encouraged partnerships with Native women, as it made for contented traders and secured tight trading relationships. Though some traders had multiple wives, each one at a different trading post, many remained wedded to the same woman for decades, finding her an indispensable helpmate and partner. Occasionally, when a trader's tenure in the wilderness was finished, he would pass his wife to another trader, or simply abandon her, which of course also meant leaving children behind, but as the years passed, this was the exception rather than the rule. And some traders brought their wives back to white society, but again, this was an uncommon practice.

An unfortunate consequence of contact between the two peoples was the use of alcohol as trading currency. Officially, the Hudson's Bay Company did not condone trading alcohol, as it felt that the practice would render the Native labour force unproductive and ultimately hurt the trade. The North West Company, however, had no compunction whatsoever about trading strong drink. By the early 1800s, brandy and rum had become major commodities of trade with the Natives, who had no long cultural tradition of alcohol consumption. The sad effect was that in many regions alcohol did significant damage to the traditional Native way of life and, among some tribes, undermined the very fabric of society. As alcohol flowed increasingly throughout the Northwest, the plight of some Native nations became increasingly acute.

One of the products of short- and long-term liaisons between traders and Native women was a new race of people, those of mixed Native and European descent. The mix of French voyageurs and Natives was known in the trade as "*les Métis*", a French derivation of *mestizo*, meaning "mixture". The mostly Scottish but also English-Native mixture were known as "Half-breeds", a term now considered pejorative. Today, many people of mixed descent in Canada refer to themselves as Métis.

While many Métis found employment directly with the two giant fur trading companies, the reception they got there varied. The offspring of Hudson's Bay Company officers and their Native wives were often educated, sometimes in Orkney or Scotland, and easily took officer-class positions, usually as clerks, when they joined the company.

In some cases, this was also true of the Nor'Westers, but the offspring of the rank and file in both companies were generally consigned to the bottom rungs of company ladders. Many Métis, however, carved out their own niche in the trade. Initially they served as voyageurs and labourers; later, even before the companies merged, they settled along the Red River in the vicinity of today's Winnipeg. There they hunted buffalo and made pemmican, a highly nutritious mix of dried and pounded buffalo meat and melted lard, sometimes augmented with saskatoon berries. High in energy, light in weight and with an almost endless shelf life, pemmican became a staple of the traders' diet, thus securing the Métis a unique and independent living in the trade for most of a century.

BISON MEAT DRIES ON RACKS IN THE RED RIVER VALLEY

WILLIAM ARMSTRONG / NATIONAL ARCHIVES OF CANADA / C-010502

By the end of the eighteenth century, the North West Company had eight times the number of men in the interior as the Hudson's Bay Company and controlled the vast majority of the trade Despite this, the HBC strategy of moving inland had met with reasonable success, and the emboldened Hudson's Bay Company now began to encroach on traditional North West Company territory in the Great Lakes watershed and the far north. The competition eventually resembled a Scottish Highland blood feud. The wily Nor'Westers used physical intimidation, sabotage and the occasional murder in an attempt to browbeat the bay men into submission. Stubborn and uncompromising, the HBC refused to quit and administered some vicious licks of its own. Ugly conflict between the two companies continued for more than a quarter-century, with the HBC slowly losing ground. By 1809, it was clear that radical steps had to be taken.

The emergence of two key Scots at this point changed the fortunes of the Hudson's Bay Company and the fate of the entire fur trade. Andrew Colvile, a shrewdly intellectual Inverness Scot, who was also a very successful sugar broker, bought a large block of HBC stock and quickly became the company's most influential committee member. At Colvile's very first London committee meeting, Colin Robertson, a rather forceful Highlander who had left the Nor'Westers over his less than stellar advancement, was scheduled to make a presentation. Wasting no time, he laid out an impressive argument to the committee: "When you are among wolves, howl!" In other words, if the Hudson's Bay Company truly wanted to compete, head to head, with a very determined North West Company, it had to adopt all its methods, and Robertson knew these methods inside out, from hiring *voyageurs* to encouraging marriage with Native women. He proposed an invasion of the rich Athabasca fur region, adopting the proven strategies of his former company. He also made two other vital recommendations: First, employees must be paid according to their performance, and second, the Hudson's Bay Company, as far as possible, should hire only Scots. Andrew Colvile was impressed and immediately engaged Robertson to revamp the stuffy Hudson's Bay Company and lead the charge to the Athabasca.

Aside from restructuring the Hudson's Bay Company to compete more aggressively, Andrew Colvile's involvement in Company affairs produced another monumentally important effect: it attracted the attention of his young brother-in-law, Thomas Douglas, a Lowland nobleman who had inherited his father's estate and title to become the 5th Earl of Selkirk. Historians have often been unfair to the young Lord Selkirk, maligning him for his utopian experiments and attempts at social engineering. Some have labelled him a quixotic fool and criticized his dangerous naiveté. Historical hindsight is, of course, often extremely clear, and therefore, sometimes unjust. Such seems to be the case with Lord Selkirk.

Thomas Douglas was in fact an intelligent, urbane and educated man. Unfortunately, he was also ill; severe tuberculosis wracked the last decade of his life. This reality, being regularly forced to cough blood into a handkerchief, served as a tragic anvil to his soaring spirit and lofty ideals.

Young Douglas had studied in France and was intimately aware of the class dynamics that were released during the French Revolution. He had also studied at the University of Edinburgh, considered by most thinkers of the day as the best university in Europe. Under the tutelage of the famous moral philosopher, Dugald Stewart, Douglas developed a strong social conscience and sense of *noblesse oblige*. He made many treks into the Scottish Highlands where he saw firsthand how the Highland Clearances were destroying the lives of many of his countrymen, and he vowed to do everything in his power to help.

Following his father's death in 1799, with the financial power of his family's estate behind him, not to mention the prestige of his new title, Lord Selkirk had the leverage to match his altruistic ambitions. In 1803, he subsidized and successfully settled eight hundred Highlanders on Prince Edward Island (see Scottish Settlements). The next year, he purchased land at Baldoon in Upper Canada and sent fifteen Highland families to live there. Unfortunately, the land proved to be too swampy for farming, and the settlers dispersed. Selkirk also learned Gaelic in order to communicate effectively with the Highlanders and in 1805 published the influential book, *Observations on the present state of the Highlands of Scotland, with a View of the Causes and the probable consequences of Emigration.* In it he argued that the only way to remedy the plight of Highlanders was to transplant them, *en masse*, into a new colony where their once-proud culture could again flourish.

Andrew Colvile's rising eminence in the Hudson's Bay Company piqued Selkirk's interest in it, and he assiduously studied the company charter. He soon came to the conclusion that it was absurd for such a colossal territory to be in the hands of an unprofitable private company that actively kept settlers out. He also noted that an original condition of the charter was to establish colonies, a secret that the HBC committee had kept to itself.

Selkirk decided that he would open the vast territory to settlement, and he began to use his wealth to purchase Hudson's Bay Company stock. Soon, he and Colvile together held a controlling interest, and in effect, Selkirk's influence gave him the leverage to do with the company what he willed. He convinced the governing committee to grant him thirty million hectares – an enormous tract of land more than one quarter the size of present-day Manitoba – in the middle of Rupert's Land for just ten shillings. He called the huge territory Assiniboia.

Colvile went along with the scheme because he too wanted to see the interior opened up, as it would allow farmers to grow food for the fur traders, provide a settlement for retired traders and their Native wives and guarantee a future labour pool for the Company. All in all, it seemed a very reasonable strategy. Selkirk agreed personally to bear the costs of settling one thousand Highland families within ten years. Then, with the paperwork done, he began to recruit.

Some historians have written scornfully about how Selkirk recklessly recruited settlers, claiming he knew almost nothing about the territory within his land grant, but this is simply not true. While the earl was unable, due to poor health, to visit his colony in what is now southern Manitoba until several years later, he had travelled to Upper Canada, Lower Canada and the Maritimes in 1808 and was very knowledgeable about the vast, imposing nature of British North America. He was also an avid student of geography and agriculture, who meticulously researched everything he undertook. In Montréal, he had met with North West Company partners and learned much about the prairies. Moreover, he had read Mackenzie's glowing accounts of the fertility of the plains, as well as those of many others. In short, Selkirk was an intelligent man, not at all given to folly. His plan to settle the Red River region of Rupert's Land was actually quite sound and history has vindicated him, for southern Manitoba contains some of the richest farmland in North America. Had Selkirk not met several unforeseen, even unimagined obstacles, his colonization project would have undoubtedly been far more successful, and historians might have hailed him as a bold and innovative hero. History, however, is not kind to failure.

When the Nor'Westers caught wind of Selkirk's plans to settle the interior, they were at first incredulous and then furious. Settlements, it was feared, would encroach upon vital supply routes, disrupt wildlife, and dislocate Native populations who were critical to the trade. Anyone could see that settlements in the eastern United States had ruined the trade altogether. The North West Company was already in a precarious position due to its ever-lengthening shipping network, and settlers would upset the fragile balance. Moreover, Selkirk's land grant encompassed several North West Company posts, including such critical provisioning posts as Fort Gibraltar at the junction of the Red and Assiniboine Rivers. Perhaps, they fumed, Selkirk's scheme was a nefarious HBC plot to destroy the North West Company.

If Lord Selkirk can be charged with a lack of common sense, such criticism should be directed at his hiring of Miles Macdonell, an incompetent, overbearing Highlander and former captain in the Loyalist Royalist Canadian Volunteers. Macdonell adhered closely to the negative stereotype of a frustrated military man whose ambition exceeds his abilities. Authoritarian by nature, his approach was to attempt to intimidate with bluster and bravado; the result was often precisely the opposite. Yet it was he that Selkirk chose to lead their displaced countrymen to their new home in Rupert's Land.

With highly exaggerated claims about the quality of life in the new colony, Macdonell managed to round up a shipload of Highlanders. The ill-fated group of a hundred hopeful Scots left home forever in the summer of 1811, heading for Hudson Bay. After two miserable months on a run-down ship, they arrived at York Factory, the Hudson's Bay Company's main shipping station. The bay men directed them to a shoddily constructed encampment twenty-three miles away over the taiga, and it was there that the newcomers spent a scurvy-plagued winter, huddling in the extreme cold. The following July, only twenty-two men were healthy enough to make the arduous two-month trek upriver to their new land.

It was therefore late summer before Miles Macdonell and his ragged, bewildered band of Highlanders finally arrived at the place just below the forks of the Red and Assiniboine Rivers, where he intended to found his new colony. Shortly after their arrival Macdonell invited all the inhabitants of the area – the Métis, Nakota and Cree, as well as the Nor'Westers from nearby Fort Gibraltar – to an arrival celebration on September 4th. With all the pomposity he could muster, he swore himself in as governor and declared that the land now belonged to the settlement and that everyone was henceforth subject to its laws. The guests raised their eyebrows and harrumphed, but no one took him very seriously, not even his cousin and brother-in-law, Alexander Macdonell, who was in charge at Fort Gibraltar.

Against all odds, the Highlanders began to scratch out a living on the land. Despite his promises of supplies and farm implements, Macdonell was often too busy enjoying his new position to think much about the settlers, and much more often than not, they had to do without. Over the next five years, 270 more Scots arrived, and what awaited them was adversity of truly biblical proportions. The Siouan-speaking Dakota, who had been pushed from their land by the fur trade, terrorized the settlers, raiding their farms and burning their homes. Wolves and winter storms killed their few cattle, and two seasons of locusts annihilated their crops. During the first ten years, the settlers produced only two decent harvests; crop-stunting drought or weather that was too cold or too wet characterized most years. The Red River flooded its banks and washed away crops, and infestations of mites, rats and birds also took their toll. Then there were the prairie winters that could last almost six miserable months. The Highlanders persevered because they had no choice. Year after year, they beat back every hardship and hung on to their fragile existence. Their tenacity and fortitude were extraordinary.

THE ARRIVAL OF THE KILDONAN SETTLERS AT RED RIVER

NATIONAL LIBRARY OF CANADA / 22647

Despite the suffering of the settlers, for the first two years there was at least a relative peace between them and the Métis and Nor'Westers. As more boatloads of settlers arrived, however, Macdonell was faced with the necessity of feeding them until they could begin to grow their own food. Since the Métis were producing thousands of pounds of pemmican to sustain the North West Company's fur traders, as well as hunting bison on what Macdonell considered Selkirk's territory, the governor came up with a disastrous plan to usurp the pemmican trade. In January 1814, he issued the Pemmican Proclamation, an edict stating that it would be henceforth illegal to export pemmican or to hunt buffalo on horseback. He also seized almost 200 kilos of pemmican that was ready to be shipped and sent it to Brandon House, on the upper Assiniboine River, for storage. Challenging anyone who did not like this arrangement, he boasted that he had enough power "to crush all the Nor'Westers ... should they be so hardy as to resist ... authority."

The edict effectively cut off the fur traders' food supply and deprived the Métis of their livelihood. And if these actions were not provocation enough, Macdonell sent notices to the commanders of all North West Company posts in Assiniboia, declaring that they must relinquish their posts within six months or be forcibly evicted.

Now any doubt on the part of the Métis or Nor'Westers that the settlers would threaten their way of life evaporated. Moreover, any chance that Lord Selkirk's noble plan would be fully realized disappeared. In one stroke of hubris, Macdonell shattered the peace and doomed many of the settlers.

The North West Company sent out Duncan Cameron, yet another Highlander, to incite the Métis against the settlers. With incendiary oratory, Cameron convinced the Métis that their very existence was threatened, claiming that it was their destiny to defend their nation, their honour, and their proud way of life. He then coached them on the best terrorist tactics, including painting themselves with war paint and pretending to be bloodthirsty Natives. Cuthbert Grant, the mixed-blood son of a Highland Nor'Wester and a Cree mother, led the Métis.

Grant had been schooled in Scotland and had learned the fur trade in Montréal under the direction of William McGillivray himself. He eventually came to identify with other mixed-bloods and so chose to work for the North West Company in the Red River Valley. There he emerged as a dynamic, patriotic leader. Following Duncan Cameron's advice, he and his band of paramilitary Métis followers embarked on a nocturnal campaign of burning barns and houses, trampling crops, stealing farm implements, and shooting at settlers. All the while, Duncan Cameron was urging the settlers to leave before real trouble began. The terrorized Scots felt they had little choice, and by the end of 1815, all but thirteen families had departed. The remaining settlers headed by boat for the temporary safety of the HBC's Jack River trading post at the north end of Lake Winnipeg. As they left, they saw the smoke rising from their burning homes. Miles Macdonell then surrendered to Cameron, and a group of Nor'Westers escorted him back to Montréal, where he had a nervous breakdown.

While in Jack River, however, the settlers ran into Colin Robertson, the feisty former Nor'Wester come enthusiastic HBC man, who was on his way to open up the Athabasca region for his company. Angered by the treachery of the Nor'Westers and the Métis, Robertson convinced the settlers to return to their farms in time for harvest. Robertson was an imposing Highlander – tall, powerfully built, with red hair and bushy sideburns. When he spoke articulately in his thick Scottish brogue, people listened. And unlike Miles Macdonell, Colin Robertson feared nothing and could not be intimidated.

Robertson led the group back to their homes and then let the Métis know, in no uncertain terms, that they had better stop hassling the settlers. Since Cuthbert Grant was absent at the time, Robertson was able to intimidate the leaderless mixed bloods. That fall, more settlers arrived, led by the new Governor of Assiniboia, Robert Semple, and the next spring, Robertson set his sights on humbling the Nor'Westers. In March 1816, he seized the North West Company's Fort Gibraltar and arrested Duncan Cameron. Searching Cameron's desk, Robertson found evidence that the Nor'Westers were plotting the complete destruction of Selkirk's colony.

Colin Robertson ordered Semple to set fire to Fort Gibraltar, having first saved the corner bastions and stockades to shore up the HBC's Fort Douglas. It was a provocative act, and greatly angered the Nor'Westers. but even worse was the pemmican blockade. Spring was the time when the year's supply of pemmican would normally be moved down the Assiniboine and Red Rivers to supply the Nor'Westers returning from their annual rendezvous at Fort William on Lake Superior. The Métis provisioners had been largely prevented from hunting by the Pemmican Proclamation. Now, once again under the leadership of Cuthbert Grant, who bore the title of Captain General of all the Half Breeds, the Métis descended on Brandon House on June 1st. Sacking the post, they took possession of the NWC pemmican being held there and organized a large escort to transport it to Lake Winnipeg.

As the brigade neared the junction of the Red River, it struck out overland to avoid confrontation with the HBC, but marshy conditions forced the heavily laden Red River carts to within two and a half kilometres of Fort Douglas. Near a clump of trees known as Seven Oaks, Cuthbert Grant and sixty-two Métis were intercepted by Robert Semple and a group of two dozen settlers. Words were exchanged between Semple and one of the Métis, and a shot rang out. Then bullets were flying in both directions, but the Métis, better armed and anticipating trouble, easily overcame the outnumbered settlers. When it was over, Semple and more than twenty of his men, as well as one of the Métis, lay dead.

Emboldened by success, Grant and his men seized Fort Douglas and imprisoned a number of settlers. The others again retreated to Jack River, while their houses were once more looted and burned.

When news of the "Seven Oaks Massacre" reached the North West Company's main depot, Fort William, the Nor'Westers cheered and celebrated. Finally, the annoying settlement had been stamped out, and the Nor'Westers could once again assume their dominant position in the region. Rum was poured

LORD SELKIRK / PROVINCIAL ARCHIVES OF MANITOBA / N10109

FORT DOUGLAS, ON THE RED RIVER.

and toasts were made.

While all this was going on, Lord Selkirk had learned that something close to a state of war existed in his beleaguered colony. In response, he travelled to Lower Canada (today's Québec), and hired four officers and a hundred tough Swiss and German mercenaries who had fought in the War of 1812 to accompany him to Red River. Though exhausted and coughing up blood, he embarked on the long journey by canoe. En route, he learned of the disaster at Seven Oaks. Devastated and outraged, he diverted his party to Fort William to confront the partners of the North West Company.

After establishing a camp near the fort, Selkirk learned that in addition to fifteen NWC partners, William McGillivray himself was there. Vowing to "cut up by the roots one of the most abominable combinations that has ever suffered to exist in the British Dominions," he stormed the fort and placed the partners, including McGillivray, under arrest. One can only imagine the response of the incredulous Nor'Westers as they were faced by the incensed, but clearly unwell, nobleman. But there was little they could do, surrounded as they were by armed soldiers.

The strain brought the earl close to collapse, and he was forced to halt his interrogation until the next day. That night, confined to the fort, the NWC partners made a blazing bonfire of all incriminating documents. Nevertheless, when Selkirk returned the next morning, a search of the fort turned up an overlooked document proving that the NWC had rewarded the Métis following the massacre at Seven Oaks. Selkirk sent the partners back to Montréal under armed guard to stand trial.

Selkirk wintered at Fort William, and the following spring sent his soldiers to recapture Fort Douglas and several North West Company posts. The appearance of the tough European troops easily subdued the Métis, and in June 1816, Selkirk arrived at his colony, saddened by the obvious hardships his settlers had been forced to endure. He spent the rest of the summer planning the future of his colony, surveying and granting land, and designing a town. In the autumn, he left for Montréal to face a barrage of counter-charges concocted by North West Company lawyers.

There are still those who believe that the dominant legacy of Selkirk's efforts was the suffering of his Highland settlers. They claim that he should have known he would be stepping on the toes of the Nor'Westers and the Métis, and that his plan was therefore ill conceived, misguided, even wacky. In fact, despite the forces that conspired against him and the settlement, Selkirk's colony did eventually succeed. Ultima Thule, one of Selkirk's original settlers, wrote in 1852, "No farmers in the world, no settlement or colony of agriculturalists can be pronounced so happy, independent, and comfortable as those in Red River."

Perhaps more important, Selkirk opened the west to settlement and, in doing so, staked a claim that signalled to the United States that Britain had transcontinental aspirations. This gave "Canada" a tenuous territorial foothold at a critical historical juncture, which held until the developing country had the will and the capacity to back up a more assertive claim to the region.

After Selkirk seized Fort William, bitter competition between the North West Company and Hudson's Bay Company intensified, and the Athabasca region became the new battleground. The HBC initiated the struggle by sending a group of traders into a region that was beyond the bounds of Rupert's Land to establish several trading posts on what the Nor'Westers had always deemed their exclusive territory. Colin Robertson had originally been chosen to lead the party, but he had been sidetracked, instead assisting Selkirk's settlers in reclaiming their devastated homes from the Métis.

In Athabasca, the Nor'Westers terrorized the bay men, each of their strategies more brutal than the last. First, they convinced the local Native people not to trade with the HBC; then they stormed and seized HBC forts. Finally, they chased all game away from the abject bay men so that some of them starved to death. The Hudson's Bay Company responded by sending the formidable Colin Robertson to the region with a force of two hundred armed men. Within weeks, Robertson had recaptured the HBC forts and not only restored but substantially augmented trade with the Native trappers.

Infuriated by Robertson's success, the Nor'Westers bided their time until they spotted Robertson alone, outside the protection of his fort. Two Nor'Westers grabbed him at gunpoint and carted him off to Fort Chipewyan, headquarters of the NWC in the region. They forced Robertson into a dark, cramped shack next to the fort's outhouse, where he stayed for eight wretched months. The following spring they set out, with Robertson under armed guard, for Montréal, but along the way the sly Scot escaped.

During his captivity, Robertson had learned a great deal about the operations of the North West Company. Now he sent a dispatch to HBC headquarters with the information that NWC wintering partners and loads of furs would soon be passing through Grand Rapids, where the Saskatchewan River flows into Lake Winnipeg. The Hudson's Bay Company sent a battalion of Selkirk's Swiss and German mercenaries and ambushed the North West Company's convoy, grabbing the rich bounty of pelts and arresting five important wintering partners. One, Benjamin Frobisher, was wounded during the scuffle. He managed to escape but starved to death in the wilderness. The rest of the partners were spirited off to York Factory, the main depot on the edge of Hudson Bay.

Outraged by the temerity of the bay men, the Nor'Westers staged their own ambush at Grand Rapids the following year, capturing none other than Colin Robertson. This time, however, his detention did not last long. During a meal break, Robertson flicked a dish full of victuals in his guards' faces, grabbed a pistol, and escaped, making his way through dense bush to the U.S. border.

Lord Selkirk, meanwhile, was fighting other battles in Montréal, attempting to justify his actions in a legal system dominated by the pervasive influence of the North West Company. Returning to London in 1818, he found he was equally unable to convince the British government that what had happened in the Canadian Northwest was the result of a conspiracy against him personally and the HBC. Ill and drained of much of his fortune, he set out for southern France, but died en route in April 1820, at the age of forty-eight.

As for the Nor'Westers, none ever faced charges, not even Cuthbert Grant, the leader at Seven Oaks. However, the acrimonious competition and lengthy legal battles took a huge toll on the company, draining its finances and distracting it from what really mattered: collecting and shipping furs. The NWC had never accumulated a significant cash reserve, depending instead on increasingly daring business exploits and higher profits to fund the lavish lifestyles of its partners. The company was therefore financially vulnerable. Further, it was finding that the fierce competition from the newly belligerent HBC, which had been significantly enhanced by recruiting Scots, had cut deeply into its profits. This, combined with vastly overextended supply lines, caused many of the company partners to see the writing on the wall. Despite protestations from McGillivray and several other senior partners, the majority of wintering partners voted to amalgamate with the Hudson's Bay Company.

Andrew Colvile, HBC director and Selkirk's brother-in-law, sensed a rift in the North West Company's ranks and assisted in driving the wedge between junior and senior partners. Negotiating a tough agreement that completely neutered the once proud North West Company, the Hudson's Bay Company officially absorbed its rival in 1821, creating an enormously powerful fur trade monopoly. No longer would Scot be pitted savagely against Scot. The blood feud between the two companies ceased.

The North West Company had expired, but its legacy to Canada would live on. "The impact of the transcontinental trading routes was pervasive enough to work the magic that helped save Western Canada from being absorbed into the United States," wrote Peter C. Newman "It was a puny scattering of tiny outposts that held the line, but it was enough."

The ubiquitous Colin Robertson eventually found his way to London to help negotiate a merger between the two titans. In many ways, he would have been an obvious choice to head the new Hudson's Bay Company, having already played a large part in the fur wars. He also knew as much as anyone about the inner workings of both companies. But Colvile wanted a fresh start and had already chosen the next governor, an unknown but indomitable young Highlander by the name of George Simpson. It was soon evident that, from a business perspective at least, Colvile could not have made a better choice for the company.

The amalgamated Hudson's Bay Company was granted exclusive trading rights far beyond Rupert's Land, all the way to the Pacific Ocean. With such an unprecedented monopoly, it was ready to embark upon a golden age of peace and profitability, but the preceding decade had been destructive. The two warring companies had let their feud preoccupy them, and the aftermath was festering bad blood between old rivals, as well as a hodgepodge of unprofitable trading posts scattered throughout the Northwest. Also, the market in Europe for beaver pelts was beginning to decline, as silk hats became increasingly *à la mode*. Imposing order on the chaos would be an almost impossible task, requiring the almost superhuman efforts of a very extraordinary man.

It has often been said that success is the product of ability and preparation meeting opportunity. George Simpson seems to be a perfect example of this axiom. Somehow, historical forces converged to place the right man, with the right abilities, at the right place and time. It is doubtful that anyone else could have not only salvaged but enhanced the fortunes of the Hudson's Bay Company the way Simpson did. Yet there is little in his early life to indicate that he was the man for the job.

His early life was either inauspicious or unknown; indeed though he was supportive to his immediate family, it is quite clear that he made considerable efforts to hide his background. He was born in Loch Broom in western Scotland in 1792 to an unknown woman and George Sr., an unremarkable ne'er-do-well. Young George was raised by his grandfather, a Presbyterian minister, and his aunt, Mary, in the northern Scottish county of Ross-Shire. Attending the parish school, he exhibited an unusual aptitude for mathematics.

When he was seventeen, an uncle offered him an apprenticeship at a sugar brokerage house in London, where Simpson's sharp, ordered mind soon brought him to the attention of Andrew Colvile. Little is known about Simpson in his early twenties, but in 1820, when Simpson was twenty-eight, Colvile enlisted him into the ranks of the Hudson's Bay Company and sent him to the Athabasca country. That winter, Simpson soaked up the knowledge and experience of the fur traders and then made plans to reorganize virtually every aspect of the company's operations. In 1821, he was named co-governor of the newly amalgamated company.

Some have contended that Colvile was actually somehow related to Simpson "on the wrong side of the blanket". This is possible, though not proven. In any case, for the next several decades, a deep bond developed between the two men, and Simpson always had the undivided attention and affection of Colvile, the HBC's most powerful director and later governor. Simpson later wrote to Colvile, "To you, I feel that I am solely indebted for my advancement in Life, and it will ever be my study that your good offices have not been misapplied."

Though personal relations were never Simpson's strong suit, he did have a keen sense of the imperative. When the two hostile companies merged, one of his first acts was to hold a large, lavish banquet at York Factory in an attempt to dispel some of the lingering bad blood between the bay men and the former Nor'Westers. As the two groups of enemies filed into the room, tension filled the air. John Tod, a clever Glasgow bay man, recorded the atmosphere in the room full of recalcitrant Scots: "... though joined together [they] would not amalgamate, for the Nor'Westers in one compact body kept together and evidently had no inclination at first to mix with their old rivals in trade." George Simpson made a speech and a toast, exhorting the two parties to come together. He then arranged the seating so that they were forced to integrate, resulting in some uncomfortable moments. Former Nor'Wester Allan McDonnell, for example, was seated near HBC veteran Alexander Kennedy. The previous season, the two had engaged in a bloody sword fight over Swan River fur catches. Tod wrote, "One of them still bore the marks of a cut on his face, the other it was said on some less conspicuous part of the body. I shall never forget the look of scorn and utter defiance with which they regarded each other the moment their eyes met ... I thought it fortunate that they were without arms ... it seemed not improbable they might yet renew the combat ..."

As the evening wore on, however, enmity between the two groups dissolved. The *soirée*, so carefully conceived by Simpson, had its intended effect. As they traded stories of their exploits, the wine and whiskey dampened the antipathy and enhanced a deep clannish admiration for one another. They chattered, gossiped, and laughed the night away, swearing allegiance with ever more mirthful enthusiasm. By the following morning, when the bash finally ended, the Hudson's Bay Company was a tight-knit clan, and George Simpson was its powerful and revered chieftain.

Though stocky and powerfully built, physically Simpson was not imposing. It was his authoritarian nature, sharp tongue, and indisputable strategic genius that earned him the nickname "the Little Emperor" after Napoleon Bonaparte. In fact, Napoleon was Simpson's hero; a painting of the egotistical general hung in Simpson's office. In temperament, ambition and tactics, the two were not at all dissimilar.

For the next four decades, Simpson ruled his far-flung empire with an iron will and seemingly unlimited energy. After uniting his employees, he set out in a birchbark canoe powered by handpicked *voyageurs.* Accompanied by a personal bagpiper to serenade him, he began a tour of inspection of his vast domain, intent on reorganizing his company's posts as he went.

C.W. JEFFREYS / NATIONAL ARCHIVES OF CANADA / C-114188

GEORGE SIMPSON AS A YOUNG MAN

Much as corporate takeovers have during the modern era, the amalgamation of the two companies had resulted in enormous duplication. Some posts were even within sight of one another. Eliminating such inefficiency was Simpson's first priority. For the next eight years, he travelled almost non-stop, visiting every post in his realm, closing down seventy-three and terminating fully half the company's employees. He was the precursor to the hands-on, micromanaging CEO who travels to his inefficient branch plants and ruthlessly downsizes in the name of corporate profitability.

Simpson was far different from his predecessors in that he knew that the key to profit was not merely to obtain more pelts but also to cut costs to the bone. He extolled the virtues of economy and slashed all company extravagances. No detail was too minute to escape his attention. He admonished his chief traders, "The table appointments throughout this country have hitherto been upon too large a scale, far exceeding the consumption of most respectable families in the civilized world and I think you may safely reduce the usual supplies by 50 per cent. Tin plates … no tablecloths … no earthenware dishes: a few tumblers which answer for wine glasses. Knives and forks ought to last at least a half a dozen years."

Simpson also penned detailed assessments of his employees and their worth to the company, forerunners of today's performance reviews. His "Character Book", however, went a step further and included incisive, often mean-spirited critiques of the traders' moral fibre. Simpson certainly knew how to turn a phrase, and he wielded his pen with the same guile as he did everything else. He described Colin Robertson as, "A frothy trifling conceited man, who would starve in any other Country and is perfectly useless here: fancies, or rather attempts to pass himself off as a clever fellow, a man of taste, of talents and of refinement; to none of which I need scarcely say he has the smallest pretension." Simpson went on to say that Robertson "is full of silly boasting and egotism, rarely deals in plain matter of fact and his integrity is very questionable. To the fur trade he is quite a burden, and a heavy burden too, being a compound of folly and extravagance, and disarranging and throwing into confusion whatsoever he puts his hand to in the shape of business."

Simpson compiled 157 of these detailed, mordant judgments. Donald McIntosh was "a very poor creature in every sense of the word, illiterate, weak-minded, and laughed at by his colleagues ... Speaks Saulteaux, is qualified to cheat an Indian, and can make and set a net ...". John Stuart was characterized as, "exceedingly vain, a great egotist, swallows the grossest flattery ...".

It is interesting to note what the formidable Scottish Chief Factor John Stuart thought of Simpson. He advised Donald Smith, his newly employed Scottish nephew, "It is his foible to exact not only strict obedience, but deference to the point of humility. As long as you pay him in that coin you will quickly get on his sunny side and find yourself in a few years a trader at a congenial post, with promotion in sight." That Smith heeded this lesson well will be borne out in a later chapter.

After several years with Simpson at the helm, the Hudson's Bay Company was running at peak efficiency, producing enormous profits. The directors were so impressed that they voted to multiply Simpson's salary by six times. Such pay increases continued during his tenure, and Simpson soon became very wealthy. His success, however, never made Simpson soft. In fact, he prided himself on criss-crossing his domain again and again, attempting each time to best his own previous speed records, though he was never known to lift a paddle. For thirty-nine years, he was in almost constant motion, traversing some of the most forbidding territory on earth: through the Rocky Mountains, over the prairies, down to the Columbia, north to Hudson Bay, over to Athabasca, and on to every other corner of his realm. No matter how remote or inaccessible the geography, the trekking never stopped. By horseback, snowshoe, dogsled and express canoe, Simpson achieved physical feats that made his employees shake their heads in amazement. They never knew where he would show up next, so they were always on guard, lest he appear unannounced and criticize their sloth.

Moving thus around his empire, preaching frugality, bolstering morale, and keeping his traders in a state of reverent apprehension, the governor appeared to require very little sleep, and his energy seemed to defy normal human limits. He would often force his tired *voyageurs* to paddle until midnight and then wake them at three or four in the morning with commands of "*Levez! Levez!*" Simpson relished cultivating his image as a superman, and such unremitting travel bordered on compulsion. He once wrote to a friend, "It is strange that all my ailments vanish as soon as I seat myself in a canoe."

During Simpson's rule, he continued to heavily recruit Orcadians to staff the posts and do much of the physical work of the trade, and while he used an elite corps of French Canadian voyageurs to speed him about his empire, he systematically eliminated many of North West Company's former French Canadian and Métis employees, either firing them outright or relegating them to isolated posts at the outer fringes of company territory. He argued that they thought themselves to be indispensable because of their excellent relations with the Natives and therefore demanded unreasonable wages.

Simpson's obsession with accounting and economy also required reasonably educated apprenticeship clerks, and recruiting from Scotland filled the bill perfectly, as the parish school system prepared young farm lads well for Simpson's brand of HBC service. As for officers, Simpson preferred fellow Scots, judging them as, "Stout strong active intelligent men who will not be above putting their hands to anything." Never satisfied, however, Simpson wrote a decade later that his Scottish employees had become, "so uppish, self-sufficient, and selfish that I must say my countrymen do not now stand quite so high in my estimation as formerly." Having said that, he continued to recruit almost entirely from his homeland.

In this way, Simpson created an empire of mind-boggling immensity. In a land in which there were no opposing checks and balances on his ego, he became a dictator. Like a Sun King of the wilderness, his every whim was realized, and the only higher power to which he had to answer was not Divinity but the HBC directors. In his domain, he was the final word, and few dared to challenge him.

While often ruthless, Simpson's tactics in the field were ingenious. Would-be rivals sometimes made attempts to encroach upon HBC lands, but guerrilla fur traders under Simpson's ruthless command were sent to deal with them. When lumber companies in the Ottawa Valley or fishermen in the Great Lakes attempted to extract a living from the HBC wilderness, Simpson waged merciless economic warfare on them, setting up rival enterprises and undercutting the competition by absorbing substantial losses. The trespassers were forced to withdraw, often bankrupted. South and east of the Columbia River, in an effort to discourage trapping and settling by American mountain men, Simpson commanded his fur trader shock troops to annihilate the fur supply by killing every possible beaver, right down to the last suckling pup. When American trappers on the southern border of HBC territory began to move northward, Simpson sent out legions of subsidized, privately licensed trappers to compete with them and drive them out of business. On the west coast, he signed a maritime agreement with the Russian-American Company and then played the two against one another, ultimately dislodging them both and assuming exclusive control himself. His dictatorial control of his territory and company and willingness to use whatever means necessary to achieve his ends helped Simpson achieve his Napoleonic aspirations.

Simpson's permanent legacy to Canada is that during his time in power, he established and extended viable trade routes throughout his domain, thus inadvertently preparing the territory for settlement. More importantly, through sheer gumption, energy, and force of will, he safeguarded British territory in a way no one else could have, until 1870 when Canada was ready to assume stewardship of the vast land.

Simpson personified many traits that have helped Scots prosper and achieve pre-eminence throughout the world: hard work, thrift, a genius for organization and efficiency, and pragmatism. Unfortunately however, on a personal level, Simpson was not a sympathetic figure. He viewed people simply as a means to achieve his own ends. His attitude, for example, toward Native North Americans may be summed up by one of his letters to London: "I am convinced they must be ruled with a rod of iron, to bring and to keep them in a proper state of subordination, and the most certain way to effect this is by letting them feel their dependence upon us." Yet, while he viewed them as inferior, he did not hesitate to take several Native country wives and mistresses to whom he referred disparagingly as his "bits of brown", "commodities" or "brown jug". With these women, he casually produced many offspring, but took no interest in the well being of most. Historian Grant MacEwan claims that Simpson studded "seventy sons between the Red River and the Rocky Mountains". While impossible to verify, this seems a hugely inflated number.

While other traders took country wives and usually established a familial relationship with them, Simpson always treated his "wives" as little more than a nuisance, never allowing any of them to take his name. He would eventually grow bored and jettison them. This flagrant flouting of the fur trading culture of the time set a socially disruptive example to the HBC employees, many of whom soon began to do the same.

A letter to one of his inner circle of employees would be all it would take to extricate Simpson from all responsibility for a liaison. One of his letters reads, "My family concerns I leave entirely to your kind management, if you can dispose of the Lady it will be satisfactory as she is an unnecessary and expensive appendage." As for his last country wife who was about to give birth to their third child, Simpson wrote, "Pray keep an eye on the commodity and if she bring forth anything in the proper time and of the right colour let them be taken care of but if any thing be amiss let the whole be bundled about their business ..."

As Simpson's wealth and prestige grew, he decided that he required a British wife, someone more socially acceptable to a man of his prominence. At forty-three, he went to England to find a mate and soon targeted his eighteen-year-old cousin, Frances Ramsay. The two married, and Simpson brought his wide-eyed bride back to settle in a large house at Lower Fort Garry on the Red River. Though she attempted to make the best of her situation, her genteel upbringing, combined with her husband's constraints, isolated her in the mixed-blood settlement. Moreover, evidence of her husband's amorous exploits was all around. Though Simpson attempted to keep his former lechery secret from Frances, she was quite aware of it. She confessed to a friend that she "was always terrified to look around her, in case of seeing something disagreeable."

FRANCES ANNE HOPKINS / NATIONAL ARCHIVES OF CANADA / C-002771

FROM MONTRÉAL TO THE GREAT LAKES, FRANCES SIMPSON WOULD HAVE TRAVELLED IN A *CANOT DU MAÎTRE*, SUCH AS THIS ONE IN WHICH ARTIST FRANCES ANNE HOPKINS PORTRAYED HERSELF.

After a difficult pregnancy, the death of a young child and declining health, Frances returned to England in 1833, where she stayed for the next five years. To entice her back to Canada, Simpson bought Alexander Mackenzie's mansion near Montréal and reinvented himself as an English gentleman, complete with a bevy of menservants. There, with Frances by his side, he enthusiastically engaged in the Montreal social scene, particularly after Queen Victoria knighted him in 1838.

Despite failing vision and declining health, perhaps due to syphilis, the desire to travel never left him, and he continued to move frenetically around his empire. When this no longer seemed challenging enough, at the age of fifty-six, Simpson sped around the world in only nineteen months, visiting many countries where he was treated as a virtual head of state. Simpson died in 1860, just days after entertaining the visiting Prince of Wales in Montréal. His energy and philosophy of parsimony had staved off his company's inexorable decline, but by the time of Simpson's death it was clear that there would be little future in continuing to harvest beaver pelts.

During the first half of the nineteenth century, British and American land claims in the western part of the continent were far from settled. After 1821, the Hudson's Bay Company held most of what is now British Columbia, but the Americans had territorial aspirations aimed at the vast Pacific territory. Furthermore, both the British and Americans had claimed the "Oregon country", comprising many of what are now the states of the Pacific Northwest. While the Hudson's Bay Company had a smattering of unprofitable trading posts in the region, the Americans contended that the area fell under its natural sphere of influence. In 1818, the two countries agreed to share the region, but each plotted to strengthen its claims. After the Hudson's Bay Company's amalgamation in 1821, the HBC Committee directed George Simpson to strengthen his hold on the Oregon territory, if only to arrest northward expansion from the Manifest Destiny driven Americans. In 1824, Simpson sent one of his most capable men, Dr. John McLoughlin, to govern the region.

McLoughlin, born in Rivière du Loup in 1784, belonged to the tight-knit Québec Fraser clan. His grandfather, Malcolm Fraser, had come to Canada in 1759 with General Wolfe and had fought on the Plains of Abraham. At eighteen, John had already passed his medical apprenticeship, and his future seemed bright. Fate intervened, however, when a drunken British officer insulted the honour of John's girlfriend, and the powerful young six-foot-four doctor, in a blaze of ire, tossed the officer into a mud puddle. Such an egregious act against His Majesty's uniform would not go unpunished, so McLoughlin chose to flee. His influential uncle, Dr. Simon Fraser, pulled a few strings with Simon McTavish and McLoughlin was hired by the North West Company. Young John was sent west a few days later.

Over the next few years, McLoughlin became a partner with the North West Company, known for his leadership abilities, intellect and fairness. He led a majority of wintering partners in the vote to join the Hudson's Bay Company, and he was an important spokesman and negotiator and when the two companies amalgamated. By the time George Simpson sent him to oversee the Oregon territory, McLoughlin had already distinguished himself in a career of more than two decades.

On the Columbia, McLoughlin quickly established his authority, planning and building Fort Vancouver on the north shore of the Columbia River, about 160 kilometres inland. Since the Oregon country was geographically isolated by the Rocky Mountains from the rest of HBC territory, George Simpson seldom visited, and McLoughlin enjoyed almost complete autonomy. Acting as a benevolent and enlightened lord of his wilderness fiefdom, McLoughlin took the initiative to diversify his operations far beyond merely collecting furs. He established farming, fishing and logging operations. He also set up sawmills and flourmills and cultivated profitable markets for his products. His operations at the fort became models of precision and discipline.

Contributing to McLoughlin's success was his egalitarian treatment of all the peoples in the region. Whether they were British, Chinook, French-Canadian, Hawaiian or American, all were treated equally. He welcomed them to the fort and treated them with respect and even-handedness, and in return, they brought him their business. McLoughlin could, however, be severe when he felt it was warranted. When Clallam warriors murdered Alexander MacKenzie, an HBC clerk, McLoughlin sent out a team of gunmen to exact revenge and teach the perpetrators a lesson. In the skirmishes that followed, his men killed twenty-three warriors, effectively ending the threat. Such occurrences were rare, however, and McLoughlin generally enjoyed enormous status among the Native peoples of the Northwest, becoming known affectionately as the "White-Headed Eagle," a reference to his mane of prematurely white hair and his great wisdom.

As difficult as it was to extract praise from George Simpson, the HBC Governor could hardly help but be impressed. On a rare five-month visit in 1828, Simpson inspected every aspect of McLoughlin's operations and concluded that "never did a change of system and a change of management, produce such obvious advantages in any part of the Indian country, as those which the present state of this Establishment in particular, and of the Columbia Department as a whole, at this moment exhibits." Simpson had reason to be pleased. All fur rivals were bankrupted, the mountain men had retreated, and the company was producing large profits in the region for the first time.

Nevertheless, over the years, despite the HBC's "scorched earth" policy toward rival fur traders, the word of the bounty of the Oregon country trickled out and would-be settlers began to arrive by the cartload from the rapidly growing United States. According to HBC edict, McLoughlin was supposed to drive them away and continue to hold a ruthless monopoly over the territory. Settlement was to be discouraged at all costs. McLoughlin, however, refused to turn anyone away from the fort and invariably lent a helping hand to anyone who needed it. At first, he absorbed many potential settlers into the ranks of the fort's servants, but eventually wagonloads of incomers threatened to overwhelm the region. McLoughlin extended credit to them and helped them obtain supplies, treating them as customers, not enemies. In so doing, he became the acknowledged *pater familias* to settlers of the area, resembling something like a Lord Selkirk of Oregon. He established more gristmills, sawmills, farms and fisheries, employing even more incomers, offered advice on establishing communities, acted as arbiter in disputes, meted out justice as required, and secured vital provisions for his people.

Some speculate that McLoughlin knew the shaky British claim to the Oregon territory might eventually crumble and that by helping settlers he was actually safeguarding the interests of the Hudson's Bay Company. Only by fostering goodwill in the region would the company be allowed to stay after the Americans took over. Whatever his motives, it is clear that McLoughlin came to think of himself as the founder of a civilized society based on the Christian principles of charity, hard work, and mutual aid. While always loyal to the company, he viewed his constituency as much broader than the profit-oriented HBC committee. In the end, then, it was almost inevitable that he would attract the scorn of George Simpson, who saw him as a rival, more interested in attracting a personal following than in adhering to company directives. The two began to lock horns over a variety of issues, and McLoughlin became increasingly incensed by Simpson's uninformed interference from afar. In 1841, Simpson overrode McLoughlin's judgement and ordered him to shut down and pack up the network of profitable trading posts he had established in the northern section of his region. Instead, the new trade would be conducted from steamboats. McLoughlin was furious but powerless to refuse.

Relations between the two men became even more bitter when McLoughlin's son and namesake was murdered at a company post in Russian Alaska, ostensibly in a fight with a drunken bay man. Simpson looked into the matter only superficially and then flippantly declared it "justifiable homicide". Devastated, McLoughlin appealed repeatedly to Simpson to initiate a proper inquiry, but Simpson refused. McLoughlin then took the case to London, where several members of the governing committee expressed sympathy. Ultimately, though, they stood behind their governor.

In 1843, the thousands of settlers in the Oregon territory voted to set up their own provisional government, independent of McLoughlin's authority.

CHARLES F. COMFORT / HUDSON'S BAY COMPANY ARHCIVES / P-405

AGAINST COMPANY ORDERS, JOHN MCLOUGHLIN WELCOMES AMERICAN METHODIST MISSIONARY JASON LEE.

C.W. JEFFREYS / NATIONAL ARCHIVES OF CANADA / C-069362

JOHN MCLOUGHLIN

Soon after, many more thousands of settlers streamed in. It was clear that McLoughlin's time as undisputed Caesar of his domain had come to an end. The following year, Simpson shrewdly demoted him, which had the desired effect: McLoughlin indignantly resigned and retired to his Oregon home.

In 1846, Great Britain, fraught with pressing foreign policy problems at home, had little interest in the Oregon territory and negotiated a swift settlement with the United States to draw a boundary at the 49th parallel. The Hudson's Bay Company would retain its rights north of the line as well as on Vancouver Island, but the vast, productive Oregon territory that McLoughlin had worked so hard to develop for settlement reverted to the United States.

On the American side of the border, McLoughlin's worth was soon better appreciated. Known today as "the Father of Oregon", he had a profound effect on establishing the international borders and his decency, active assistance and benevolent paternalism ultimately laid out the foundation for western U.S. settlement. With the region full of American settlers, the United States had an undeniably powerful claim to the Oregon territory, which it exercised during ensuing negotiations with Great Britain.

While McLoughlin was for many years the uncrowned sovereign of the Oregon territory, another Scot, James Douglas, was his closest consort and most able administrator. Douglas would eventually leave Fort Vancouver to oversee British Columbia's rapid transmutation from remote HBC fur territory to British Crown Colony and finally to Canadian province. His contributions to the developing Pacific region would earn him the title of the "Father of British Columbia".

James Douglas was born out of wedlock in the West Indies in 1803. His father, John Douglas, was a successful Glasgow sugar plantation owner, his mother a Creole woman, the Barbados equivalent of a country wife. The couple produced James and his two brothers before John Douglas abandoned his family in 1809 to return to Scotland. He soon married and began a new family, but to his credit, he always supported his first three sons, and when James was nine, his father sent him and his brothers to be educated in Lanark, Scotland. There, James received a solid education, learning the writing and accounting skills that would later serve him in the fur trade.

At sixteen, he was employed by the North West Company, which had been actively recruiting Scots. Amalgamation took place shortly after, and the HBC sent the young clerk to the New Caledonia trading post of Fort St. James in what is now central British Columbia. He served with distinction for many years, but circumstances and his temper intervened in 1830.

Despite his early Caribbean upbringing, Douglas was a typical Scot – ambitious, diligent, industrious, pragmatic and disciplined. Although very formal, often appearing stiff and sometimes pompous, he was not above rolling up his sleeves to do difficult or unpleasant jobs. His frugality bordered on stinginess, and he proved himself to be a skilled manager of money and resources. In his "Character Book", George Simpson described him as "a stout, powerful, active man of good conduct and respectable abilities", but also one who could become "furiously violent when aroused".

NATIONAL ARCHIVES OF CANADA / C-014554

SIR JAMES DOUGLAS

This side of his temperament came through in an incident involving the local Dakelh or Carrier people who inhabited what is now central British Columbia. Two Carrier men had murdered a pair of bay men in nearby Fort George in 1824. When one of the murderers showed up near Fort St. James four years later, young Douglas and two other employees took it upon themselves to bring him to justice. They searched the area and finally found him hiding in the lodge of the local clan leader, Qua, who was absent at the time. As they tried to detain him, the fugitive stabbed Douglas with an arrow. In a blaze of fury, the bay men dragged him from the lodge and brutally killed him.

When Qua heard what had happened, he was livid, for tradition protected anyone who sought refuge in the chief's lodge. He gathered a party of warriors, stormed Fort St. James and soon had Douglas splayed on a table with a knife at his throat.

Here, versions of the story diverge. The "official" version is that Douglas' mixed-blood wife, Amelia, saved him by tossing gifts from a balcony and pleading for his life. The Carrier version says that it was Qua's grandsons who convinced him to let Douglas go, reminding him that killing was the job of the warrior chief and that murder would tarnish his reputation as clan leader. The result either way was that Douglas was immediately shipped out to Fort Vancouver, to keep him from further trouble. And there he swiftly became John McLoughlin's right hand man.

In 1842, George Simpson was fully aware that the Hudson's Bay Company would probably lose the Oregon territory to the United States. As a strategic move, he sent James Douglas to survey the southern tip of Vancouver Island and establish a trading post so that the company could claim "prior ownership" in any future border negotiations. Douglas built the fort on a spot he considered to be "a perfect Eden" and eventually named it Fort Victoria after the queen.

Simpson's pre-emptive strategy worked. Negotiations with the United States in 1846 had resulted in a division of the continent at the forty-ninth parallel, with the exception of Vancouver Island, which dipped well below. The HBC's "prior ownership" was recognized for the time being, but sovereignty was certainly not permanently secure. An influx of American settlers could result in annexation by the United States, just as had happened in the Oregon territory. The Crown and James Douglas had no intention of letting Vancouver Island and the rest of the Pacific region north of '49 go by default to land-hungry Americans.

In 1849, Vancouver Island became an official Crown colony and was handed over to the Hudson's Bay Company, the only body with an established

James Douglas, right, examines the plans as Fort Victoria rises behind him.

Robert John Banks / BC Archives / PDP-792

presence able to administer the vast land mass. The company's job was to oversee orderly colonization for several years so that Britain could secure its claim. Britain also sent Richard Blanshard to help govern the new island colony. By this time, however, James Douglas had been the undisputed ruler of the island for most of a decade, and he had no inclination to share power. Douglas made sure the young governor had nothing – no proper residence, no money, no staff and no real duties. Blanshard resigned in exasperation and headed back to England.

Having no other viable option, the Crown appointed Douglas as governor, thus merging the fur trade and the power of the Crown into one autocratic position, despite the obvious conflict of interest. Douglas began to receive two large pay cheques and with his wealth grew his haughtiness. Joseph Watt, an Oregon immigrant, commented, "Douglas would step around in a way as much as to say: 'you are not as good as I am, I don't belong to your class.'" His love of titles and position soon prompted him to sign documents as, "His Excellency, James Douglas, Governor of Vancouver Island and its Dependencies, Commander-in-Chief and Vice-Admiral of the same." Unlike McLoughlin, Douglas was not beloved by his followers.

Despite his social airs, Douglas was an able administrator. Britain demanded that some sort of representative assembly be set up on the island, but the dictatorial Douglas largely ignored such demands and went about the business of developing a social and economic infrastructure. He was opposed to universal male suffrage and felt that only the "ruling classes" were qualified to govern. Since he was doing his job well, and perhaps in part due to the isolation of the island, Britain did not press Douglas with any real conviction.

When coal was discovered on the northwest coast, near modern Prince Rupert, Douglas recruited hundreds of Scottish miners and sent them to extract coal from the region, as well as from the Queen Charlotte Islands. The coal veins turned out to be disappointing, however, and the operations were soon dismantled. Most of the miners stayed in the Pacific region and soon found work when a giant coalfield was discovered near Nanaimo. The mine operated profitably for the next hundred years and gave Scottish mining families an economic foothold on the island.

Douglas continued to administer his colony and run the fur trade until 1858, when gold was discovered on the banks of the Fraser River. Soon, thirty thousand mostly American miners from the waning California rush were tramping through the streets of tiny Victoria on their way to the fields of the vast mainland interior region. The town was transformed overnight from a quiet colonial backwater to a vibrant, rambunctious, chaotic saloon town. Within weeks, it became a sort of muddy Dodge City of the Pacific. Douglas complained that Victoria had far too many "merchants, transients and saloons and a considerable

F. WHYMPER / BRITISH COLUMBIA ARCHIVES / PDP00607

FORT YALE ON THE FRASER RIVER

shortage of accommodation, water, women and good roads."

Nor were the lessons of the Oregon territory wasted on Douglas. He knew that the Americans could jeopardize British claims to the region by settling in large numbers and then demanding political autonomy, and he acted resolutely to stop this from occurring. He issued a proclamation stating that the gold fields were British territory and that all miners had to purchase licenses from Victoria. Even though he had no formal authority on the Pacific mainland, he assumed it and hired HBC constables to enforce the law. He also decreed that all supplies had to be bought from Fort Victoria, Fort Langley or from the decks of HBC ships. Thus, he was able to establish British and HBC control over a vast, unruly region.

With American miners pouring into the mainland, it became clear to Great Britain that a new colony had to be established in an effort to prevent an erosion of sovereignty, and who better to govern it than the imperious James

Douglas? By this time, British officials were not vehement about representative government, as the miners were "so wild, so miscellaneous, and perhaps so transitory" that the authoritarianism of the rigid Scot seemed suddenly desirable. A second Crown colony was declared on the mainland and named British Columbia, with New Westminster as its capital. James Douglas became absolute ruler of both colonies, although he was forced to give up his HBC position of chief factor.

Douglas threw his energies into maintaining law and order and building bridges, schools, roads and lighthouses for the two colonies, although he seldom set foot on the mainland. By 1860, a bigger and even more lucrative gold rush took hold in Barkerville, in central British Columbia. Douglas decreed the construction of an enormously difficult and expensive road, cut out of dense forests and solid rock, into the previously impassable interior to facilitate the movement of people and supplies and to open up the wild region to trade. Barkerville, with its several thousand inhabitants, became the biggest city north of San Francisco and west of Chicago.

During his entire time as governor, Douglas took every possible step to ensure that miners eventually either left the colonies or submitted willingly to British authority. Many chose the latter, staying and settling in the interior, on the lower mainland or on the island, and the population of the province swelled, with more colonists arriving all the time. By 1863, however, the height of the gold rush was past, and it was clear that Douglas' brand of ruling by proclamation was *passé*. While he had deftly kept the entire Pacific region firmly British, times were changing and pressures were mounting from all sides to establish a representative assembly. Douglas was ordered to arrange an election. Peeved at the notion of placing power into the hands of rabble and giving up his unquestioned authority, Douglas resigned in a sulk. He remained irked even after the British granted him a knighthood.

In 1866, the two colonies were fused into one. Shortly after, John Tod visited the retired Douglas at his estate near Victoria. In a letter to a friend, Tod wrote of Douglas: "You probably think me unjustly severe on our old friend, but it is with sorrow I say it, that to all those who have known him for years, he has appeared cold, crafty and selfish; and justly merits the reward he now reaps of isolation and desertion of all who have know him from early times." The "Father of British Columbia" died in 1877, inflexible and bitter to the end.

In addition to helping define Canada's southern and western borders, Scottish fur traders also charted much of the north. By far the most well known arctic explorer of the era was Orkneyman John Rae.

Born in 1813 not far from Stromness, Rae was well educated, both in a formal sense – after a solid public education in Orkney, he studied medicine in Edinburgh – and informally, becoming a skilled climber and sailor during his youth. On graduation from university, he joined the Hudson's Bay Company and was posted initially to Moose Factory at the bottom of James Bay. Ever the student, he quickly learned both the fundamentals of the fur trade and also the wilderness skills of the local Cree population.

Rae appears to have been remarkable in many ways. Ken McGoogan, author of *Fatal Passage*, an award-winning biography of Rae, writes: "Physically almost superhuman, Rae became legendary as a snowshoe walker; once, returning from a house call, he covered 166 kilometres in two days. In 1844, HBC Governor George Simpson appointed Rae to complete the geographical survey of the Arctic coast of North America – part of the centuries-old quest for the Northwest Passage. That winter, to learn surveying techniques, Rae snowshoed from Red River (Winnipeg) to Sault Ste. Marie, covering nearly 2,000 kilometres in two months."

Over the next decade, the young doctor charted Canada's northern coast, served as second-in-command to Sir John Richardson in a search party for the missing Franklin expedition (comprised of two ill-fated British ships, last been seen in the summer of 1845, sent on a mission to explore the Arctic), led another search in 1851 and finally, in 1854, learned the final fate of Franklin's party – all had died and the last survivors had resorted to cannibalism. At the same time, Rae continued charting the north coast, finally proving that the final link in the Northwest Passage, now called Rae Strait, was impassable for the ships of the day because of ice.

KEITH ALLARDYCE / STROMNESS MUSEUM

DR. JOHN RAE

During all this time, Rae lived as the Inuit had for millennia, wintering primarily in igloos and travelling with dog sleds. When his news of the fate of Franklin reached London, he was met with disbelief and was ostracized. Lady Jane Franklin, Captain John's Franklin's widow, led a fierce campaign to discredit him that included the likes of novelist Charles Dickens, who, as McGoogan writes, "castigated him for accepting the 'Eskimo savages' as credible witnesses."

Rae revolutionized Arctic travel and solved two great mysteries of the nineteenth century, the fate of the Franklin expedition and the final link in the Northwest Passage. Yet Rae was the only major

British explorer never to be knighted. He died in London in 1893 and is buried in St. Margaret's Cathedral in Kirkwall, the capital of Orkney.

By the time George Simpson died in 1860, the fur trade as a major industry was in steep decline. Silk hats had supplanted those of beaver, and demand for North American pelts had all but dried up. Through his constant cost cutting measures, Simpson had managed to keep the industry alive, but at his death, the writing for the fur trade was on the wall. The timing was nearly perfect, for within a decade, Canada would be confederated and soon after, would begin to dream of a nation from sea to sea.

The leaders of the new country, confederated in 1867, knew they must settle the vast HBC lands or ultimately forfeit them to the Americans. When the Hudson's Bay Company's hegemony was gone, the government knew it had no choice but to step in and fill the vacuum. As early as 1865, John A. Macdonald wrote, "I would be willing, personally, to leave the whole [HBC] country a wilderness for the next half century, but I fear if Englishmen do not go there, Yankees will." In 1870, Canada purchased the vast territory for three hundred thousand pounds, making the new country transcontinental in one bold stroke.

The fur trade, run by Scots, was a vital step in Canada's nation-building process for three critical reasons. First, the trade was Canada's first large-scale enterprise, to which most other commerce was related. Shipping, manufacturing, banking, and merchandizing all initially revolved around the fur trade or evolved from it. The trade, in essence, served as Canada's commercial foundation upon which other industries were built and from which they evolved. Second, the fur trade opened up the vast hinterland of the north and west. Fur traders mapped and developed an impressive transportation matrix and network of trading posts throughout the daunting wilderness, which ultimately served as the blueprint for settlement. When Canada was ready to assume stewardship of the land, much of the difficult legwork had already been done. Trading posts often evolved into towns, as settlers built on the organizational and transportation structures developed by fur traders. Third, fur traders fiercely guarded their territorial monopolies, and this in the end meant that the northern half of North America was kept in British hands. Because of the crafty and determined territorialism of the fur traders, the seemingly unstoppable American aspiration of Manifest Destiny was never able to take hold. In a very real sense, Canadians owe their very sovereignty and independent culture to a small group of profit-driven, predominantly Scottish fur traders.

It was during the fur trade that Canada took on its character resembling a Scotland of North America. The Scots instinctively understood the importance of resisting a grand imperial power to the south, and Scottish fur traders carried on this tradition in British North America for two hundred years, ostensibly to protect their profits but also to protect their autonomy. Moreover, while individual Scots, such as Simon McTavish, Alexander Mackenzie, Lord Selkirk and George Simpson, as we have seen, each made an enormous mark on Canada's development at a critical historical juncture, the collective influence of Scottish fur traders also made a profound and indelible imprint on Canadian culture.

It has often been said that colonial nations take on the character of their earliest active immigrant populations – hence, Australia's somewhat renegade national character might be said to stem from its origins as a penal colony, while the zealous and sometimes dogmatic nature of many Americans could be the result of the United States' origin as a haven for Puritans. This theory might explain the moderate, accommodating and pragmatic Canadian temperament, since for two centuries the fur trade, run almost entirely by Scots, was Canada's only national enterprise. And though we have seen that individual Scots exercised enormous authority – appeared to enjoy it – as a group they were deferent and law-abiding, which might also account for Canadians' general tendency to defer to authority, to emphasize collective interests rather than individual pursuits, and to place faith in rules. This was, after all, the culture of the Scottish fur traders, all of whom were company men, as opposed to the rugged, individualistic settlers of the United States.

Aside from such ruminations, it is perfectly safe to say that the Scottish fur traders, to an incalculable extent, both individually and collectively, laid out much of the foundation for Western Canada. When the fur trade had run its course, the Scots, already used to positions of leadership and prominence, moved into other areas of endeavour in Canadian society, where they not only continued to excel but to dominate.

Shaping the Political Landscape

For centuries the Scots suffered political oppression under the English. Despite their relatively higher collective level of education, and despite the Scottish Enlightenment of the eighteenth century, which produced some of Europe's most radical and progressive political ideas of the time, Scotland lived under the political yoke of its much larger and commercially more powerful neighbour to the south.

SEAFORTH HIGHLANDERS KILT, MACKENZIE OF KINTAIL TARTAN, COURTESY OF HARRY MARDON / SPORRAN, KILT HOSE, SHOES AND BELT COURTESY OF THE SCOTTISH CROFT / SYDNEY, BC

When Scots arrived in British North America, however, they found themselves in a much different situation. For the first time, they had the opportunity not only to become politically active but also to play a major role in shaping the political landscape of their new country. Primed with impressive educations and a Scottish tradition of civic responsibility, politically articulate Scots made an impact in Canada from the outset of their arrival. And their achievements were impressive indeed. It is no exaggeration to say that the Scots were primarily responsible for structuring the Canada we know today. The unified, transcontinental federation of provinces that recognizes and respects cultural and regional differences, while maintaining a strong central administration, is largely a Scottish creation. Canada's political culture, which leans towards social democratic values and equality of opportunity, while simultaneously promoting free enterprise, also bears the ineffaceable stamp of the Scots. In terms of the actual work of nation building, Scots politicians proved themselves to be bold, innovative and indefatigable architects.

Because of the sheer number of Scots who excelled at politics in Canada and for the purposes of this chapter, we must be highly selective. Indeed the Scots are the single most over-represented group of politicians in our nation's history, having held every level of office far out of proportion to their actual numbers. We must therefore limit our discussion to only those Scots who contributed to building the Canadian federation, excluding all but the most prominent of the many accomplishments of provincial and municipal politicians. We will highlight only the most notable Scots, whose actions as governors, political reformers, Fathers of Confederation and prime ministers created the political structure of Canada. Yet even this brief survey of Scots politicians in Canada reveals their truly astonishing pre-eminence and dominance.

The political rise of the Scots came as soon as the British conquered New France. In 1759, when the victorious General Wolfe died on the Plains of

Abraham, his Scottish second-in-command, James Murray, took charge. He and his sick and starving soldiers, many of them also Scots, held the city of Québec all winter. There, half of them died; the remaining forces were nearly defeated by French General François Gaston, duc de Lévis and his army from Montréal. In the spring of 1760, however, British reinforcements arrived, the French retreated, and Murray and his remaining men were saved.

Half a continent changed hands when the French gave up New France, and British North America was born. Aware that he would not be popular under the circumstances, Murray imposed martial law. Three years later, he was sworn in as Governor of Québec, overseeing 65,000 French Canadians and a handful of newly-arrived British merchants, most of whom were seeking fur trade profits from bases in Montréal.

James Murray was, on the surface, a contradictory figure. He was born in 1712 into an aristocratic Scottish Lowland family and entered the British military while still a teenager. Though small in stature, his toughness and courage soon distinguished him, and his career evolved in a series of successful campaigns and military honours, though not without cost. At his death in 1794, more than a few musket balls were extracted from his body prior to embalming. In short, he was considered to be one of the best military officers of his generation.

Yet this quintessential military man was also fair and compassionate. A contemporary commented, "As a soldier he stood foremost in the army, and had won his way by his own merit and by his own good sword, owing nothing to influence. As a genuine Christian officer, he was esteemed by all good men, and ever distinguished for his humanity and readiness to relieve the oppressed." This sympathetic nature and even-handed manner became his enduring legacy to Québec and shaped the future of Canada at a critical juncture in its history.

His task after the Conquest was a difficult one. He found himself in charge of a proud and patriotic population with its own unique history and culture. Unfortunately, the French Canadians were also poverty stricken and ill-educated, for their French rulers had exploited and mismanaged the colony for years. Moreover, the whole French population had been subjugated by force of arms and were apprehensive about what British rule would mean. At the same time, the small band of English-speaking merchants in Montréal had every expectation that they would be allowed to benefit fully from the spoils of conquest. It was Murray's job to rebuild a workable government from this smouldering and potentially volatile social wreckage.

The Royal Proclamation of 1763 was intended to open the doors for British immigration into British North America and to forcibly assimilate the French inhabitants by erasing their institutions. It specified that the colony would henceforth institute British law, do away with Québec's feudalistic land ownership system, recognize only the Protestant faith, organize an all-British ruling assembly, and conduct its affairs in English only. Montréal's small enclave of English merchants could not have been happier; they were fully prepared that, though numbering only about 200, they would rule the vast French majority.

Murray, however, would have none of it. He had come to admire the French Canadians and refused to enforce a system that was patently unfair. He ignored the Royal Proclamation and delayed calling an assembly. He also instigated a French court, which preserved French law and social customs, and worked with the Catholic clergy, defending its role as an important component of Québec's social fabric.

Many historians have surmised that it was James Murray's Scottish sensibilities that impelled him to champion the French Canadians and their way of life. As a Scot, he could empathize with a proud culture whose rights were about to be trampled under the political and economic boots of Great Britain. Moreover, in many ways Scottish laws and intellectual traditions resembled those of France far more than those of England. This gave Murray an instinctive understanding of and sympathy for the French Canadians. He wrote to London:

> … nothing will satisfy the licentious fanatics trading here but the expulsion of the Canadians who are perhaps the bravest and the best race upon the globe, a race, who could they be indulged with a few privileges which the laws of England deny to Roman Catholics at home, would soon get the better of every national antipathy to their conquerors and become the most faithful and most useful set of men in this American empire. Unless Canadians are admitted on juries and are allowed judges and lawyers who understand their language, his majesty will lose the greatest part of this valuable people.

Not surprisingly, the British merchants in Montréal were furious over Murray's obvious siding with the French against their interests. Led by Thomas Walker, an Englishman who had come to Montréal from Boston, they lobbied to have Murray fired as governor. In 1766, London recalled the general and, in a parliamentary inquiry, grilled him on his loyalty to Britain. Though he articulated his position and was quickly exonerated, he would never return to Canada. He continued to serve with impressive distinction throughout the Empire until his death in 1794.

However, to the disbelief of the Montréal merchants, Murray's replacement, Governor Guy Carleton, agreed with Murray and continued to implement reforms that recognized French rights. In 1774, the Quebec Act formally returned and entrenched most of the rights and institutions the French had enjoyed before the Conquest.

Murray is a case of the right man at the right time in history. His Scottish aversion to political oppression, his concept of plurality and fairness, and his courage to follow the dictates of his own conscience resulted in the preservation of French Canada's linguistic and cultural distinctiveness. At a key point in the nation's development, he chose an enlightened path that established French Canadians not as a conquered people but as legitimate and worthy British citizens. It was a critical step towards recognizing French Canadians as partners in nation building.

During Governor Guy Carlton's tenure, the American Revolution broke out, and British North America found itself in a bitter struggle with the thirteen American colonies. Throughout the dozen years following the Revolution, approximately 50,000 Loyalists poured into British North America, about half settling in the Maritime colonies, and the other half choosing "Canada", a huge territory that would one day become Ontario and Québec. Before long, this new influx of English settlers, uncomfortable with French traditions, began to demand institutions and government that more closely resembled Great Britain's. Britain responded with the Constitutional Act of 1791, which carved the territory into two colonies, English Upper Canada (which eventually became Ontario) and French Lower Canada (which eventually became Québec). By cleaving the colonies along cultural and linguistic lines, Britain ruled out any possibility of ever assimilating the French. It also assured itself that cultural and linguistic tensions between English and French would be a perpetual issue. At the same time, it placated not only the French but also the English, each group settling into a recognizable society with familiar laws.

The governor essentially ruled all of British North America, and a lieutenant governor administered each of the colonies. Each colony also had an appointed council and an elected assembly comprised of male landowners. In practice, this political structure was an oligarchy ruled by conservative elites, with little resemblance to a true democracy.

However, under this arrangement, the Scots held inordinate influence, not only in the Maritime colonies and Upper Canada, but in Lower Canada as well, where the British continued for the most part to rule the French. Historian A. Margaret MacLaren Evans writes:

> ...in the young colonies of the late eighteenth century and the first years of the nineteenth century, Scots had had little reason to be political reformers since they practically controlled the governments: for example, John Fraser, William Grant, Hugh Finlay, James McGill, John Richardson, John Young, James Stuart, in the councils of Lower Canada; and John Munro, Robert Hamilton, Alexander Grant, John McGill, Thomas Scott, William Dickson, James Crooks in those in Upper Canada. In fact, in the latter province around the turn of the century, Scots so predominated in the government that it was called 'the Scotch faction' or 'the clan.'

The War of 1812, fought against the United States, only further entrenched the stiff conservatism of the ruling class. Any suggestion of political reform towards a more responsible, democratic form of government was immediately condemned as "Yankee republicanism." In Upper Canada, the group of ruling elites who tightly controlled the government councils, senior bureaucratic positions and courts became known disparagingly by reform-minded individuals as "the Family Compact." In Lower Canada and the Maritimes, the situation was much the same. The exclusiveness of these ruling groups resulted in strong reactions and violent reform movements that marked the next phase of Canada's political development.

It is interesting to note that the Scots can almost never be pigeonholed, and this was certainly the case during the reform movement. Scots led the causes of Tory conservatism and radical reformism with equal zeal. It seems that the only generalization one can make about them is that they seemed invariably to emerge as leaders wherever they went and in whatever cause they chose to espouse.

The leader of the Family Compact was a stodgy, dour Scot named John Strachan, who powerfully reigned in the executive and legislative councils of Upper Canada. Strachan had immigrated to British North America from Aberdeen in 1799 and had become an Anglican priest shortly after. He and his followers held land grants in Upper Canada in an iron grip, refusing to allow land to those who did not adhere to their values and placing huge tracts of land in idle crown and clergy reserves. This infuriated many would-be settlers.

The first strong voice for reform came from an energetic Scottish writer, Robert Fleming Gourlay, who had come from Edinburgh in 1817 hoping to secure land in Upper Canada to help settle other Scots. As a writing project,

Gourlay distributed questionnaires to Upper Canadians asking what factors they thought retarded the progress of the colony. The questionnaires became a catalyst for much popular criticism, and the irate Family Compact, branding Gourlay a radical, refused to grant him any land.

Gourlay was at first shocked and then incensed. He wrote newspaper articles criticizing the unopposed authoritarian power of the rigid oligarchy. The Family Compact in turn slapped him with two lawsuits for libel. When these proved ineffective, they charged him with sedition and, with the help of judges they controlled, banished him from Upper Canada in 1819.

The Family Compact's pompous and condescending attitude was summed up perfectly in a letter written by John Strachan: "A character like Mr. Gourlay in a quiet colony like this where there is little or no spirit of inquiry and very little knowledge may do much harm and notwithstanding the check he has received he has done harm by exciting uneasiness and irritation and exciting unreasonable hopes." Having dealt with the troublemaker, the Compact's exclusive rule continued uncontested for years afterward.

It would eventually meet its match, however, in the form of an acid-tongued little firebrand from Dundee, Scotland. William Lyon Mackenzie's grandfather had fought at Culloden and had been persecuted by the English, and young William's father, a weaver, had died shortly after he was born, forcing the family to live in poverty afterwards. His family's circumstances as well as his diminutive stature – he was just five feet tall – likely contributed to his self-perception as an underdog. Even as a boy, he displayed a fiery temper and a contrary nature; essentially he began life with a chip on his shoulder, and it stayed with him for the rest of his days.

As a young man in Scotland, Mackenzie launched a general store, but it soon went bankrupt in the wake of the Napoleonic Wars. He then wandered around France for several months, soaking up revolutionary ideas and working at low-paying, temporary jobs. At the age of twenty-five, he emigrated to Upper Canada and it was there that he found a legitimate way to channel his rebellious energies. In 1824 he founded the reformist newspaper, the *Colonial Advocate*, and began to write inflammatory editorials against the Family Compact. With no training, Mackenzie had a remarkable ability for political hyperbole and muckraking, and he wielded his pen with ever increasing levels of venomous criticism.

At first the Family Compact ignored the blazing little Scot, but as his popularity grew, a group of Tories was sent to smash his printing presses and threaten him. Of course, this only made Mackenzie more popular, and when a court awarded him damages to replace his presses, he stepped up his vitriolic

NATIONAL ARCHIVES OF CANADA / C-024937

WILLIAM LYON MACKENZIE

campaign. He harangued against the appointed council that continuously blocked the initiatives of the elected assembly, which consisted of a majority of reformers. He wrote that the council was, "The most extraordinary collection of sturdy beggars, parsons, priests, pensioners, army people, navy people, placemen, bank directors, and stock and land jobbers ever established to act as a paltry screen to a rotten government. They cost the country about £40,000 a year and the good laws by which it might benefit, they tomahawk."

Though Mackenzie's blistering speeches and editorials offended many in Upper Canada, his popularity grew. He won election to the Assembly in 1828, but the fed-up Tories expelled him in 1831 on the grounds that he was "unsuitable" for office. Re-elected by the voters of York, he was expelled again. In fact, Mackenzie was expelled no less than five times, and each time he was re-elected by his constituents. In 1834, when the town of York became the city of Toronto, Mackenzie was elected its first mayor.

A year later, Mackenzie sent a 500-page document, the *Seventh Report on Grievances,* to London, lambasting the government in Upper Canada and demanding a more democratic system. The exasperated Tories did not know what to do about the relentless troublemaker. Lieutenant Governor Sir Francis Bond Head met with him in an attempt to placate him but came away rattled. Head wrote, "Afraid to look me in the face, he sat, with his feet not reaching the ground, and with his countenance averted from me ... with the eccentricity, the volubility, and indeed the appearance of a madman, the tiny creature raved in all directions about grievances ..."

In the 1836 elections, Head's active campaigning influenced the vote, resulting in a Tory win in the Assembly. Watching his reform movement slipping away, Mackenzie wrote, "Ye false Canadians! Tories! Pensioners! Churchmen! Spies! Informers! Brokers! Gamblers! Parasites, and Knaves of every caste and description, allow me to congratulate you! You may plunder and rob with impunity – your feet are on the people's necks ..." He now believed that the only way to achieve reform was through revolution, just as the Americans had done.

Meanwhile, a similar reform movement was taking place in Lower Canada, revolving around leader Louis-Joseph Papineau and his French Patriotes, who demanded many of the same reforms as Mackenzie. The Lower Canadian version of the Family Compact was the Chateau Clique, named for the excessive amount of time that members spent socializing at the governor's chateau. Another powerful group was the anglophone business elites, a majority of whom were Scots, who let it be known that they would not tolerate any form of insurrection in Lower Canada. Speaking before a crowd of 4,000 in Montréal, Peter McGill, the fabulously wealthy Scottish president of the Bank of Montreal, said of the Patriotes, "We must admit their constitutional right to meet and discuss ... and to petition and remonstrate ... if they feel themselves aggrieved, but any and all of them who overstep the bounds prescribed by the laws in doing so, who outrage the feelings of loyal and well disposed peaceable citizens by overt acts verging on rebellion, ought to be made to understand, that such conduct can no longer be tolerated with impunity." The Montréal Scots had no intention of relaxing their tight grip on power.

The Patriotes rose up in armed rebellion in 1837, but the British Army, sent from Upper Canada, quickly crushed the revolt. In a series of separate pitched battles, almost 300 Patriotes were killed or wounded, and many, including Papineau, were forced to flee to the United States, where they remained in exile for several years.

For weeks in the summer and fall of '37, Mackenzie travelled tirelessly throughout the countryside, organizing meetings among farm folk and delivering incendiary speeches. He also recruited a couple of aging ex-military officers as lieutenants in his militia, and they began to put the ragtag, ill-equipped volunteers through a series of military drills in preparation for future battles.

A mere week after the Patriotes had fought their first battle against the British army, Mackenzie decided to stage an armed rebellion of his own. It is interesting to note that instead of fearing the obvious British resolve to quash any armed revolt, the intrepid little Scot saw a perfect opportunity to strike while the British army was preoccupied in Lower Canada. His call to arms was a pamphlet, distributed throughout the rural areas, inciting rebellion with these words: "Up then Brave Canadians! Get ready your rifles and make short work of it … now's the day and the hour! Woe be to those who oppose us, for 'In God is our trust.'"

Mackenzie instructed his rebels to meet at Montgomery's Tavern near Toronto on December 4th. Throughout the day and into the night, hundreds arrived, poorly armed and ill prepared, many carrying only picks and axes. The next day, the mob of several hundred insurgents marched down Yonge Street, where twenty Tory militiamen met them. The two sides traded pot shots. Mackenzie wrote this account of what happened next: "Colonel Lount and those at the front fired – and instead of stepping to one side to make room for those behind to fire, fell flat on their faces. The next rank did the same thing. Many of them country people, when they saw the riflemen in front falling down and heard the firing, they imagined that those who fell were killed by the enemy's fire, and took to their heels. This was almost too much for the human patience. The city would have been ours in an hour, probably without firing a shot. But 800 ran, and unfortunately the wrong way."

Two days later, a thousand well-armed citizen militiamen, loyal to the government, met Mackenzie's 400 remaining dispirited rebels. As government troops put their field artillery in place, a few of Mackenzie's men began to break ranks and run, and as the cannons thundered, the rest dispersed in panic, many jettisoning their weapons in the pandemonium that followed. The battle had not lasted more than a few minutes, but any hopes of a successful armed insurrection died then and there. Government troops proceeded to Montgomery's Tavern and burned it to cinders. Mackenzie was forced to make a run for the United States with a large price on his head.

Remarkably, the colonies granted William Lyon Mackenzie and Louis-Joseph Papineau amnesty, and the two men returned to their respective homes in 1849. By this time, however, the radical reform movement had run out of steam, and few in the colonies seemed to have much appetite for radicalism of any sort. Mackenzie was re-elected to the Legislative Assembly, but his cantankerous nature made it impossible for him to build another following, and now his extremism seemed anachronistic to a younger generation. He finally retired from politics, disillusioned and bitter, in 1858 and died three years later.

"Mackenzie was a rebel rather than a statesman," writes eminent historian George Woodcock. "It was always difficult to say what he stood for but never difficult to say what he stood against: authority in general and its inherent liability to be abused." Nevertheless, Mackenzie's actions proved important, and ironically, they did galvanize reform, although in ways that he himself would never have predicted. Historians J.W. Chafe and A.R.M. Lower write, "The Rebellions were American Revolutions in miniature, and though at the time they seemed to have failed, they cleared the way for self-government; and just beyond self-government stood national life."

Meanwhile, the colonial rebellions caught the attention of Great Britain, which dissolved the assemblies of Upper and Lower Canada and sent over a veteran politican and diplomat with temporary dictatorial powers to see what the commotion was all about. Lord Durham held the title, "High Commissioner and Governor-General of all Her Majesty's provinces on the continent of North America", and his observations in the colonies and subsequent recommendations to parliament back home had enormous consequences. Durham's *Report on the Affairs of British North America*, tabled in January 1839 after he had returned to London, advocated that the colonies be given the power to run their own internal affairs and the institution of responsible government; in short elected assemblies would be in control. He also suggested that as long as the French in Lower Canada maintained a degree of governmental independence, British North America would be plagued with cultural and linguistic tensions. He proposed that Upper and Lower Canada be merged into one large colony, with English as the official language of government, though the French population was much larger. Under this system, Durham believed the French would eventually be assimilated. The idea seemed logical to the high commissioner, who stated, "The superior political and practical intelligence of the English cannot be, for a moment, disputed."

Durham had suggested representation according to population, as he was certain that as English Canada grew, the French would ultimately become overwhelmed in Parliament. Great Britain, however, chose to allot the same number of seats to both English and French Canada, choosing to under-represent the French right away. In 1841, the two Canadas were united under one government. Upper Canada became "Canada West" and Lower Canada became "Canada East." Under the new system, however, Durham's call for responsible government was ignored.

The British plan to submerge the French backfired spectacularly. Under the new system, like-minded French and English reformers were brought together, forming coalitions to fight for common causes. The two leaders who emerged during this era were Louis-Hippolyte LaFontaine and Robert Baldwin.

GREAT CANADIAN POLITICAL CARTOONS: 1820 TO 1914

THE GOVERNMENT THIMBLERIG.

THE ACT OF UNION MOVED THE CAPITAL FROM KINGSTON TO MONTRÉAL AND FINALLY TO TORONTO. IN THIS PERIOD CARTOON, MR. PUNCH TRIES TO GUESS WHERE IT WILL MOVE NEXT.

In the 1848 election, Lafontaine and Baldwin won a majority of seats in the assembly, though up to that time, the assembly had held very little true power. At this critical point in Canada's history, Lord Elgin, Lord Durham's son-in-law, was the newly appointed Governor of British North America.

Elgin, a Lowland Scottish aristocrat from a powerful family, was the very embodiment of fairness and progressive thinking. Like many Scottish nobles of his generation, his ideas had been profoundly influenced by the Scottish Enlightenment, which promoted egalitarian principles and a belief in the universality of human nature. Elgin's duty as governor was to appoint members to the powerful executive council, the locus of real power in Canada.

Much to everyone's surprise, he appointed LaFontaine and Baldwin, recognizing their legitimacy as the top vote getters in the assembly. This unprecedented move outraged the Tories, who wailed and moaned in disbelief. Lord Elgin, however, held firm, stating that he wished "to establish a moral influence in the province which will go far to compensate for the loss of power consequent on the surrender of patronage to an executive responsible to the local parliament." Elgin's faith in responsible government and his appointment of LaFontaine and Baldwin are considered by many historians to be cornerstones in "the birth of Canadian democracy". And Elgin is another example in Canadian history of the right Scot in the right place at the right time.

LaFontaine and Baldwin soon passed a bill that lifted the ban on the French language in government. When parliament opened the following January, Lord Elgin delivered his Speech from the Throne in English. He then paused, smiled and delivered the speech again in fluent French. This act held enormous symbolic significance, and sewed the seeds for official bilingualism.

In the spring of '49, Lafontaine and Baldwin proposed a bill that would compensate the Patriotes for damages they had suffered during their rebellion. This was simply too much for the Tories of Canada East. Democracy had gone too far and was resulting in mob rule. Lord Elgin faced a very difficult dilemma. He did not personally approve of the bill, and he did not want to alienate the Tories of Montréal, many of whom were fellow Scots. At the same time, Elgin did not want to undermine the practise of responsible government in Canada. To his everlasting credit, Elgin swallowed his personal reservations, chose democracy, and signed the bill.

The outraged English-speaking merchants of Montréal threw stones, eggs and rotten vegetables at Lord Elgin as he exited the parliament building. They then went on a frenzied rampage, burning reformers' homes and finally burning the beautiful Montréal Parliament Building to the ground, along with its valuable art collection and library. Lord Elgin, ever the model of restraint, refused to call in the troops, aware that such action would only escalate the crisis. He chose instead to let the riots wind down on their own. What saddened him most was not the torching of parliament, and not the vicious attack on him, but the fact that he had recognized so many of his countrymen – men whom he thought were "citizens of good standing" – in the rioting horde.

Like Governor James Murray a century before, Lord Elgin found the Anglo-merchant-dominated Montréal "rotten to the core". Canada's seat of government was pulled out of Montréal and until 1857, when Queen Victoria named Ottawa, nicely situated in the middle of colony, as the capital, it was moved to Toronto. Lord Elgin left the colonies in 1854, having established the important legacy of responsible government in Canada.

Shifting coalitions between various factions in parliament marked the decade prior to Confederation in 1867. Pre-eminent Canadian writer George Bowering comments, "Even reading about the political scene in Canada from 1856 to 1866 is frustrating. It can give you a headache … In those ten years governments were basted together only to come apart at the stitching." Suffice it to say that Scots dominated. Three Scots sat as the longest serving prime ministers of the period: the rigid Tory Allan MacNab, the reformer John Sandfield Macdonald and the political dealmaker John A. Macdonald (who would later become the Dominion of Canada's first prime minister).

This politically turbulent political phase also saw the emergence of the "Fathers of Confederation", most of them Scots, who would play such an important role in inventing the larger Canadian nation.

By the 1860s, it seemed obvious that the British colonies in North America must be united. As separate colonies, they were facing problems that could seemingly only be solved by coming together to form a new, bigger, stronger nation. But the parliament of United Canada was perpetually in the throes of gridlock between its French and English halves. English Canada West had become more populous, but French Canada East still held half the seats in the assembly. As a result, many English Canadians felt that the French minority was unfairly dictating their affairs. A new constitution was needed to get the political process moving. At the same time Britain, growing tired of constantly propping up and defending its expensive colonies, made it clear that the colonies were going to have to take more responsibility for governing and defending themselves. London let it be known that it was not opposed to a constitutional shake-up.

Meanwhile, bloody civil war (1861–1865) was raging in the United States. Yankee politicians, resentful that Britain clearly favoured the rebellious South, began to make threats that as soon as the war was over, British North America would be next. Fears of the mighty, battle-hardened Union armies marching north, artillery in tow, probably did more than anything else to bring about Canadian union. Moreover, the irate Americans refused to renew their free-trade agreement with British North America, so forging a northern free-trade union with the disparate British colonies seemed the best way to ensure economic survival.

Finally, before the 1860s, the daunting magnitude of British North America had discouraged union. It had been simply impossible to move goods and people freely throughout the immense, rugged land. During the sixties, however, railroads seemed to shrink the intimidating geography down to a more manageable size. For the first time in history, it became feasible to bind the vast colonial regions together with railways, which could facilitate free trade and rapid troop movements. Logistically, union no longer seemed to be such a far-fetched notion.

The most important "Fathers of Confederation", the actual architects of the new unified Dominion of Canada, were predominantly Scots. Eight out of ten of these paternal figures were either born in Scotland or of recent Scottish extraction, including John A. MacDonald, George Brown, Alexander Galt, William McDougall, Oliver Mowat, Charles Tupper, Leonard Tilley and John Hamilton Gray. Only George-Étienne Cartier, a French-Canadian, and Thomas D'Arcy McGee, an Irishman, were not Scots. Together, this impressive group of statesmen planned, argued and negotiated a new constitution and a new country into being.

In Canada West, John A. Macdonald headed the "Liberal-Conservative" party, a moderate conservative coalition that eventually evolved into the Progressive Conservative Party. George Brown led the Reform Party, nicknamed the "Clear Grits", which had previously advocated a sweeping American-style of reform, and which evolved into the Liberal Party of Canada. To this day, the Liberals are often referred to as "Grits". Interestingly, Canada's two main political parties, which dominated the political scene in Canada for the next century and beyond, can be traced back to the leadership of these two influential Scots.

George Brown and John A. Macdonald were arch political rivals. Brown, born near Edinburgh, was a tall stately fellow whose appearance and intelligence commanded natural respect. He was a strict Presbyterian, suspicious of French-Canadian Catholics and resentful of their over-representation in parliament. Brown was also founder of the *Globe,* still Canada's most influential newspaper, which he used to blast his political enemies, none more frequently and

ENTITLED "GEORGE BROWN'S STATUS QUO", THIS EDITORIAL CARTOON RAN IN QUÉBEC'S *LA SCIE*.

personally than Macdonald. Brown's paper would often print cartoons of Macdonald with a red, bulbous nose and dishevelled hair, a half-empty booze bottle sticking out his pocket. This was, of course, a clear reference to Macdonald's legendary fondness for strong drink.

In one instance, after Macdonald had attended a formal state dinner wearing a British civil uniform with a ceremonial sword, Brown wrote, "A great deal of time has been wasted by John A. Macdonald in learning to walk, for the sword suspended from his waist has an awkward knack of getting between his legs, especially after dinner." The witty and gregarious Macdonald responded in his next speech that voters "would rather have a drunken John A. Macdonald than a sober George Brown." Such jousting had gone on between the two for years.

In 1862, overworked and exhausted, George Brown went to Scotland to recuperate. There, he met Anne Nelson, the daughter of a well-known Scottish publisher, and the forty-three-year-old bachelor fell headlong in love. The two soon married and boarded a ship to Canada. People who had known Brown before his marriage could not believe how mellow and contented he acted, his spirit seeming to have taken a great leap towards magnanimity. He said that he had returned to Canada, "with a better knowledge of public affairs and with more ardent desire to serve."

John Macdonald had been giving stirring speeches in favour of colonial union, but the gridlock of Canada West's parliament made it impossible to build a coalition that would pass the required laws. On June 24, 1864, the kinder, gentler Brown did the unthinkable: he agreed to join forces with his Tory nemesis, John A. Macdonald, seeing a united federation as the best way to end the over-representation of the French and to expand into the west before the Americans did. Although it was hard to team up with political enemies he had previously condemned as "Corruptionists", Brown swallowed his pride, saying he hoped the two sides could "forget our merely political partisanship and rally round the cause of our country." With this courageous act, Confederation moved forward.

The three premiers of the Maritime colonies, Charles Tupper, Leonard Tilley and John Hamilton Gray, were somewhat suspicious of colonial union, fearing that their influence as smaller "provinces" would be overwhelmed by the much larger Canada. In an attempt to assuage their fears, the Canadians arranged a conference in Charlottetown, Prince Edward Island, on September 1, 1864. For days, the delegates drank enormous quantities of champagne, wine and port, ate delectable foods, chatted through the night, attended dances, traded jokes and slapped each other on the back in the spirit of inebriated fraternity. During the day sessions, Macdonald and Cartier outlined the main advantages of Confederation, Brown explained the constitutional mechanics of union, and

Alexander Galt, the immigrant son of famous Scottish novelist John Galt, explained his vision of how the union's finances would operate. Finally, Thomas D'Arcy McGee tugged everyone's heartstrings, giving a rousing speech about the glory of the new nation. When the conference was over, the delegates resembled a mutual admiration society. Most fears had disappeared, replaced by feelings of friendship, goodwill and an overall desire to see confederation succeed. The delegates agreed to meet a month later in Québec City.

The Canadians brought with them seventy-two resolutions, outlining how the new country would be governed under the new constitution. Though the other "Fathers of Confederation" had contributed to the document, John A. Macdonald conceived and wrote most of the resolutions, building in his belief that Canada should possess a far stronger central government than that of the United States. Of the seventy-two resolutions, Macdonald had penned fifty. He declared to his friend, Sir James Gowan, "Not one man, except Galt in finance, has the slightest idea of Constitution making. Whatever is good or ill in the Constitution is mine." Not only was John A. Macdonald literally the author of Confederation, he was the central figure who manoeuvred through the difficult obstacle courses presented at the conferences, building alliances and negotiating compromises that ultimately led to colonial union. Moreover, his passion and indefatigable work to achieve his political vision are in themselves singular and remarkable. In a very real sense, he deserves his figurative title as the "Father of Canada."

The main delegates spent the winter of 1866 and '67 in London refining the Quebec resolutions. Finally, on March 29, 1867, the British Parliament passed the British North America Act and Canada was born. The colony of United Canada was split up, Canada West becoming

NATIONAL ARCHJIVES OF CANADA / C-127864

A YOUNG JOHN A. MACDONALD, CIRCA 1842

the province of Ontario and Canada East becoming Québec. The provinces of New Brunswick and Nova Scotia joined them in the new federation, while Prince Edward Island and Newfoundland chose, temporarily, to remain independent. John A. Macdonald, the acknowledged leader of the Confederation movement, was called by the Queen to form an interim government and become Canada's first prime minister. He soon called an election and won a majority in the House of Commons. He then began to mould his new nation in unexpected ways.

John A. Macdonald, perhaps the most famous and important Canadian Scot of them all, was a true paradox, both personally and professionally. His administration was known in its day as much for its scandals as for its accomplishments. Indeed, the Macdonald era was a tempestuous period, a time when the very survival of Canada was in doubt. Despite huge challenges, however, Macdonald continued, against considerable odds, to realize the grand dream of a transcontinental nation.

John Alexander Macdonald was born in Glasgow to Highland parents in 1815. His father was an unsuccessful cotton broker, perpetually down on his luck. In 1820, the family moved to Kingston, Ontario, where Macdonald's father was no more successful than he had been in Scotland. He opened a store that soon went bust, set up a mill that failed, and opened another unprofitable store. Finally, broke and disgusted, he gave up and became a bank clerk for the rest of his working life.

Young John, a voracious reader, left school at the age of fifteen and became a clerk in a law office. At twenty-one, he took and passed the bar exam, becoming a full-fledged barrister. He was soon an eloquent public defender, known for his energy and wit. At the age of twenty-eight, he was a Kingston alderman, and the next year he was elected to the Assembly of Canada West. Macdonald rapidly rose in prominence, due largely to his ability to conciliate and build consensus. He once jokingly referred to his profession as "cabinet-maker".

Macdonald was not at all an ideologue. In fact, he was the epitome of Scottish pragmatism, doing what needed to be done in the most efficacious manner to achieve his goals. Although he was suspicious of the French, he was aware that he could make no political headway without their help. He thus proceeded to build one of history's great political coalitions with the multi-talented George-Étienne Cartier, a lawyer, politician, and railway promoter, who was purportedly a descendant of Jacques Cartier.

Though Macdonald was a conservative, he had no fondness for the Family Compact and its outdated grip on power. This is not to say, however, that he did not know how to make alliances with its members from time to time. He was anti-republican (and anti-Yankee) and was certainly opposed to any sort of radical social reform, but he was concerned with social justice and open to liberal ideas. In a very real sense, he was a progressive conservative.

Macdonald's personal life was no less enigmatic. He was a workaholic, routinely putting in twenty-hour days, often working through the night and skipping sleep altogether. This sometimes made him appear unkempt and frazzled, an appearance aptly noted by political cartoonists. At the end of a gruelling workday, Macdonald would frequently make his way to the pub, where he would drink hard for several hours, trading ribald jokes with cronies and laughing raucously until the wee hours of the morning. The next day would find him seated in parliament tired and hung over, his hair shooting out in all directions.

Macdonald's fondness for stiff drink was well known, and he would sometimes appear intoxicated in parliament or at public events. When confronted with a major political or personal crisis, Macdonald would invariably disappear for several days, leaving both colleagues and opponents guessing. He would then resurface and resume his duties, seemingly not the worse for wear. Despite this weakness for alcohol, his political contemporaries and even his political opponents were willing to cut Macdonald a good deal of slack, as everyone recognized his intellect and his almost superhuman ability to outwork and outperform virtually anyone. Moreover, no one who knew him could question either his love for Canada or his sense of public duty.

Macdonald's family life was sad. In Scotland in 1843, Macdonald met and married his cousin, Isabella Clark, and brought her to Canada. Within a year, she was afflicted with a strange malady that no doctor could accurately diagnose, but which left her chronically fatigued and bedridden for the next thirteen years. Her condition wore Macdonald down, year after year, but he remained devoted and attentive to her dying day. Ever worried, Macdonald accompanied Isabella many times to the United States, hoping drier, warmer weather would do her good, but nothing seemed to help.

Isabella gave birth to a son, but the frail baby boy died when he was a year old, permanently scarring the normally resilient Macdonald. The couple eventually produced another son, Hugh John, who was forced to live mostly with his aunt, due to his mother's chronic infirmity and his father's long absences. Though rather shy and nervous in public, Hugh John Macdonald followed his father into public life and served briefly as Premier of Manitoba, but he was more an intellectual than a politician and was never close to his father.

Isabella died in 1857, and Macdonald found solace in the Confederation cause. For the next ten years, he punished himself with unrelenting cycles of work and drink, seldom sleeping through an entire night. In 1867, he married

NATIONAL ARCHIVES OF CANADA / C-097287

NATIONAL ARCHIVES OF CANADA / C-047927

SIR JOHN A. MACDONALD, JUST AFTER CONFEDERATION, WITH (INSET) EARNSCLIFFE, HIS HOME IN OTTAWA. TODAY IT IS USED BY THE BRITISH HIGH COMMISSIONER.

an intellectually curious and able woman named Susan Bernard, and Macdonald's cheerless personal life began to look promising. The couple, however, soon had a daughter, Mary, who was born mentally handicapped and never learned to speak well or walk. Macdonald's sadness over his daughter's condition consumed him, and just as he had done with Isabella, he spent much of his personal time anxiously attending to the needs of his little girl.

The Macdonald era was marked by enormous political achievements as well as colossal blunders. Macdonald's first major test after Confederation was the threat of secession. Shortly after Nova Scotia had entered political union with Canada, the people elected a government, led by reformer Joseph Howe, which felt Confederation had been foisted upon Nova Scotians without proper public consultation. Howe threatened to pull out of Confederation, and some of the province's most prominent citizens even talked of joining the United States. Macdonald outflanked the secession movement by quickly promising better financial terms for the province and Howe, its powerful and vocal leader, eventually accepted a cabinet position in the new federal government.

Macdonald's next major challenge was what to do with the vast Hudson's Bay territory west of Canada. Although he was reluctant to take on the enormous task of opening up the west for settlement, he knew that he must act or let the vast territory be annexed by a "peaceful invasion" of American settlers. The Americans, he knew, were "resolved to do all they can, short of war, to get possession of our western territory, and we must take immediate and vigorous steps to counteract them." To counter this, he convinced the British Parliament to exert pressure on the Hudson's Bay Company to sell its land to Canada. In 1869, the HBC reluctantly agreed to sell its land for $1.5 million, a real estate deal that outstripped even the Louisiana Purchase of 1803. In one stroke, everyone in the North-West Territories (the HBC's Rupert's Land and North-Western Territory) would become Canadians, whether they wanted to or not.

Macdonald was aware that the transaction might cause problems with the Métis and First Nations living in the western lands. He remarked to Cartier, "All these poor people know is that Canada has bought the country from the Hudson's Bay Company and that they are handed over like a flock of sheep to us." Macdonald's fears were soon realized when government surveyors, sent west to divide up the prairies for future settlement, were met by the young Métis leader Louis Riel and seventeen of his men. Riel literally put his foot down on one of the surveying chains and ordered the surveyors off Métis land.

Riel's stature quickly grew among the Métis and First Nations for having courageously stood up to the Canadian government. When word reached Macdonald of the Métis' act of defiance, he was perturbed. "These impulsive half-breeds," he exclaimed, "must be kept down by a strong hand, until they are swamped by an influx of settlers." He later mused to George Brown that it was going "to require considerable management to keep those wild people quiet." It was a comment typical of the times, but ignorant of the reality, for Riel had been classically educated in Montréal and though a firm believer that the rights of the Métis and mixed-blood majority should be respected, he was a democrat and a man who would – and did – go to great lengths to avoid violence.

Macdonald appointed his Scottish colleague, William McDougall, as first Canadian lieutenant governor of the North-West Territories, but aware that he intended to overthrow their democratically elected council, a group of armed Métis barred McDougall from entering Métis territory. Powerless and frustrated, McDougall returned to Canada spitting contempt for the "half-breeds." Meanwhile, Riel and 120 Métis riflemen rode to Fort Garry, the administrative centre of the Red River region, and seized it from William Mactavish, Governor of Rupert's Land, a man who was dying of tuberculosis. They then set up a provisional government and made a list of demands to the Canadian government, stating that they would consider becoming Canadians provided that they were assured of property and language rights and freedom of religion. Their demands were given extra weight by the fact that they held forty-five Canadian prisoners.

Among the prisoners was a loud-mouthed Irishmen named Thomas Scott, who let everyone know he was going to kill Riel at the first opportunity following his release. Despite these threats, and violent action against his men, Riel made a number of attempts to reason with Scott, but failed to temper his outbursts. Finally, charged with inciting a counter-rebellion and treason, Scott was tried and hastily convicted. Though Riel pleaded with the six-member military tribunal to show mercy, four of the six voted for the death sentence. Scott did little to assist in his own defence. When one of the members of the tribunal suggested exiling Scott would be better than handing down a death sentence, and even offered to escort him to the American border, the defiant Scott, who had repeatedly threatened to shoot Riel, retorted, "Take me there if you will. I will be back as soon as you."

During the night that followed the sentencing, members of the English-speaking community repeatedly pleaded with Riel to commute the death penalty, something he had done previously for the commander of the insurrection, Captain Charles Arkoll Boulton. But, perhaps believing Scott's threats and under pressure from his Métis guards, Riel agonized long and hard before eventually determining to proceed. "We must make Canada respect us," he said.

At noon on March 4, 1870, Scott said farewell to the other prisoners, and a short prayer with a Protestant minister, then was led out into the courtyard of Upper Fort Garry and blindfolded. In *The Canadian Crucible,* her acclaimed assessment of Riel's government, Frances Russell writes, "[Scott's] non-stop insults and bravado had all now completely evaporated. "This is horrible. This is cold-blooded murder," [he] sobbed as he was pushed down to kneel in the snow … all six executioners fired. With a ghastly groan, he sank to the ground in a pool of his own blood."

But Riel had made a serious miscalculation, for with the execution he gave up the moral high ground and undermined his credibility. When word of the execution reached English Canada, there were calls for revenge against the cold-blooded "half-breed" killer and his apparently flagrant defiance of Canada. Macdonald, ever the pragmatic conciliator, did not wish to see the Red River Rebellion escalate into a much larger revolt and upset his dream of a nation from sea to sea.

The previous December, Prime Minister Macdonald had sent Donald A. Smith to negotiate with Riel and the Métis provisional government. Smith, a Scot, had worked his way up from his initial posting as a clerk in the Hudson's Bay Company to become its chief representative in Canada; he would later be named Lord Strathcona and would become president of the Canadian Pacific Railway.

Officially, Smith was named "Special Commissioner" to inquire into the situation at Red River. Unofficially, he was apparently privately authorized by the prime minister to attempt to buy off the Métis who supported Riel with money and jobs. Smith did manage to weaken support for Riel among the Métis population, and eventually forced the Métis to negotiate. He then proposed sending a delegation to Ottawa, assuring Riel that they would receive "a very cordial reception". On May 12th, following vigorous debate in the House of Commons led by Deputy Prime Minister George-Étienne Cartier standing in for the prime minister who was seriously ill with gallstones, the HBC territory was formally sold to Canada. On the same day, Manitoba was born as Canada's fifth province, a much smaller version than it is today, with 1.5 million acres or 600,000 hectares set aside for the Métis. With the deal sealed and the political dust settling, Riel was forced to flee to the United States in order to escape being taken prisoner.

In 1870, British Columbia too was considering joining Canada, and the colony sent delegates to Ottawa to negotiate terms. Hoping to get Canada to build some sort of primitive wagon trail from British Columbia to the East, the BC delegation was dumbfounded when the Macdonald government offered them a full-blown railroad and an impossible and irresponsible promise. Railway construction would begin within two years and be completed within ten. B.C. jumped at the offer and joined Canada in 1871, becoming the nation's sixth province. Against enormous odds, Macdonald had realized his dream of a transcontinental dominion.

Still, there was a lot of space between British Columbia and Manitoba, and Macdonald realized that he had to exert law and order not to mention Canadian sovereignty on the immense North-West Territory. His solution was the North-West Mounted Police, the "Mounties." In 1873, 300 policemen, clad in dashing red uniforms spread out throughout the territory, establishing peace and order as well as a reputation for duty and fairness. From the outset, they were not only extraordinarily successful, but also the primary reason the Canadian West evolved with a very different character than the raucous and often lawless American West. In 1920, the force was reorganized and named the Royal Canadian Mounted Police, an iconic Canadian institution that still has an international reputation for even-handedness and moderation.

Following British Columbia's example, Prince Edward Island saw that Macdonald was ready to give away the farm, so to speak, and the government of the tiny island decided to reconsider its independence. Macdonald offered to soak up the colony's enormous debts and assist in ordering its finances. The deal was too good to pass up, and Prince Edward Island joined Canada in 1873, becoming Canada's seventh province.

But promising a railroad from east to west had been easy; delivering the promise turned out to be far harder. Technically speaking, the project was almost unimaginably difficult, and the cost would be astronomical. Many eastern voters couldn't see why they should be forced to bear such an inordinate burden. Macdonald, however, realized that without a railroad, the idea of confederation was only a theory. There must be a physical link between the provinces; otherwise the disparate regions could never truly form a lasting nation. Macdonald, however, would be cast out of office before having to deliver on his promise.

Meanwhile, two of his Scottish friends, the powerful businessman and senator, David Macpherson, and the Montréal financier and shipping tycoon, Hugh Allan, were vying for the lucrative cross-country railroad contract. Behind closed doors, Macdonald tried to convince the two stubborn Scots to cooperate and share the contract, but Macpherson refused. In a smoke-filled room well out of public view, Macdonald then promised Allan the contract on the conditions that no American money would finance the railway and that Allan would contribute generously to Macdonald's re-election campaign. Allan gave assurances that he would get rid of the American backers, but in fact he only shuffled papers to create the illusion of exclusive Canadian investment. He then proceeded to funnel $350,000, an enormous sum in those days, towards the Conservative campaign. Hard pressed by the Liberals, Macdonald wasn't paying close attention to Allan's manoeuvrings. Instead, his focus was the campaign, which he barely won.

The victory, however, was short-lived. Evidence that he had accepted bribes from Allan soon made its way into the newspapers; the *coup de grâce* was a leaked telegram that Macdonald had written to Allan: "I must have another ten thousand. Will be the last time calling. Do not fail me. Answer today." The scandal was blown wide open, and to make matters worse, it was soon revealed that Yankee dollars made up a significant part of the backing for the proposed railway. Macdonald rose in parliament to declare, "These hands are clean!" but it was soon proved that they were not, and in 1873, his government fell. Macdonald disappeared for most of the winter; his political career seemed to have ended in ignominy.

The Liberals won the 1873 election, and Canada's second prime minister was – surprise! – another Scot. Alexander Mackenzie came to power in the wake

THIS *GRIP* CARTOON REFLECTS THE PUBLIC'S GROWING CYNACISM.

of the "Pacific Scandal" largely because he was the antithesis of John A. Macdonald. Although history has recognized Mackenzie as a competent and upstanding prime minister, his rise to prominence came at one of the most turbulent periods in Canadian history, and exacted a heavy toll on him both politically and personally.

Mackenzie was born in the Scottish Highlands near the city of Dunkheld. He had little formal education, but had learned the stone cutting trade at an early age. At twenty, he packed up his tools and moved to Canada, following his sweetheart whose family had emigrated several years earlier. Once in his adopted land, he set up a contracting company, and through thrift, diligence and hard work, he prospered, his company gaining ever-larger contracts until Mackenzie was considered one of the most dependable and successful contractors in Canada East. Unlike Macdonald, who was always broke, Mackenzie was stereotypically "Scotch". He seldom engaged in luxuries, choosing instead to live a parsimonious and disciplined life, and he became wealthy.

But there was one similarity between the two men, for Mackenzie's personal life was also filled with tragedy. Two of his three children died before their first birthday, and the birth of Mackenzie's third child damaged his wife's health to such an extent that she was bedridden for two years until her death at the age of twenty-seven. Unlike Macdonald, who drowned his sorrows in politics and gin, Mackenzie found solace and strength in prayer.

After having established himself as a successful businessman, Mackenzie became friends with George Brown, who encouraged the young stonecutter to run for office. Mackenzie won a Liberal seat in the assembly, and his moral rectitude and unwavering honesty soon won him the respect of his peers. During the Pacific Scandal, the upright Mackenzie was one of the most effective critics of Macdonald's corrupt government and became a potent symbol of integrity, something that the Conservatives obviously lacked. On the collapse of Macdonald's government, the Liberals swept into power in the 1873 election, and Mackenzie found himself, much to his astonishment, prime minister of Canada.

He held power reluctantly, exhorting George Brown to take the Liberal leadership off his hands, but Brown refused. Brown knew, perhaps, that the country was on the brink of a profound economic depression, and like other Liberals, he wanted neither the job nor the political fallout. As fate would have it, John A. Macdonald's exit from office had turned out to be a lucky dodge of a deadly political bullet. Mackenzie was forced to face the depression alone, with only half-hearted support from members of his own government.

Mackenzie's political philosophy may be summed up in four basic tenets: responsible financial management, equality of opportunity for all Canadians, faith in natural market forces (Mackenzie was a disciple of Scottish philosopher and economist Adam Smith), and always telling the truth regardless of political consequences. These noble beliefs ended up costing "honest Sandy," as he was dubbed, his political life.

Mackenzie decided to put a stop to the transcontinental railway, believing it would bankrupt the country. He opted instead to build a network of railways, one stage at a time, so as not to further damage the nation's flagging economy. This made British Columbia furious, and it threatened to pull out of Canada.

Unlike Macdonald, who loved to dress up in dapper clothes, including wildly chequered pants, tailed coats and top hats, Mackenzie invariably wore plain but tasteful dark business suits. While Sir John A. had revelled in the knighthood bestowed on him by the Queen after Confederation, Mackenzie's egalitarianism and desire to set a good example led him to refuse knighthood. Throughout his term, Mackenzie also let the governor general and Great Britain know that Canada was an independent nation ruled according to a constitution, and it was the prime minister, not the Queen's man in the colonies, who would run things. After years of wrangling, Britain accepted this assertion, for the most part.

The depression during Mackenzie's term was long, intense and global. Mackenzie knew, however, that markets had natural cycles, and he kept assuring Canadians that they simply had to be patient. Better times would come, as they always did. In the meantime, he attempted to pass a free trade agreement with the ailing United States in an attempt to stimulate the economy. A Conservative senate, however, blocked his bill.

Mackenzie did manage to create some enduring Canadian institutions, including the Supreme Court of Canada, the office of Auditor General to oversee government spending, and the secret ballot, designed to stop political bribery, pressure tactics and outright intimidation.

Despite his obvious achievements, "honest Sandy" was rather too honest for his own good. One might argue whether John A. Macdonald was a better prime minister, but he was certainly a better politician, and by 1876 he sensed a political comeback. He began to appear in parliament, sober most of the time, to slam Mackenzie, declaring, "Liberal times are hard times." He then offered a panacea to the country's economic ills with his "National Policy,"which was essentially a call for higher tariffs and interprovincial trade. It certainly had a nice ring to it, and it sounded like an action plan. Disgruntled voters, desirous of better times, began to believe. Mackenzie, having a great faith in the common sense of the electorate, didn't take Macdonald's criticism seriously. After all, hadn't Macdonald proved he was corrupt? Surely the electorate would be able to see through his desperate political grandstanding. But Mackenzie had overestimated the good judgement of voters, and in 1878, Macdonald achieved an implausible return to power.

George Bowering offers the following assessment of Alexander Mackenzie's term as prime minister: "A person has to feel affection and sympathy for this unlucky Baptist idealist, even if he was a market man. He brought us the secret ballot and *Hansard.* He refused to wear the gaudy rewards of the British Crown. His actions sprang out of democratic belief rather than political opportunity. He chose loneliness over image-building. He gave his fellow citizens more credit than they knew what to do with. He had the grace to be a bad politician to the end." Overall, despite his trials, the sincere Highlander made a lasting impression on Canada's political culture.

John A. Macdonald stormed back to power in the election of 1878. Incredibly, no sooner had he been sworn into office than the depression began to lift. Himself once again, Macdonald announced, "Conservative times are good times," and who could argue with him? Banks again wanted to lend money, making it possible once again to plan a transcontinental railway. Though the Liberals still branded the project "an act of insane recklessness," Macdonald pushed ahead.

To realize his grand vision, Macdonald summoned an impressive line-up of Scottish talent. Historian A. Margaret MacLaren Evans remarks, "Macdonald was fortunate to secure the aid of a sagacious group of men, all Scots by birth, for the syndicate with whom the contract was made to build the railway: George Stephen of the Bank of Montreal, his cousin Donald A. Smith, who had first-

GREAT CANADIAN POLITICAL CARTOONS: 1820 TO 1914

ABOVE: SIR JOHN A. MACDONALD AND LIBERAL LEADER EDWARD BLAKE TRY TO DRIVE THE CPR HOG AWAY FROM THE PUBLIC TROUGH.

hand knowledge of the West, the wealthy businessmen Duncan McIntyre and Robert B. Angus, and John Rose, formerly Macdonald's Finance Minister, who was now a member of a London banking house. The skilful chief engineer, Sandford Fleming, was also a Scot."

This talented group of Scots worked hard on the audacious project, but the vast Canadian land mass quickly ate up the first $25 million that the government had committed. Taxpayers again began to grumble about the inordinate cost of the railway, and the Liberals again vociferously pointed out the lunacy of such an irresponsible policy. It seemed that Macdonald's dream of a ribbon of steel tying the provinces together was about to die.

During Macdonald's hiatus from power, Ontario settlers, as well as those from the United States and many European nations, had been pouring into Manitoba and the North-West Territory, pushing the Métis and First Nations farther west. Outside Manitoba, the Métis had no recognized property rights, and both they and the First Nations began to suffer miserably due to declining numbers of bison. In part this was due to a treacherous campaign on the part of the American government to starve the Native peoples of the plains into submission. For several years in the early 1880s, they hired buffalo hunters to commit wholesale slaughter on the enormous herds. It was said that so many animals were killed that it was possible to travel for miles by jumping from one carcass to the next. Most of the hundreds of thousands of animals killed were left to rot in the sun. And soon the Lakota, the Cree, the Blackfoot and many other western plains nations were on the brink of starvation.

They issued petitions to Ottawa for help, but Macdonald refused to take their pleas seriously. If the federal government doled out material or money, he said, they would "drink it or waste it or sell it." As government surveyors began to move into the vast territories of the west, the Métis and First Nations became more desperate, for their proud way of life was obviously doomed.

In 1884, the Métis sent for Riel, who for years had been living in exile in the United States. Riel had been a symbol of defiance and hope for the Métis and had helped them secure valuable rights in Manitoba. Perhaps he could help them again. Returning to Canada, Riel sent a petition to Ottawa demanding provincial status, a recognized regional government, and property rights. Still Macdonald did nothing. He harboured a good deal of antipathy towards Riel as a result of their last clash years before, and he was not about to recognize the troublemaker as a legitimate leader.

When it was clear that Macdonald would not budge, Riel and a group of Métis declared a provisional government in March 1885 in the small village of Batoche on the South Saskatchewan River about halfway between the modern cities of Saskatoon and Prince Albert. Later that month, a small party of North-West Mounted Police travelling from nearby Fort Carlton were fired upon. Such a flagrant violation of Canada's authority could not go unanswered, and the government sent fifty-six Mounties and forty-three settlers to confront the Métis and restore order. At Duck Lake, near Batoche, the two forces clashed in a short, intense firefight that resulted in the death of twelve Mounties and five Métis. The Mounties were forced to retreat, and the Métis celebrated their victory in the hope that their abject situation was about to change.

Ironically, the Northwest Rebellion solved at least one of Macdonald's political problems. No longer did the enormously expensive Canadian Pacific

GREAT CANADIAN POLITICAL CARTOONS: 1820 TO 1914

A RIEL UGLY POSITION.

ENGLISH AND FRENCH CANADIANS WERE DEEPLY DIVIDED OVER THE FATE OF RIEL.

Railway seem such a foolish white elephant. Instead, both the public and the Members of Parliament saw the high-speed railway as a vital component of Canada's national security. Canadian troops could reach the West in just over a week, compared to the three months it would have taken without a railway.

Heavily armed soldiers boarded the train and headed west.

Now the government was able to inject another huge infusion of cash into the beleaguered railway project with virtually no opposition. Once again, Macdonald had managed, through remarkable luck, to dodge another potentially deadly political bullet. Historian Donald Creighton wrote, "The crisis of the railway and the crisis of the rebellion coincided. Each solved the other. The rebellion ensured the completion of the railway; the railway accomplished the defeat of the rebellion."

The troops from Canada placed the Métis under military siege at Batoche, where the two sides traded bullets for four days. Eventually, the Métis were forced to flee, and the rebellion was suppressed. Riel surrendered, was tried and found guilty. Though the jury recommended clemency, and there was great sympathy in Québec for the French Catholic Riel and his cause, Macdonald refused to pardon the Métis leader, saying "He will hang, though every dog in Quebec barks in his favour." Riel was executed in Regina on November 16, 1885. To this day, his execution is considered extremely controversial and continues to be hotly debated.

That same month, the powerful Scot Donald Smith drove the last spike in the Canadian Pacific Railway at Craigellachie, B.C. The place was named for a rocky crag in Morayshire, Scotland, where Smith had grown up. Though hundreds had died during its construction and government coffers had been more than drained dry, Canada was now a viable physical union, spanning the continent from sea to sea.

In 1891, Macdonald finally died. Many historians have used the adjective "flawed" to describe John A. Macdonald, and undoubtedly he was. But he was also the greatest nation builder in Canadian history, and it is unlikely that anyone else could have achieved what he did when the embryonic Canadian nation most needed a strong and visionary leader. He did more than anyone else to bring about Confederation, he oversaw the addition of three subsequent provinces, his government purchased the vast HBC territories, and he was the driving force behind the Canadian Pacific Railroad. In short, this self-made man from Glasgow clearly deserves the respect most Canadians accord him.

After the formative Macdonald era, Scots continued to play a role in Canadian politics, far out of proportion to their numbers. A revealing study by historian Richard Van Loon showed that the Scots had "a proclivity for gaining the seats of the mighty". Between the Macdonald era and the Second World War, Scots comprised an average of one-quarter of Canadian Members of Parliament, making them by far the largest ethnic group in the House of Commons. Moreover, they were vastly over-represented as cabinet ministers. According to Van

Loon, twenty per cent of Wilfred Laurier's appointees were Scots, 13.3 per cent of Robert L. Borden's, almost twenty-seven per cent of Arthur Meighen's, 23.9 per cent of William Lyon Mackenzie King's, and 28.6 per cent of R.B. Bennett's.

In the twentieth century, there were countless high-profile Canadian politicians of Scots descent; a list of them reads like a role call at a gathering of the clans. Their achievements, however, lie largely beyond the scope of this book, which concentrates on those who were Scots by birth or clearly by culture. There are, however, several notable exceptions, including William Lyon Mackenzie King, Canada's longest-serving prime minister; Agnes Macphail, Canada's first female Member of Parliament; Tommy Douglas, Canada's first elected socialist leader and the first leader of Canada's New Democratic Party, and Pierre Elliott Trudeau, one of the dominant figures of the twentieth century in Canada.

King was born in 1874 in Kingston, Ontario. He was the grandson of the 1837 rebel, William Lyon Mackenzie, and this fact was a significant factor in shaping his consciousness and political ideology. King served as prime minister longer than anyone else in the history of the British Commonwealth, and historians increasingly recognize him as one of the most successful prime ministers Canada has ever produced. Serving more than twenty-one years from 1921-1926, 1926-1930 and 1935-48, King seemed to have had a permanent lock on the Prime Minister's Office. And when he was not prime minister, he was leader of the Liberal Party and serving as head of the Loyal Opposition in Parliament.

The most important influence on young Willy King was his dynamic mother, Isabella Mackenzie, daughter of the rebel of Upper Canada. Isabella deified her dead father and told her young son, virtually every day of his life, magnificent stories of William Lyon Mackenzie's heroic exploits on behalf of Canada's underdogs. These romantic vignettes had a profound effect on young Willy, who read extensively about his seditious grandfather.

As a result, despite being a pudgy, bookish mamma's boy, Mackenzie King grew up with a sense of destiny. As a young man, he wrote in his diary that he believed God had big things in store for the Great Rebel's grandson, and he waited for "the fulfillment of the purpose for which I was created." He kept his diaries throughout his life, and expressly ordered that they be burned on his death; instead they made their way into the public domain, revealing his most personal thoughts. One shudders to think what embarrassing thoughts might be written down when a person believes his diaries will always be completely private. Yet it is only thus that we get a glimpse into the private world of a highly intelligent and talented man, but also one who was repressed, lonely and enormously superstitious.

King believed that the spirits of dead people were all around, watching and giving signs that expressed appreciation, approval or displeasure. When his mother died in 1917, he created a shrine to her and honoured her memory in a way that bordered on obsession. In fact, many historians agree that his fixation on his mother, before and after she died, warped his personal and social development in many ways. King's only real friends were his beloved dogs, and when his favourite one died, he would sometimes skip important meetings to sing hymns to the dead "angel" canine. Most importantly, King initiated spiritual contact with his recalcitrant grandpa, mainly through paranormal séances. This is worth mentioning because through King, figuratively speaking, William Lyon Mackenzie's influence continued to reverberate throughout much of the twentieth century.

It is perhaps unfair to judge a man by the private scribblings in his diaries, and many have focused more on King's idiosyncrasies than on his contributions to Canada. To be fair, during his life, King kept most of his eccentric ideas to himself, and his conduct as prime minister was generally proper and appropriate.

A fascinating aspect of King is that he believed himself to be, as his grandfather's scion, a reformer, but the methods he used could not have been more different from his muckraking ancestor. Educated at the University of

MACKENZIE KING EMPHASIZED CANADA'S ROLE AS A BRIDGE BETWEEN BRITAIN AND THE U.S.

Toronto, University of Illinois and Harvard, King was one of Canada's most intelligent and well-educated prime ministers, and he knew that reform often takes place most effectively through evolution, not revolution. He was greatly concerned with social welfare, and early in his political career he argued for the eight-hour workday. He also penned an influential book, *Industry and Humanity*, in which he recognized capitalism as the main engine for social progress, providing governments legislated against capitalism's inherent tendency to abuse workers. Unchecked capitalism, he believed, had brought "desolation to the very heart of the human race."

William Lyon Mackenzie King's career was far too long and varied to chronicle here. Suffice it to say, through his moderate politics of compromise and his continuous seeking of middle ground, he was able to achieve social reforms that would have made his recalcitrant granddad proud. He led Canada through a period of transition from being a relatively submissive and undeveloped colony to a modern, industrialized middle power. But he is often best remembered as the father of the Canadian welfare state. He brought in groundbreaking social programs "to guarantee basic minimums of dignity," including Family Allowance, Unemployment Insurance and Old Age Pension, thus steering Canada towards a social democratic political culture that endures to this day.

Another Scottish reformer was elected the first year Mackenzie King became prime minister. Agnes Macphail became a Member of Parliament in 1921, in the very first federal election in which women were allowed to vote. For the next nineteen years, she worked for better working conditions for farmers and farm women, as well as for economic

JOSHUA STANTON

AGNES MACPHAIL

and social equality for women, almost always as the only woman in the chamber. It wasn't easy, but determined and quick-witted, Macphail more than held her own.

When one of her male colleagues shouted to her, "Don't you wish you were a man?" she immediately shouted back, "Don't you!"

Agnes Macphail was born in Grey County, Ontario, on March 24, 1890 to Henrietta Campbell and Dougald MacPhail, both Scots who had come to Canada as teenagers. Her parents were poor farmers and even as a young child Agnes was determined to ease the lot of others like her parents, for whom life was a never-ending struggle.

Agnes excelled at school and became a teacher in the small Ontario hamlet of Kinloss. Here, local men gathered around the pot-bellied stove in the local store to talk politics. Since the storekeeper was also her landlord. Agnes was soon joining them and it was here that her interest in politics was born. Initially a Liberal, she soon joined the United Farmers of Ontario and began speaking in farm communities about the plight of farm women. By 1921, she was a veteran of two years of public speaking and during the campaign, she gave nearly sixty speeches. And she never wore a hat or gloves, a departure from the expected norm that caused considerable controversy.

Hat or no hat, Macphail (she changed the spelling of her name during the campaign) was among twenty-four UFO candidates elected as part of the Progressive party. The rule that women had to wear hats in the House of Commons was soon abandoned.

Over the next two decades, though the UFO's fortunes faltered, Macphail won election after election. But in parliament, she was always wary of abandoning her principles. When Mackenzie King, lacking the numbers to form a government in 1925, offered her a cabinet post in return for her support, she declined. The Liberals, she felt, were hypocritical. Indeed, she thought the same thing of the Conservatives. Instead, she soldiered on alone, always working for the betterment of women and children. She encouraged public education on childbirth, childhood education and better working conditions for farmers and miners and labourers. As the years passed, she became more interested in international affairs. Writing in her weekly newspaper column, she thumped for an end to Canada's colonial status.

In 1929, she was appointed as Canada's first female delegate to the League of Nations. Travelling abroad, she realized the advantages conferred by bilingualism, and insisted that ministers travelling abroad be better briefed. During the Depression, far ahead of her time, she began to work for prison reform, and opposed the death penalty.

She was finally defeated in the election of 1940, but was elected provincially the following year, the first woman to be elected to the Ontario Legislature. She served there, except for a three-year period, for the next decade. She died on February 13, 1954, a feisty woman who had made a difference under difficult circumstances.

But the person who took William Lyon Mackenzie King's social reforms to the next level was Tommy Douglas, a Scottish Baptist minister who became one of the most eloquent and respected politicians of his day. Douglas is best remembered as the father of socialized medicine in Canada, but his most significant overall influence was moving the nation's political culture much farther to the left than it had ever been before. Many Canadians consider the social democratic paradigm that he helped introduce to be an inviolable aspect of Canadian life. Indeed, when journalists and polling firms ask Canadians what they believe to be the essence of Canadian identity, the average Canuck invariably points to high-profile social programs that Tommy Douglas helped to create. Socialized medicine, for example, has become a potent symbol of Canada's "kinder, gentler" social democratic political culture, and whenever politicians propose modernizing or streamlining the cumbersome system, they usually end up paying a heavy political price.

Tommy Douglas was born in 1904 in Falkirk, Scotland to proud, working class parents. There were two major influences in his early life that would shape his political thinking as an adult. When he was seven years old, he contracted a potentially fatal bone disease in his right leg. Since Douglas's parents were poor, they could not afford the required medical treatment, and it appeared that the lad might have to have his leg amputated. Fortunately, a magnanimous doctor offered to treat the disease free of charge, and young Tommy was eventually cured. This experience had a profound effect on Douglas and shaped his ideas on universal health care.

The second major influence was Douglas' Scottish grandfathers, who taught him Christianity was an agent for social change, not meant only to secure a better afterlife. They also taught young Tommy to debate, to appreciate Robert Burns, and to continually educate himself. The Douglas family moved to Winnipeg in 1919, just in time for the impressionable boy to witness the Winnipeg General Strike, a powerful spectacle of labour unrest and working class solidarity.

Douglas, despite having quit school to go to work as a printer at the age of fourteen, decided at age twenty to study at Brandon College in Manitoba and then enter the Baptist ministry. During this period, the short, vibrant little Scot became a champion boxer and a powerful orator and debater. He also developed radical ideas, which he called the "Social Gospel", meaning that the princi-

NATIONAL ARCHIVES OF CANADA / C-036220

TOMMY DOUGLAS IN 1961

ples of Christianity were worthless unless they were used to bring about much needed social change. Thus Douglas built on the teachings of his grandfathers.

After graduation, Douglas moved to Weyburn, Saskatchewan, in 1930 and became the town's minister. This brought him into close contact with the worst hardships inflicted by the Depression and soon made it clear that the best way to fulfill his Christian duty was through active political action. In 1935, as a member of the fledgling Cooperative Commonwealth Federation, he ran in a federal election and found himself on his way to Ottawa as a Member of Parliament.

It took little time for him to become known as one of the most effective and likeable debaters in parliament, and although many Canadians were deeply suspicious of the socialist agenda, Douglas was able to disarm them with his wit, humour and logic. The ravages of the Depression made his arguments seem reasonable, and Douglas attracted an ever-larger following. When Canada entered the Second World War with King at the helm, Douglas pointedly commented, "Surely, if we can produce in such abundance in order to destroy our enemies, we can produce in equal abundance in order to provide food, clothing and shelter for our children." Later, he attacked the war economy itself: "We [Canada] went from spending $580 million a year, which was the Canadian budget, to spending over five billion dollars a year, and we didn't borrow a dollar from outside Canada. We put every person to work and put people into uniform who made tanks and guns and planes, who could just as easily have been making houses, building hospitals, recreation centres, daycare centres. We could have done all those things. We didn't do it." Canadians listened more and more attentively to Douglas' pointed criticisms, and many historians feel that Douglas' views greatly influenced the already reform-minded King.

An interesting element of Douglas' politicking was that, although he was a staunch socialist, he never spoke in revolutionary or Marxist terms, which would have been unpalatable or even frightening to most Canadians. Instead, he employed the sensible, folksy language of a country preacher, appealing to people's sense of fairness and decency. This made Douglas almost impervious to political attack, and although many politicians disagreed with his views, their criticism was never vicious or personal. Douglas seemed the very antithesis of a radical socialist, and a majority of his constituents in Saskatchewan adored him. He came to believe, however, that he could affect more change at the provincial level, and in 1944, he was elected Premier of Saskatchewan, giving the province the first socialist government in North America. He soon implemented his socialist agenda with a dizzying barrage of legislation aimed at improving the quality of life of the average worker. Among his many initiatives were establishing publicly owned utilities, such as Saskatchewan Power and Sask Tel, which provided rural areas with power and phone services they'd never had before; expanding educational opportunities; imposing a minimum wage; recognizing collective bargaining, establishing workers' compensation and supplying medical insurance for all. Douglas' reforms continued throughout his five terms as premier, but his biggest program was Medicare, the publicly funded universal health care system, which was finally passed in 1962. The other provinces as well as the federal government took notice, as did ordinary Canadians. Medicare soon proved that socialized medicine could work, and Canadians in other provinces began demanding similar programs. Within a decade, all the other provinces had fallen in line, and all Canadians became entitled to universal medical coverage, a radical and fundamental step in the emergence of a welfare state.

Douglas resigned as premier in 1961 to lead the federal New Democratic Party, a socialist alliance between organized labour and the old Cooperative Commonwealth Federation. The NDP, Canada's third national political party, was decidedly left of centre, and gave Canada's workers a distinct political voice. Douglas led the party until 1971 and continued as a parliamentarian until 1979 – a remarkable career that included forty-three years in either federal or provincial politics.

Over the decades, other political parties were forced to adopt social democratic policies and move towards the political centre and in a very visible way, Douglas and his socialist movement changed the ideological landscape of Canadian politics. His death in 1986 inspired glowing accolades from across the country, including many from political opponents.

Influenced by Douglas, Canada continued to expand its social democracy, which reaching a apogee during the sixteen-year leadership of Pierre Elliott Trudeau. The brilliant son of a successful Québec businessman and a mother of Scottish descent, and educated at the Université de Montréal, Harvard and the London School of Economics, Trudeau was fluently bilingual and at home in both cultures, though decidedly more comfortable in the upper echelons of society than among working class Canadians. He was, nevertheless, a true liberal and when he became Lester Pearson's Minister of Justice in 1967, just two years after being elected to parliament, he wasted no time in liberalizing the laws on divorce, abortion and homosexuality.

He had to be convinced to contest the Liberal leadership in 1968 and was elected only on the fourth ballot, but his popularity in the ensuing general election was unprecedented in Canada. Though a private and rather undemonstrative person, he was a superb speaker and had about him an aura of mystique. Perhaps for these reasons, he was welcomed like a rock star in many places in Canada, with enormous crowds and screaming fans, during the 1968 campaign. He won a majority and went on to serve longer than any other prime minister, with the exception of the two Scots described above – Sir John A. Macdonald and William Lyon Mackenzie King.

Trudeau's achievements included official bilingualism, the repatriated Constitution and the Canadian Charter of Rights – accomplishments that assisted significantly in Canada's coming of age, but when he left office in 1984, Canadians were deeply divided in their feelings about him and the country itself was as divided as it had been in decades.

WESTERN CANADA PICTORIAL INDEX / A1715-56168

PRIME MINISTER PIERRE TRUDEAU GREETS QUEEN ELIZABETH II IN JULY 1970.

Since the birth of British North America, Scottish political achievements in Canadian history have been unparalleled in terms of their scope and ramifications. Indeed it is not unreasonable to claim that the Scots' political acts, in a very true sense, created the Canada we know today. Governors General Murray and Elgin, Scottish nobles influenced by the egalitarian ideals of the Scottish Enlightenment, helped to preserve the French culture in Canada, paving the way for bilingualism and the thriving French culture within the federation. Reformers Gourlay and Mackenzie served as agitators in Upper Canada that indirectly and ultimately led to responsible government in the colonies. The founding fathers, mostly Scots, negotiated and constructed a uniquely Canadian constitution that created a transcontinental nation. The first two Scottish prime ministers, Macdonald and Mackenzie, put into place permanent Canadian institutions that helped the nascent Canadian nation govern itself effectively at a critical time. Macdonald went on to become the driving force behind building the CPR, which served as a viable economic link between the unlikely federated provinces. Moreover, his patriotic National Policy gave Canada an alternative to falling under the inordinate influence of the United States during the country's formative years. King, Douglas and Trudeau moved Canada towards a social democratic political model that serves, in part, as a central cornerstone of Canadian identity. Overall, the Dominion of Canada is indeed predominantly a product of Scottish political engineers.

THE MILITARY

There is widespread belief, both at home and abroad, that Canada is a harmonious dominion, a peaceful nation that evolved in a calm and measured fashion. Indeed, many Canadians assert with pride that, unlike the United States for example, Canada is not the product of war and social upheaval. This great serene northern land, embodying civilized values and inhabited by a population of enlightened pacifists, is a stereotype that is both popular and surprisingly persistent.

QUEEN'S OWN CAMERON HIGHLANDERS TARTAN KILT, COURTESY OF JAMES W. BURNS / SPORRAN AND KILT HOSE COURTESY OF HONOURARY COLONEL DOUG LUDLOW/ BELT AND SHOES COURTESY OF THE SCOTTISH CROFT, SYDNEY, BC

Many Canadians tend to feel a certain moral smugness knowing that Canada's history reveals a path of peaceful progression rather than one of confrontation and conflict. Unfortunately, such self-righteousness stems from ignorance. In truth, Canada's history is full of bloody conflict. In fact, no historical force has forged and altered the Canadian nation more than war. And no other ethnic group has borne more of the brunt of war than the Scottish Highlanders, who brought their martial culture to Canada and fought in most of the battles that shaped the country. Through war, Canada endured a series of crucibles, eventually emerging as a modern, independent and self-confident nation, and in this dialectical historical process, the Scots played an enormous role.

The Scottish Highlands produced a breed of men who for centuries were known as some of the world's best soldiers. The cold, wet, barren Highlands did not forgive weakness of any sort, and only the most hardy were able to survive the harsh climate, scant crops and unremitting poverty of the region. Over centuries, Highlanders developed a martial culture based on honour, interdependence, loyalty to a clan and chieftain, indifference to physical hardship, and courage. They also acquired skill and fierceness with weapons that truly terrified their enemies. The very qualities that allowed them to thrive in the bleak Highlands made them excellent professional soldiers.

After the Battle of Culloden in 1745 and the subsequent Highland Clearances, a majority of Highlanders was forced to leave home and construct new lives. In many ways, the world beyond northern Scotland was unfamiliar: Britain was industrializing, and factory smokestacks began to spike up and sully the air throughout the countryside. A worldwide empire of colonies was opening up, and ships laden with goods from distant lands filled busy British harbours. Commercial society was growing rapidly, supplanting old feudalistic traditions. Thrust into this changing world, the Highlanders were forced to find a market for their skills. It soon became apparent to many of them that their martial talent was their greatest asset, and many signed on with the British army.

Although traditional Highland weapons, such as the broadsword and axe, and Highland garb, such as the kilt and tartan, had been outlawed after Culloden, English generals decided to lift this ban for their Highland soldiers. They recognized that traditional weapons and garb would boost morale and effectively tap into the Highlanders' ancient fighting skills. They also understood the Highlanders' clannish nature and made a point, whenever possible, to compose certain regiments entirely of Highlanders, led by a Highland commander, a chieftain figure for whom the loyal troops would be ready to lay down their lives. Organizing Highland regiments according to pre-existing cultural traditions was a stroke of genius, which resulted in courageous teams of crack warriors, among the most effective the world has known.

Scottish troops made their first appearance in North America during the Seven Years' War (1756–63), a bitter struggle between the imperial powers of Great Britain and France. Before this conflict, however, "Canada" had seen a great deal of war. Intertribal warfare had been a way of life among many First Nations peoples for countless centuries. Moreover, after 1608, when Champlain established the stronghold of Québec and the colony of New France, the French had been constantly at war, first with the Iroquois, then with the English over territorial hegemony. By the time the Seven Years' War came about, New France had been at war for almost a century and a half.

The Seven Years' War began in North America when it became clear to the French, who claimed all lands that drained into the Mississippi River, that the English colonists in America desired to expand west into territory claimed by the French. To solidify their claims, the French set up Fort Duquesne in the Ohio River Valley. The American colonies interpreted this as a flagrant attempt to block English expansion and sent a military force under commander George Washington to expel the French. Washington ambushed a French patrol, killing ten men and sparking a bloody war that would last for years. The infuriated French answered by laying siege to and defeating Washington's army at his outpost, Fort Necessity.

The humiliated British in the thirteen American colonies made a decision to do away with the French threat once and for all. They would send a large army of 2,500 men to the Ohio Valley, engage the enemy, and take the region. The French, however, had been living among First Nations warriors for decades and had adopted their guerrilla tactics. They had also managed to ally themselves with several Native nations who saw land-hungry English settlers and farmers as far more of a menace than French traders. Instead of arranging the soldiers in standing formations and marching headlong into volleys of enemy fire, the French had learned to scatter, hide in the dense foliage, and pick off their enemies from a distance. They also learned how to lure an army into an ambush where it could be surrounded and cut down from all sides.

The French and their Native allies bushwhacked the large colonial army in the Ohio Valley, killing 977 men and losing only twenty-three. Although New France had only 60,000 inhabitants while the thirteen American colonies had a population of well over a million, the French were a united and experienced fighting force that won battle after battle. At Niagara, Oswego and at sea, they drove the British back.

In 1756, the first regiment of Scots, the Black Watch, was sent over to America to engage the French. That winter, the Highlanders underwent extensive guerrilla warfare training. Their traditional tactic of lobbing cannon fire on opposing armies, followed by directly charging their disoriented foes while shouting and hacking furiously with broadswords and axes, was obviously going to be of little use against the elusive French and Native bush fighters.

Finally, in 1758, the Black Watch engaged the famous General Montcalm and his army at the French outpost of Fort Carillon on the shore of Lake Champlain. After trading shots for several frustrating hours, the Highlanders fell back on their traditional battle tactics and charged the fort. The unruffled Montcalm, well prepared behind the walls of his stronghold, essentially cut them to pieces with organized volleys of fire. The raging Highlanders again charged only to be slaughtered by French muskets. Their Celtic blood boiling, the Highlanders screamed for vengeance and again charged the fort, some even managing to evade the rain of musket balls and scale the fort's walls, only to be bayoneted by the waiting French soldiers. Five times the wild Highlanders charged, but it was futile. All the wrath and fury in the world could not shake the experienced French, and after four cruel hours, the Black Watch was forced to accept defeat. Six hundred fifty men, half the regiment, had been killed or wounded, but it was a valuable, albeit painful, lesson. The Highland regiments thereafter adapted themselves extremely effectively to the realities of fighting in the wilds of North America and seldom lost another battle.

The same year, another Highland regiment, the Montgomery Highlanders, led the attack to take Fort Duquesne in the Ohio Valley. The Highlanders suffered heavy casualties but were ultimately successful. The French retreated, abandoning their doomed claim to the Ohio Valley, which marked a critical point in the war. It was the turning of the tide for the French, who would lose most subsequent battles and eventually the whole continent. The British renamed the captured fort after Prime Minister William Pitt, and it eventually became the city of Pittsburgh.

A key to defeating New France was to take the formidable naval fortress Louisbourg on what is now Cape Breton Island. The heavily fortified stronghold stood guard over the St. Lawrence Seaway, New France's route inland to its principal cities, Québec and Montréal. If Louisbourg could be captured, the path would be clear to attack the heart of New France.

In June 1758, 12,000 British troops sailed from Halifax to Louisburg.

Brigadier-General James Wolfe led the attack along with the Fraser Highlanders regiment. Wolfe had fought against Highlanders at Culloden and was initially apprehensive about fighting alongside them. However, he soon came to appreciate their toughness, determination and loyalty, and at Louisbourg and Québec, Wolfe came to depend on the Scots to do the most difficult, dangerous fighting. Some historians contend that Wolfe had a death wish, desiring to fall in glory on the battlefield. This would explain his recklessness in the face of overwhelming fire. Whether this is true or not, Wolfe was indeed courageous to the point of foolhardiness, and he needed troops as fearless as he was. He found them in the Highlanders. He and his Highlanders made a daring charge against a vital French position, shells bursting all around, capturing it and clearing the way for a British landing. The British put Louisbourg under a terrible siege, blasting it relentlessly for seven weeks until the beleaguered French commander was forced to capitulate.

Unopposed, the British made their way the following spring into the interior of New France. The awesome spectacle of 140 British war ships sailing up the St.

HENRY R.S. BUNNETT / NATIONAL ARCHIVES OF CANADA / C-113709

WILLIAM WOOD / NATIONAL ARCHIVES OF CANADA / C-002164

GENERAL JOHN SMALL, ABOVE, COMMANDED THE 42ND REGIMENT AT CARILLON IN 1758.

LEFT: THE 5TH ROYAL SCOTS OF CANADA, PORTRAYED IN THE 1880S.

Lawrence caused panic among the French *habitants* whose farms lined the riverbanks. Wolfe, who had just been promoted to full general, anchored near the virtually impregnable citadel of Québec and planned his next move. The city was perched on a cliff high above the river, and there seemed to be no way for British soldiers to reach it. On an elevated precipice on the opposite side of the river from Québec, the British set up long-range cannons and began mercilessly to bombard the French. Although the destruction was enormous and French civilians died by the dozen, the outgunned Montcalm held out. Wolfe became increasingly frustrated and sent raiding parties along the riverbanks to lay waste to *habitant* farms. Still, nothing happened. As the summer began to slip away with no victory in sight, Wolfe became increasingly aggravated. British ships would soon have to withdraw from the St. Lawrence to avoid freeze-up.

In a last desperate act on September 13th, Wolfe assembled 700 of his best troops, mostly Fraser Highlanders, and under cover of darkness, sailed upstream to scale a remote cliff to the plains above. Climbing the sheer fifty-metre rock face was almost impossible, but amazingly, the men, many of whom were used to ascending the flinty Highland mountains, were successful. As they approached

NATIONAL LIBRARY OF CANADA / 22642

THE FRASER HIGHLANDERS STORMING THE HEIGHTS OF QUÉBEC.

several French sentries, a French-speaking Highlander, Captain Donald Macdonald, convinced them that fellow French soldiers were approaching. The British were thus able to overpower the sentries and position themselves for the bloody battle to come.

As daylight broke on the Plains of Abraham, Wolfe arranged his troops in battle formation with the Fraser Highlanders in the front rank led by the Scottish General James Murray. An incredulous Montcalm marched his troops to meet them, and the two armies exchanged fire. After several vicious volleys that tore through the flesh and shattered the bones of both armies, the Fraser Highlanders threw down their muskets, drew their broadswords, and charged savagely.

"I can remember the Scotch Highlanders flying wildly after us," wrote Joseph Trahan, a French soldier, "with streaming plaids, bonnets, and large swords – like so many infuriated demons – over the brow of the hill. In their course was a wood in which we had some Indians and sharpshooters, who bowled over the Scotch savages in fine style." Once again, the Highlanders paid a heavy price for charging headlong into enemy fire, but they also caused the French to panic and retreat and were primarily responsible for winning the battle.

The British had won the fateful battle on the Plains of Abraham, but Québec was by no means secure. Both Wolfe and Montcalm had been hit by enemy fire and died, and the tough little Scot, James Murray took charge. He took over the city, nursed his bloodied troops, and braced himself for a cruelly cold winter with few provisions. During the months that followed, more than 1,000 of Murray's men died of cold, starvation, and sickness. The following April, the skilled French General Lévis assembled his troops outside the walls of Québec, ready to re-engage the wretched, emaciated British troops. This was an ironic role reversal made doubly ironic when Murray made the same mistake that Montcalm had made, marching his men outside the city to meet his enemy head-on. The well-rested French army quickly shot down dozens of British soldiers before the rest retreated inside city walls and prepared for a dreadful siege. Fortunately for Murray and his men, the British had decimated the French navy in Europe, and a large armada of British ships soon appeared on the St. Lawrence to occupy New France. The French had no choice but to surrender to overwhelming British might, and on September 8, 1760, New France ceased to exist.

The battles near Québec were the culmination of the Seven Years' War in North America, also known as the "Conquest" (a singularly tactless term), when it became clear, once and for all, that half a continent would be turned over to British hands. Throughout the long, bloody war, Scottish regiments played an inordinately large role in key battles, which ultimately and profoundly influenced the future course of Canada as well as the United States.

After the official birth of British North America in 1763 when peace seemed likely for the foreseeable future, the Highland regiments were disbanded. The Scottish fighters were given a choice either to return home or to stay in North America. Those who chose the latter would be given a land grant in the upper part of British North America in recognition of their valuable services during the war. Since Scotland was plagued with unemployment and the Highlands were by that time being ruined by the Clearances, the majority of soldiers decided to stay. Thus, from very early on in Canada's history, the Scots established themselves as landowners with a vested interest in their new country. For the next century, Gaelic would be the third most widely spoken language in what would become Canada.

Peace in the colonies did not last long, however. After the war's end, General James Murray remarked prophetically, "If we were wise, we would return Canada to France. New England needs something to rub up against." In other words, in the absence of a French threat, the independent-minded American colonies of New England would begin to clash against their mother country. Such fears were realized in 1775 when the thirteen American colonies held a Continental Congress to coordinate a common strategy against Great Britain. The "Americans" invited the northern colonies to attend the Congress, but there seemed to be little revolutionary fervour in the upper part of the continent. This is due probably in large part because the English-speaking subjects were happy with the land grants the British had bestowed upon them, and they did not want to rock the boat, and the French were suspicious of coming under the influence of yet another foreign country. At least under General Murray and Governor Guy Carleton, the French had been treated relatively well.

The Continental Congress decided to attack the British northern colonies, and in September 1775, an American army, led by Benedict Arnold, assailed Québec City, and another, led by Richard Montgomery, marched on Montreal. The French generally stayed neutral, neither resisting nor aiding the Americans, and Montréal was soon under martial law. Montgomery then moved his troops to Québec City to aid Arnold.

During the build-up of hostilities between Great Britain and her American colonies, more Highlanders were called into military service. The old regiments in North America were revived as well, and a new one was formed and called "the Royal Highland Emigrants".

When Montgomery and Arnold attacked Québec City, the tough and disciplined Highland Emigrants met them. Montgomery was shot dead at the outset, and a musket ball ripped through Arnold's leg, forcing him to retreat. The American army pushed into the city in the midst of a blinding snowstorm, where they fought hand to hand with the Scots. This, of course, was exactly the kind of fighting the Highlanders were famous for, and the Americans never stood a chance. Under commander Allan Maclean, the Highlanders killed more than 100 Americans

NATIONAL ARCHIVES OF CANADA / C-005420

TODAY, AS IN THE LATE NINETEENTH CENTURY, SCOTTISH REGIMENTS IN DRESS UNIFORM ARE EASILY IDENTIFIED AMONG THE CANADIAN FORCES.

and took 400 prisoners. The Scots lost only three men.

The American troops pulled completely out of Canada by the summer of 1776, and various Highland troops were stationed along the border to repel any future attacks. Such attacks, however, never came, as the United States declared itself an independent nation that same summer. It is interesting to consider that the Declaration of Independence brought about not one country but two. While the American colonies had made clear their intention to become a single sovereign nation, they also tacitly recognized that the upper half of North America would go its own direction and not fall under U.S. influence. This was, of course, a critical point in Canada's history. Repelling the American army at Québec had been crucial to maintaining "Canadian" independence from our powerful southern neighbour.

After the American Revolution, between fifty thousand and sixty thousand loyalists poured into the shrunken "British North America". Many of these loyalists were Scottish military men who received land grants from the seemingly endless supply of *terra firma* that existed in the colonies. The Scottish troops in Canada, such as the Royal Highland Emigrants, were disbanded and granted still more land for their services.

Though the American Revolution had ended with a peace treaty, feelings of hostility between British and Americans simmered just below the surface for a quarter century. During the Napoleonic wars in Europe, Britain blockaded France and banned all countries, even neutral ones, from trading with the French. This hurt the American economy and became a major irritant for Americans, many of whom began to call for war. Meanwhile, many American politicians saw war with British North America as a way to absorb the northern colonies into the American union. During this period, few Americans thought "Canada" could remain neutral indefinitely, and most believed that most "Canadians" actually wanted to join the U.S. Furthermore, Great Britain would be unable to defend its North American colonies because its military was already stretched thin in Europe. Thomas Jefferson asserted that taking British North America would be "a mere matter of marching".

All British North America contained only 80,000 inhabitants, while the United States was a far more populous nation of more than seven million. It seemed unlikely that the sparsely populated, disparate northern colonies could offer much resistance to the superior might of the United States of America. In July 1812, the Americans declared war on Great Britain and marched an army of 2,500 men into Upper Canada.

Because of Great Britain's preoccupation with Napoleon, it could not send soldiers until 1814. In effect, "Canada" had to fend for itself in the face of staggering odds. The Scottish Glengarry Regiment of Light Infantry Fencibles was created in Upper Canada and fought skilfully in major engagements against the Americans. Most Scots, however, blended in with the local militias, with Highlanders usually commanding. A glance at the names of Upper Canada's militia commanders reveals the extent of Highlander prominence: Neil Maclean, William Fraser, Thomas Fraser, Alexander MacMillan, Allan Macdonell, Allan Maclean, John Macdonell, Archibald Macdonell, John Ferguson, Matthew Elliot, William Graham, William McKay and Aeneas Shaw.

The brilliant British General Isaac Brock and his Native ally, Tecumseh, instead of fighting defensively, immediately took war to the enemy. First, they employed a clever ruse to make the American General Hull at Detroit believe that British-Native forces were far greater than they actually were. Terrified of a massacre, Hull surrendered. Brock and Tecumseh then took Fort Dearborn (now Chicago) and much of the American western frontier. Brock died later that year at the Battle of Queenstown Heights where he pushed the American army back from the Canadian side of the Niagara River. Tecumseh died the following year when the U.S. Cavalry defeated a British-Native army near present day Chatham, Ontario.

In November 1812, an American army of 1,700 entered the poorly defended city of York (Toronto). The scant local militia set fire to a building containing a large gunpowder store to prevent it from falling into American hands. The ensuing explosion killed the invading American General and set off several furious days of American troops sacking and plundering before they eventually left the ruined city.

In August 1813, the Americans initiated a two-pronged attack against

Montreal. A militia consisting of French, British and Native Canadians ambushed the first prong at Chateauguay, forcing the Americans to retreat. Another British militia chased the second prong, overtook and engaged it near what is now Cornwall, and defeated it handily. Again, the American armies had failed to attain their military objectives and were compelled to withdraw.

By August 1814, professional British troops, including the Glasgow Lowland Division, had finally arrived in North America. In direct retaliation for what the Americans had done to York, the British army sailed to Washington and burned the American President's official mansion. They then ransacked and torched much of the city before moving on to Baltimore and wrecking it as well. The Americans were stunned. No one, least of all President Madison, had believed that the British could be so audacious. After the British were satisfied and had pulled back, the President's official residence was quickly rebuilt and whitewashed to hide the fire damage. It would be known thereafter as the "White House".

During the War of 1812, the Americans won several battles in Canada, but by and large, British forces stopped them cold. In effect, the United States lost the war, failing completely to obtain its political objective of conquering and absorbing British North America. With the dream of easily annexing the North at an end, the Americans began to focus their energies on expanding west. For Canada, the War of 1812 was critical. It confirmed and solidified the fact that British North America was determined to develop on its own, which ultimately paved the way for the creation of an autonomous Canadian nation.

The next significant military crisis in the Canadas came in 1837 when Scottish political agitator William Lyon Mackenzie King and French reformer Louis-Joseph Papineau instigated armed rebellions against the Crown (see Shaping the Political Landscape). Although there were many Scots among the rebels in Upper Canada, there were even more in the loyalist militias. Indeed, the dormant Highland regiments responded to the British call to arms with great alacrity and formed roughly one third of the militia that suppressed Mackenzie's uprising. They also made up half the British troops that put down the Patriote revolt in Lower Canada. This prompted a British officer to report glowingly that the group of Scottish military reserves in Upper Canada had "on every occasion been distinguished for good conduct, and will, in any emergency, turn out more fighting men in proportion to its population, than any other in Her Majesty's Dominions."

Until the Dominion of Canada was formed in 1867, the British kept garrisons of soldiers near the U.S. border to defend the colonies' sovereignty, as U.S. territorial ambitions were always a perceived threat. In fact, the fear of American invasion, probably more than any other single factor, led to Canadian Confederation. During the American Civil War, the Union Army had greatly increased in power, and some American politicians, annoyed at Great Britain for supporting the

South, were grumbling against Canada. Many Canadian politicians argued that only a unified Canada could assemble an integrated and significant deterrent to American invasion. The Scottish George Brown, one of the most prominent Fathers of Confederation, summed up Canada's fears in an 1865 confederation debate: "The Americans are now a warlike people. They have large armies, a powerful navy, an unlimited supply of warlike munitions, and the carnage of war has to them been stripped of its horrors. The American side of our lines already bristles with works of defence, and unless we are willing to live at the mercy of our neighbours, we, too, must put our country in a state of efficient preparation. And how can we do this so efficiently and economically as by the union now proposed?"

Canadian fears seemed to be realized when in 1866, a group of primarily ex-union Irish-American soldiers calling themselves the Fenian Brotherhood, launched border attacks in New Brunswick, the Niagara Peninsula, and the Red River region. Their political agenda was to free Ireland from British rule, so they struck the closest British target to the north while the U.S. government turned a blind eye to the whole affair. Canadian volunteer militias, again composed largely of Scots, clashed with the invading Fenians. Battles amounted to little more than nasty skirmishes with a few dozen men dying on each side, and soon, the Fenians, fed up with fighting, eventually pulled out of British North America, unable to achieve a victory or provoke a political response from Great Britain. The Fenian raids, however, had an enormous effect on confederation. Historian Desmond Morton calls the Fenians a "blessing" to Canada and asserts, "They united the country as nothing else could."

The Dominion of Canada was conceived and created, in no small part, as a response to the threat of war with the United States. Canadians were very aware of the American doctrine of Manifest Destiny, and the predominantly Scottish Fathers of Confederation thus sold the idea of a united Canada, to a great extent, as a defensive alliance.

After Confederation, Canada became responsible for its own defence, and the emergent federal government assembled a new national professional army. The Canadian military's enthusiasm and respect for British North America's Scottish military tradition was evident when a majority of the new regiments were given Highland names, such as the Highland Battalion of Infantry, the 94th Victoria Highland Provisional Battalion of Infantry, the 48th Highlanders of Toronto, the 91st Highlanders of Hamilton, the 72nd Highlanders of Vancouver, the 79th Highlanders and Queen's Own Cameron Highlanders of Winnipeg, and the Royal Scots Fusiliers of Montréal. While these regiments possessed Scottish names and a disproportionate number of Scots still served in the military, Highland regiments were no longer comprised exclusively of Scots. Canadians of many different ancestries proudly blended in, espousing and carrying on the martial spirit of the Highlanders.

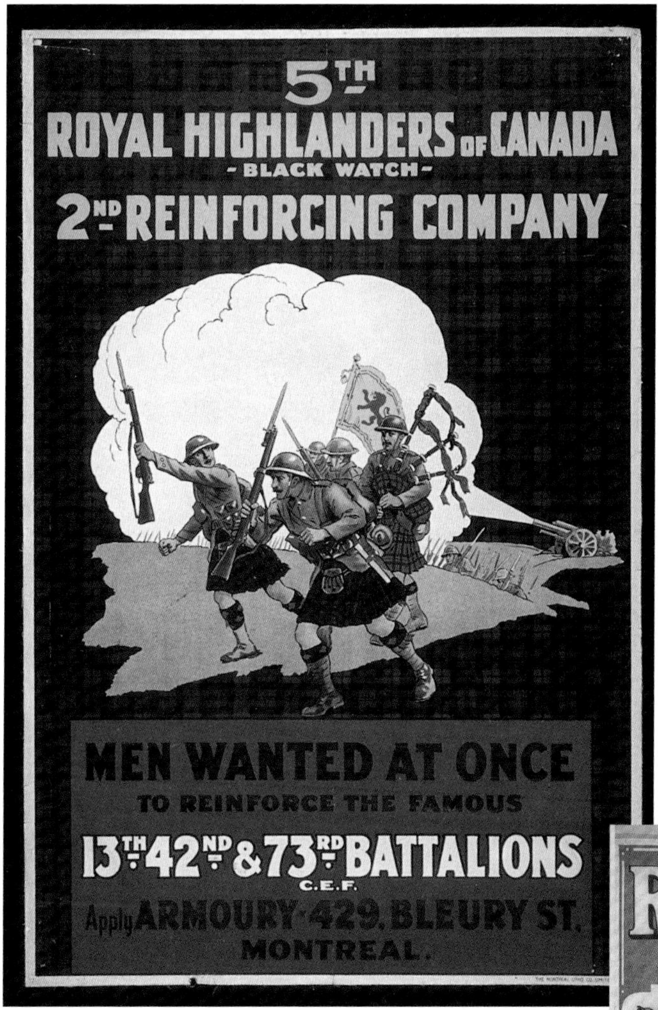

NATIONAL ARCHIVES OF CANADA / C-095391

New methods of mechanized warfare, the more utilitarian sensibilities of an industrial age, and an increasingly multicultural mix of soldiers all contributed to the demise of the kilt, tartan, broadsword, and bagpipe, except for ceremonial purposes. The Canadian Army became an efficient, no-frills, modern fighting force that reflected the emerging industrial culture of the day.

RECRUITING POSTERS USED HIGHLAND DRESS TO GOOD EFFECT DURING WORLD WAR I.

NATIONAL ARCHIVES OF CANADA / 095741

When World War I (also known as the Great War) broke out in Europe, Canada, as part of the British Commonwealth, found itself automatically at war. Caught up in the pre-war spirit of nationalistic enthusiasm and British patriotism, 30,000 Canadians immediately volunteered to fight for the mother country. Of these volunteers, two-thirds were recent British immigrants, many of them Scots. The excited lads from Canada began shipping out in October 1914, not knowing they were about to face one of the most horrific tribulations in all of human history.

All illusions concerning the glory of war were soon shattered during the

Canadians' first major engagement in which three Highland regiments came under the infamous German gas attack at Ypres. The terror of modern industrial warfare was ruthlessly unleashed on the wide-eyed Canadian boys, many of

WALTER CHESTERTON / NATIONAL ARCHIVES OF CANADA / C-013143

PREPARING FOR AN UNANTICIPATED HORROR, TROOPS DRILLED AT MCGILL UNIVERSITY IN 1915.

whom had never been far from the family farm. They suffered unspeakably from the horrid yellow gas, but refused to break their defensive line and ultimately thwarted the advancing Germans. Time after time, the Canadians distinguished themselves in equally horrifying battles that still ring with meaning today, such as the Somme, Vimy Ridge and Passchendaele. Allied commanders soon came to recognize and rely on the Canadians as among the toughest, most fearless, most effective soldiers of the war. In the final three months of the conflict, the battle-hardened Canadians led the charge through enemy lines, breaking one after another and occupying vast tracts of enemy-held territory. At the cessation of hostilities in November 1919, it was widely acknowledged that Canada's contribution to the allied effort had been far beyond its numbers.

After World War I, Canada would never be the same. Over 600,000 Canadians had served in the war. More than 60,000 had died and more than 170,000 had been wounded, many dreadfully disfigured or dismembered. War-weary Canadians had paid an enormous price, proportionally higher than any other allied country, to defend British imperialism. Much of the pull and glamour of the mother country had diminished, and Canadians became resolute that they were going to run their own affairs. The Great War, if nothing else, had earned them the right of self-determination.

Canadian Prime Minister Sir Robert Borden forced the British to recognize Canada as an "autonomous nation" within the British Commonwealth, and Canada signed the Treaty of Versailles, the World War I peace treaty, as an independent country. Canada also signed on with the League of Nations as a sovereign nation. These steps were symbolically extremely important, marking the fact that Canada had finally come of age and was a full fledged, self-governing nation state with its own unique identity.

In 1939, Canadians again answered the world's call to arms to defeat fascism in Europe and Asia, and once again, the country paid a disproportionate and terrible price to defend its ideals. Canada's proud Scottish military tradition, embodied and honoured in its Highland units, continued during the Second World War. Among the Canadian regiments that served with distinction were the 48th Highlanders, the Seaforth Highlanders of Canada, the Essex Scottish, the Black Watch of Canada, the Calgary Highlanders, the Queen's own Cameron Highlanders, the 1st Battalion Canadian Scottish, the Highland Light Infantry of Canada, the Stormont, Dundas and Glengarry Highlanders, the North Nova Scotia Highlanders, the Argyll and Sutherland Highlanders, the Cape Breton Highlanders and the Perth Regiment, the Lanark and Renfrew Scottish, the Toronto Scottish, the Lorne Scots, the Prince Edward Island Highlanders and the Scots Fusiliers. By the time the war drew to a close in 1945, Canadians had sacrificed more than 45,000 soldiers, and another 55,000 had been wounded, often horribly so.

During the Cold War, Canadian troops, as usual, served with honour and distinction, most notably in the Korean theatre. And since the worldwide collapse of communism, Canadian soldiers have established themselves as the world's pre-eminent peacekeepers serving in a remarkable number of United Nations peacekeeping missions throughout the world. While military budgets have shrunk steadily over the past two decades, the Canadian military has continued to preserve and pay tribute to its Scottish military tradition through its Scottish Highland regiments. Although many have been downsized, amalgamated or disbanded, the following Scots regiments still carry on their proud traditions:

The Black Watch
The Royal Highland Fusiliers of Canada
The Lorne Scots
The Stormont, Dundas and Glengarry Highlanders
1st Batallion, The Nova Scotia Highlanders
2nd Batallion, The Nova Scotia Highlanders
The Cameron Highlanders of Ottawa
The Essex and Kent Scottish Regiment

48th Highlanders of Canada
The Argyll and Sutherland Highlanders
The Lake Superior Scottish Regiment
The Queen's Own Cameron Highlanders of Canada
The Calgary Highlanders
The Seaforth Highlanders of Canada
The Canadian Scottish Regiment

Scottish prominence in Canada's military history is reflected by the fact that one third of Canada's regiments proudly bear Scottish names.

Canada, throughout its history, has been shaped enormously and undeniably by conflict and combat. The Seven Years' War, which culminated in the "Conquest", was, in essence, the birth of English Canada. The American Revolutionary War largely established what is now Canada as a permanent fact in North America, and the Loyalist migration gave the country a much-needed infusion of people. The War of 1812 solidified "Canada" and sent a clear signal to Americans that Manifest Destiny would not be accepted without a violent struggle. Confederation, modern Canada's very existence, came about as a response to the menace of war with the potent United States. Finally, the two world wars earned Canada its true independence from Great Britain as well as the respect of the world, and the crucible of those two horrid conflicts helped forge a pan-Canadian identity.

Canada, contrary to an all-too-popular belief, did not evolve peacefully. The modern Canadian nation emerged largely as a result of a series of brutal struggles, throughout which the Scots invariably played leading roles. From the outset of the Seven Years' War, Highlanders brought their military culture from the glens and heath-covered mountains of their homeland and transplanted it in what would become Canada. They fought and won vital battles that shaped the nation and bore the burden, more than any other ethnic group, of horrific casualties. The Scottish military tradition in Canada runs exceptionally deep and is thus appropriately preserved, honoured and embodied in Canada's present day military institutions.

Scottish Settlements

When writing about Scottish contributions to Canada, it is far too easy to concentrate solely on the brilliant achievements of individual Scots. Indeed, the more one learns about Canadian history, the more one is stunned at the ubiquity, prominence and profound impact of individual Scots on the nation. But this approach reveals only part of the story.

MACINNES TARTAN (ANCIENT DRESS), COURTESY OF DONALD MCINNES, DDS / SPORRAN, KILT HOSE, SHOES AND BELT, COURTESY OF THE SCOTTISH CR0FT, SYNDNEY, BC

For every famous Scot, whose success is supported by volumes of historical documents, there were untold thousands of ordinary Scottish immigrants who sought to make a better life in what is now Canada. Though their struggles were not, on the whole, imprinted on the nation's collective memory, these immigrants nevertheless made contributions to Canada's national fabric far out of proportion to their numbers. This "Scottish phenomenon" in Canada is due to three principal reasons: first, the Scots, by and large, had little choice but to emigrate. Their prospects at home were often less than hopeless, and many thus embraced the immigrant life with a vigour and motivation that virtually ensured success. Second, in general the Scots possessed particular attitudes and skills that helped them adapt successfully to the harsh realities of life in "Canada", while other immigrant groups seemed to not fare as well. Third, as they established themselves as some of Canada's earliest and most energetic immigrants, they were in a unique position to set the cultural tone during the nation's subsequent development. A brief survey of early Scottish settlements illustrates how Scottish culture was able to gain such an early and vital foothold and effectively lay much of Canada's cultural and social foundation.

Canada's first Scottish immigrants may have come to the new world much earlier than most Canadians realize. In 1965, one of Canada's finest writers, Farley Mowat, published *Westviking*, laying out evidence that Norse boatmen had settled in Newfoundland hundreds of years before the arrival of John Cabot in 1497. At the time, the academic community considered the book a piece of historical heresy and scoffed at Mowat's theories, but since then, impressive evidence has vindicated him, and his theory has become mainstream history. In 1998, however, Mowat threw a new wrench into the existing theoretical framework with his book, *The Farfarers*, claiming that the "Albans", a Pictish people who originally inhabited Orkney, the Hebrides, and parts of what is now mainland Scotland, preceded the Norse Vikings in North America by a full century. According to Mowat, aggressive Viking raiders drove the seafaring Albans ever west, compelling them to seek refuge first in Iceland, then in Greenland, and finally on Canada's eastern coast, in Baffin Island, Labrador and Newfoundland.

Drawing on four decades of research, Mowat points to very persuasive evidence such as ancient fifty-foot roofless stone houses, tapered at each end, which closely resemble ancient Alban houses in Scotland; the buildings were designed so that upturned boats could be used as roofs. Such structures are scattered throughout Baffin Island, Labrador and Newfoundland, and Aboriginal peoples claim that they were built not by their ancestors but by strangers who had come by boat and settled long ago. Mowat also cites other artifacts, such as numerous ancient stone cairns similar to those of Alban design, as well as an iron axe head, apparently of Pictish manufacture, which has been dated to the tenth century AD.

If Mowat's paradigm-busting theories are correct, the first Europeans to "discover" and settle in North America were not Norse but Alban. In effect, the initial European immigrants in Canada may very well have been Scots, although it remains to be seen if mainstream scholarship will eventually subscribe to this notion. As to what became of the Albans, Mowat believes that in some places they eventually blended in with local Native cultures and ceased to be a distinct people. In Newfoundland, however, Mowat theorized that the Alban people were driven inland, to the remote centre of the island, where their descendents may be living today. Perhaps DNA testing may someday offer conclusive evidence.

The first recorded influx of Scots immigrants into what is now Canada came at the beginning of the seventeenth century when the imperial powers of Europe were competing aggressively with one another to establish colonies in the New World. There was a New Spain, a New France and a New England, but there was no New Scotland. In 1605, the French had established their first successful North American colony at Port Royal (now Annapolis Royal, Nova Scotia). They had also claimed most of what is now most of Canada's east coast, calling it "Acadia". In 1613, however, the English captured Port Royal and seized all of Acadia with it. In 1621, William Alexander, a Scottish Lowland nobleman, poet and visionary came up with the idea that Scotland too deserved her own empire, and he convinced King James VI to grant him the land between New England and Newfoundland in order to form a New Scotland. To lend a legitimate and poetic ring to the project, Alexander called the new colony by its Latin name, *Nova Scotia.*

After Nova Scotia was made a legal reality, the problem was how to get anyone to settle there. Undaunted, Alexander came up with a scheme to sell noble titles, the "Baronets of Nova Scotia", to any Scot willing to clear and settle a 16,000-acre (or 6,400-hectare) chunk of wilderness. Some well-to-do, title-hungry Scots jumped at the opportunity, and in 1629, William Alexander's son and seventy newly-minted Scottish nobles sailed to Nova Scotia. For three years, they suffered severe winters, hacked through dense forests, and attempted to till the virgin soil.

In 1632, just when it seemed that some of the Scottish settlers might eventually meet with success, Nova Scotia was handed back to the French under the terms of a peace treaty, forcing the fledgling colony out of existence. While a handful of Scots did decide to stay under French rule, the disgruntled majority returned home. Despite the colony's failure, its royal charter gave Nova Scotia its name, coat-of-arms and flag. More importantly, it established in the minds of many Scots that there lay somewhere beyond the sea a "New Scotland", and a century and a half later, when Scots began to emigrate in large numbers, many chose Nova Scotia as much for the promise its name implied as any other reason.

Scottish emigration took off in the mid to late 1700s, primarily due to Culloden and the Highland Clearances that followed, but also because Britain's wars abroad gave many Scots a lucrative market to sell their fighting skills. Moreover, in 1763, British North America was born, which sparked excitement and hope among potential émigrés searching for a better life. During this period, there were three distinct modes of Scottish settlement in the upper half of North America: military settlement of retired soldiers who were granted land in recognition for service in assorted wars; proprietary settlement, usually organized and financed by charitable organizations or businessmen; and free settlement, initiated by individual Scots without help of any kind.

While military and proprietary settlement always brought Scottish immigrants directly to the land, free settlement usually required an immigrant to go through a period of dues paying and earning before he was able to acquire land. Regardless of which mode of settlement brought them to Canada, one thing is clear: to the Scots, land represented security and independence, and virtually all of them sought to own a piece.

After the Seven Years' War, Great Britain was faced with several nagging problems. It had a great number of battle-hardened Highland soldiers on its hands, and many English legislators did not relish the idea of trying to integrate them back into Scottish civilian life. Such a dangerous and volatile force, it was thought, might upset the peaceful equilibrium achieved in Scotland after Culloden. In North America, the British had a new colony consisting primarily of French Canadians who were potentially hostile to their new overlords. Britain would need to keep a loyal army close at hand to stamp out sedition of any kind if required. Finally, the American colonies in the southern half of North America were already grumbling rebelliously, and the British felt it necessary to have forces ready to counter any serious insurgence. To all these problems, the obvious solution was to settle disbanded Highland regiments in "Canada", enticing them with land grants and calling them into service whenever needed.

The first major group of Scottish settlers in Canada were members of the dissolved Fraser Highlanders and Black Watch. Many settled in Québec near

Murray Bay, while others chose Nova Scotia, primarily near Mount Murray. Both settlements were named after Scottish General James Murray, who had granted each of the soldiers 100 hectares of land. The land grants delighted the Highlanders and cemented their loyalty. Officers, of course, were granted much more.

Recipients of military land grants had several advantages that put them in a position to make their farms successful: the government provided them with the basic tools and seed they needed to sow and harvest their initial crop; they had no mortgages on their land, and most had saved enough of their military pay to see them through the first two or three years before the farm was productive. Within several years, most Scottish former soldiers had become prosperous, self-sufficient landowners, something almost undreamed of back home.

NATIONAL LIBRARY OF CANADA / 22644

AT GLENGARRY, THE NEWCOMERS TRANSPLANTED THEIR SETTLEMENTS, "UNALTERED, UNADULTERATED AND UNSULLIED", ACCORDING TO ONE OBSERVER.

At the end of the American Revolutionary War in 1784, the British again doled out land to disbanded Highland regiments. More than three thousand ex-soldiers settled in what are now Ontario and Québec, in places such as the townships of Glengarry, Lancaster, Charlottenburg, Cornwall, Osnabruck, Chatham and Williamsburg. Many others chose to homestead on land throughout Nova Scotia and what is now New Brunswick. While carving farms from the raw terrain was arduous in the extreme, the Highlanders generally banded together and helped one another through the difficult trial of the first several years. Indeed, their clannishness was another major factor in their success, giving them a sense of common purpose, community and fraternity as they struggled against the unforgiving Canadian bush.

As the Highlanders set down roots, their communities became close approximations of villages back home, albeit with a far more egalitarian flavour and with less dependence on a chieftain figure. Governor General Francis Bond Head, speaking of the Glengarry community, stated, "As [they] speak nothing but Gaelic, there is scarcely a stranger among them." He also remarked, "Their religion, language, habits and honour have continued there ... unaltered, unadulterated and unsullied." Indeed, as pockets of Highland culture in British North America spread, Highlanders were increasingly drawn to the New World to join family and friends. This is not to imply, however, that the Scots stayed entirely in their own communities, mixing only with others of their kind. In fact, one of the most interesting and peculiar aspects of the Scots was how easily they blended in with anyone and everyone whenever it suited their purposes, picking up languages and adapting to whatever circumstances they encountered.

At the end of the War of 1812, Britain realized that her hold on British North America was tenuous at best. Historian K.J. Duncan writes, "It was widely believed that only the loyalty of the inhabitants of the central and eastern parts of the colony, particularly the Scots between Kingston and Brockville, had prevented the Americans from occupying everything west of Montreal." Britain was therefore determined to settle ex-soldiers on land where they could be readily called into service, and the Crown doled out property to Highlanders near Perth, Richmond, Lanark and Drummondville. While some Scottish ex-soldiers, through inexperience or poor management, were not able to succeed as farmers, the majority prospered, establishing themselves very early in the colonies as privileged land owners, unfettered by debt. Their early advantageous position in a budding Canadian society was likely a major factor in their subsequent success and inordinate influence.

Proprietary settlement, which usually involved an individual or group acquiring a large piece of land and then actively recruiting immigrants to live on and work it, was an important mode of settlement that brought many Scots to British North America. In most cases, the proprietors' motives were altruistic, but

ROBERT R. MCIAN'S "J. MACALISTER, PASSENGER FOR CANADA" WAS DRAWN ABOUT 1850, BUT REPRESENTS THE YOUTHFUL HOPES AND TREPIDATION OF GENERATIONS OF SCOTTISH EMIGRANTS.

unfortunately, there were several nasty cases of unscrupulous behaviour that took a terrible toll on hopeful and unsuspecting immigrants.

After the Conquest, the British took control of Prince Edward Island and expelled the French. They then parcelled the whole island into sixty-seven townships of 8,000 hectares each, which they promptly granted to military officers and other nobles to whom they owed favours. Some of the nobles quickly sold their grants, and within a few years, wealthy Scottish Lowlanders held a majority of the island's townships. Most of them cared little for their land, and few ever set foot on it. Because there was no Crown land on Prince Edward Island, farms had to be either purchased or settled under contract with a proprietor.

There were several attempts to settle Prince Edward Island in the late 1700s. Captain John MacDonald, a noble Scottish military man, sold his holdings in Scotland and bought two island townships. His intention was to provide the Highlanders with a better life, but he also wanted to establish a sort of benevolent feudalistic estate with MacDonald as lord. Between 1770 and 1773, he managed to recruit 300 Highland families to work the land, but the arduous nature of clearing virgin bush and better prospects in the military caused many to bail out of their arrangement with him.

George Mendez Roe / Courtesy of the BMO Financial Group

THOUGH FARMING PRINCE EDWARD ISLAND'S RICH, RED SOIL WAS THE PRIMARY OCCUPATION OF ITS SETTLERS, FISHING, PARTICULARLY FOR COD AND LOBSTER, HAS LONG BEEN AN IMPORTANT INDUSTRY IN P.E.I., JUST AS IT IS IN NEIGHBOURING NEWFOUNDLAND.

Other would-be Scottish lords, such as Chief Baron Montgomery and Peter Stewart, endeavoured to settle Scots on the island. Between them, 200 families were transplanted, but again, the settlements did not initially proliferate. The American Revolutionary War attracted many Highlanders away from the buccolic island, and settlement was slow for decades. In 1779, only sixteen of the sixty-seven townships had any form of settlement; the rest were still wild. Despite this faltering progress, the Scots did manage to establish themselves on Prince Edward Island before anyone else, and their presence attracted a steady trickle of their kinsmen. Thus, from very early on, Prince Edward Island took on a decidedly Scottish character.

In 1803, Thomas Douglas, Lord Selkirk (see Blueprint for a Nation), bought several P.E.I. townships and brought 800 Highlanders to the land. Selkirk's settlement was well planned and organized. Land was carefully divided and communities were clustered together to ensure maximum convenience and interdependence among clan members, which was vital to the long-term success of the colony. Selkirk also made sure that his settlers had the proper tools, seed, and information to allow their farms to flourish. Unlike many other proprietors, Lord Selkirk had no interest in personal gain and spent his life and fortune attempting to help his countrymen. He encouraged his settlers to buy their land, offering them extremely favourable terms and extending generous credit. He also provided them with the leadership they needed to help them overcome the difficult stumbling blocks all new immigrants inevitably had to face. Selkirk, in effect, became a magnanimous chieftain who benevolently ruled his colony from afar.

In 1804, Selkirk brought several hundred more Highlanders to the island, this time having hired crews to clear the land ahead of the settlers. By any measure, the Selkirk settlements on Prince Edward Island were unqualified successes; the relocated Highlanders generally prospered and were unanimously grateful to their benefactor. Selkirk was deeply gratified and fulfilled by the triumph of his colony, and determined to continue on an even larger scale. Unfortunately, no more land on Prince Edward Island was available, so Selkirk set his sites on Upper Canada.

In 1804, after having to surmount many obstacles set out by the Family Compact, Selkirk finally obtained land near Lake St. Clair in Upper Canada. He hired Alexander McDonell to oversee the new settlement of Baldoon and brought twenty Highland families to inhabit the land.

Alas, from the outset, the Baldoon settlement was a disaster. McDonell viewed the independent, high-spirited Highlanders as an undisciplined rabble, while they saw him as a meddling tyrant. Furthermore, the settlers had arrived too late in the season to plant their first crop, resulting in an extra year of miserable hardship. Adding to the mix of problems, the soil at Baldoon turned out to be poorly drained and swampy, rendering normal methods of agriculture marginal at best. Sick of the whole debacle, a majority of Highlanders abandoned Baldoon.

A disappointed Selkirk gave them money to start afresh elsewhere and then began to focus on the great fertile plains of the Red River region.

As discussed in this book's fur trade chapter, Selkirk's Highland immigrants in the Red River Valley endured unimaginable and unforeseen hardships. Nevertheless, Selkirk was eventually vindicated. His settlers did ultimately prosper, opening the West to future settlement. The Scots also imprinted their character on the prairies in a way that endures to this day. Overall, the high-minded Scottish earl, despite many hindrances, did manage to resettle many of his countrymen and thus helped to introduce a strong Scottish spirit to Canada's developing multicultural mix.

Proprietary settlement did not always stem from altruistic impulses. In 1822, a roguish conman named Archibald McNab abandoned his wife and children in Scotland and fled to Upper Canada to avoid his creditors and debtors' prison. Like most successful scam artists, McNab was charming and a master of manipulation. On arrival in Upper Canada, he met with many members of the Family Compact and in an amazingly short time had wormed his way into the colony's most powerful clique. Convinced that he was an old-school Tory of the highest calibre, members of the Family Compact made McNab justice of the peace and granted him 2,000 hectares of prime land at Arnprior on the Ottawa River. McNab immediately began to recruit hopeful Scottish families to work the land for him.

In all, McNab recruited twenty-eight families of trusting Scots and coaxed them into signing agreements with him stating that they would pay high rents and fork over a significant percentage of their crops. In return, as soon as he deemed they had fulfilled their end of the bargain and settled the land properly, they would receive deeds to their farms. It soon became clear that McNab had no intention of ever handing over the promised deeds. He began to bully the generally illiterate Highlanders, most of whom were completely ignorant of their rights under Canadian law. McNab clearly desired to establish himself as a feudal lord, living from the labour of his indentured serfs. He even insisted that members of his clan were not allowed to leave their farms, even for a few hours, without his consent.

For fifteen years, the hated McNab oppressed his workers, and when the Highlanders mustered the confidence to challenge his authority, he used his influence with the Family Compact's corrupt courts to slap them down. It was only after the Rebellion of 1837, led by William Lyon Mackenzie, that the lieutenant governor took complaints against McNab seriously. The swindling Scot was finally stripped of his power and fled first to Hamilton, where he lived for several years, and then to Orkney.

Fortunately, proprietors like McNab were the exception, and proprietary settlement was, by and large, an important and effective means of relocating Scottish immigrants. William Dickson, for example, successfully transplanted 6,000 of his Scottish countrymen in the Township of Dundee in Upper Canada. Various church

CHARLES MILLS SHELDON / NATIONAL ARCHIVES OF CANADA / C-003363

HIGHLAND SETTLERS ARRIVE AT PICTOU, NOVA SCOTIA, FROM THE *HECTOR*, IN 1773

and charitable organizations were also responsible for bringing Scots to the land, though usually on a much smaller scale. But by the mid-1800s, proprietary settlement had waned, and from then on most immigrants were free settlers.

Free settlement was the mode adopted by the vast majority of Scottish emigrants. Simply put, free settlement consisted of booking passage to the colony, going there and then doing whatever it took to become established. For the most part, Scottish immigrants did not randomly pick a spot on the map. They usually joined friends or family members, so once Scots settled an area, further Scottish immigration invariably followed. This is a major reason Ontario and the Maritimes contain a relatively high proportion of inhabitants of Scottish descent.

One location that attracted Scots like a magnet was Pictou, Nova Scotia. Immigration to the region began in the early 1770s, and successful settlements led to further immigration. By 1830, settlements around Pictou boasted a population of more than 21,000 inhabitants, a very large number for the time. From Pictou, succeeding waves of immigration spread north to Cape Breton Island. Nova Scotia's proximity to Scotland itself, the rocky landscape and ocean reminiscent of home, and the presence of large numbers of kinsmen all made Nova Scotia a preferred destination for many Scottish emigrants.

Because of the unfavourable conditions in Scotland in the 1800s, especially in the Highlands, virtually every Scottish town had an emigration society that helped raise money for ship passage, provided information on the colonies, and offered advice on how to be a successful immigrant. As a result, most immigrants had a fair idea of what to expect in the New World. Moreover, letters from friends and family members in the colonies helped paint generally accurate (though sometimes overly rosy) pictures of immigrant life.

THOMAS DE VANY FORRESTALL / COURTESY OF THE BMO FINANCIAL GROUP

FROM THE EARLIEST SETTLEMENT PERIOD IN NOVA SCOTIA, THE APPLE HARVEST WAS OF GREAT IMPORTANCE. NOVA SCOTIA BEGAN EXPORTING APPLES TO GREAT BRITAIN IN 1849. HERE PICKERS WORK BELOW THE FIRST BUILDING OF ACADIA COLLEGE NEAR WOLFVILLE, ABOUT 1860.

After 1825, land companies sprang up throughout the eastern half of what is now Canada and played a large part in settling many thousands of immigrants. Such companies would obtain huge tracts of land, survey and parcel them, and then sell the land to immigrants, offering mortgages of various terms, usually twenty years or more. Although land companies generally made little profit, they did help plant settlers on plots of semi-prepared land, some with small houses, which vastly increased an immigrant's chances for success. Some land companies even sent agents to recruit in Scotland, offering free transport for those willing to enter into a mortgage. For many thousands of Scots, such an arrangement seemed a viable escape from grinding poverty. While some companies did not deliver on their promises, and a few took advantage of immigrants, most conducted business fairly and were responsible for significant numbers of immigrants.

The thought of early Scottish immigration to Canada usually creates images of a tough Highlander getting off a boat, heading into the bush and hewing logs to build a home. After several years of hard toil, clearing the land and planting, the immigrant is a self-sufficient farmer. Such images are mostly myth, though a tiny percentage of immigrants did succeed against overwhelming odds at this kind of independent settlement. For the most part, however, homesteading in the bush was next to impossible, as it required very specialized pioneering skills. The vast majority who attempted to attack the daunting Canadian wilderness failed

NATIONAL LIBRARY OF CANADA / 22643

IT TOOK AN EXPERIENCED WOODSMAN, LIKE WILLIAM DAVIDSON OF NEW BRUNSWICK, TO CONQUER THE OLD-GROWTH FORESTS. HERE DAVIDSON AND HIS CREW CUT MASTS FOR THE BRITISH NAVY.

miserably because they had neither the required expertise nor the considerable capital required to bring even a small farm into production. A successful homesteader needed to know how to cut timber, build a house and clear land, and all had to be accomplished by one man. He also needed a pair of oxen, a yoke, a logging chain, several months' supply of food, a plough, etc., all very costly. Thus independent homesteading, contrary to much Canadian folklore, was seldom undertaken by immigrants. Successful homesteaders were almost always Canadian or American born woodsmen who had years of pioneering behind them.

Almost all Scottish free settlers who ended up owning land bought farms already in production. While some purchased farms from land companies, the majority usually obtained employment and worked for several years in their new country, while saving a significant portion of their wages. When they had accumulated enough money, they purchased a small farm outright. Although the amount of time it took to earn enough for a farm varied, a study in Upper Canada between 1840 and 1860 revealed that the average Scot was able to do it in eight years. Interestingly, the Scots, far more than any other immigrant group, were able to save their money consistently over a long period of time. This undoubtedly was a significant factor in their rise to dominance. Their innate independence, excellent work ethic, parsimonious lifestyle, and loathing of debt all contributed to their prosperity, which later translated into disproportionate influence. The "Scotch" ability to delay gratification and handle money wisely gave them a definite advantage over others.

While many Scottish immigrants worked in urban centres and never sought to own land at all, most desired land, and in the late 1700s and through the 1800s, the Scots owned an astonishingly large amount of land in what is now Eastern Canada. While the majority did eventually buy small farms, most farmers continued to work at least part time at an occupation other than farming. Because so many Scots came to British North America with marketable skills, many were in the unique position of being able to diversify their income sources. Thus, the modern notion of supporting a family farm with an outside job is in fact very much a Scottish-Canadian tradition.

Patterns of Scottish settlement in the West differed greatly from those in the East, primarily because there was virtually no settlement at all in the West before 1870 (except in Manitoba, as discussed earlier, and in British Columbia, beginning about 1850) when the Hudson's Bay Company sold most of its vast land holdings to the Canadian government. Of course, between 1770 and 1870 the Scots had controlled the fur trade, establishing trading posts and mapping vast regions of the country. They were also responsible for the first real western settlement, the Red River colony, which in effect became a gateway for a later westward exodus. In essence, the Scots laid the foundations for western settlement.

After 1870, however, when a tide of immigrants from many countries poured into the West, few predominantly Scottish communities were established. Instead, Scots blended into Canadian communities and prospered through hard work and active involvement in business and public affairs. Their actual numbers in most communities seldom deviated from an average of fifteen or sixteen per cent.

Because the Scottish fur traders had already been active in the West for a century, they were used to being in charge, and they naturally assumed many of the important public sector and business roles after Hudson's Bay Company lands were opened up to settlers. In short, Scottish prominence and even dominance established itself early in the West, just as it had done in the East. For example, a large majority of the early premiers of Canada's western provinces and territories were Scots. Scots were also inordinately overrepresented as municipal politicians and government agents who oversaw Western development. Scottish businessmen, many having had a head start in the West due to the fur trade, used their knowledge and fur trade profits to launch into other enterprises. It is little wonder, then, that the Scots had such an influence on the character of the emerging West.

As for average Scottish settlers, the same qualities that allowed them to prosper in the East permitted them to thrive in the West. Most Scots intrinsically desired land and worked diligently to save in order to acquire it, usually avoiding debt. Between 1870 and the turn of the century, Scots held more land in the West than any other ethnic group. Though no such study has been undertaken, it would be interesting to see a breakdown of the ethnic origins of Canada's present landowners. Extrapolating from trends set out in the late 1800s, it would not be surprising if most land is still controlled by Canadians of Scots extraction.

The story of the Scots' success in Canada is truly astonishing, not only in terms of their dazzling individual achievements but also in terms of their collective success. And, satisfactorily explaining the paradox of the Scots is a challenge. How did a minority of relatively poor immigrants to Canada become so powerful and influential? A partial answer is that many Scots were pushed out of their homes precisely when the new colony of British North America was in its first stages of development. Many emigrated and became landowners in the new colony through military, proprietary, and free modes of settlement, obtaining a vested stake in a nascent Canadian society much earlier than other immigrant groups. In brief, they got in on the ground floor, and this gave them subsequent power and influence far beyond their numbers. In addition to coming to Canada early and often, most Scots came with winning attitudes. Their ability to delay gratification and work toward a future goal, their unwavering commitment to their new country, and their enthusiastic and active participation in public and business affairs made them stand out. Moreover, their tradition of disdaining debt, their desire for land, and their ability to live simply and handle money judiciously translated into long-term prosperity. Overall, Scottish patterns of settlement, which laid much of Canada's cultural and social foundation, help to understand its diligent, earnest, and sometimes sober national character.

As the next chapters will further illustrate, Scottish domination of virtually all forms of Canada's industry and in all parts of the country continued well into the late 1800s and early 1900s. For example, Alexander Graham Bell, perhaps the most famous Scottish-Canadian of them all, invented the telephone while living in Canada, making his first successful call between Brantford and Paris, Ontario in 1874. The young native of Edinburgh had moved to Ontario at the age of twenty-three but soon accepted a teaching position at Boston University. He later established his titanic Bell Telephone Company in 1877. Despite his necessary sojourns in the United States, Bell considered Canada his "home" and continued to spend every summer in Brantford and on Cape Breton Island, where most of his inventions were conceived and tested, including aeronautic equipment, sonar distillation and detection, and hydrofoil technology. It is fitting that Canadians, the world's most frequent users of the telephone, should be able to claim Alexander Graham Bell as one of their own.

Bell once summed up his philosophy of success – one that might just as easily apply to many of the Scottish enterprisers of his era:

> Leave the beaten track occasionally and dive into the woods. Every time you do so you will be certain to find something that you have never seen before. Follow it up, explore all around it, and before you know it, you will have something worth thinking about to occupy your mind. All really big discoveries are the results of thought.

Scottish Enterprise

For two and a half centuries, in Canada and elsewhere, the term "Scotch" has been synonymous with miserly frugality. It was, no doubt, employed by those who remarked with envy that Scots immigrants generally seemed to land on their feet more quickly and acquire wealth more rapidly than anyone else.

ANGUS TARTAN, COURTESY OF JOHN ANGUS / SPORRAN COURTESY OF BOB VANDEWATER / KILT HOSE, SHOES AND BELT COURTESY OF THE SCOTTISH CROFT, SYDNEY, BC.

THE STEREOTYPE OF THE RIGID, TIGHT-FISTED SCOT who saves and invests his way into prosperity actually has a good deal of basis in fact. The vast majority of Scottish capitalists in Canada came from inauspicious beginnings but, through steely discipline and a stiff work ethic, acquired enormous fortunes and built enterprises on a monumental scale.

The purpose of this chapter is neither to offer a detailed economic history of Canada nor to chronicle the achievements of every successful Scottish businessman – that would require a tome too heavy to lift. Once again, we must be highly selective. Our purpose here is to examine a small assortment of notable Scottish entrepreneurs who dominated Canada's industrial development and thus literally built the nation.

"Canada" attracted all stripes of Scot for many different reasons. The stoic Orcadians found employment in the fur trade long before and well after the Conquest. After 1760, and as a result of Culloden and the subsequent Highland Clearances, many Highlanders were attracted to British North America's expanding fur trade as well as opportunities in the military. Lowland Scots, generally better educated than their Highland brothers, immediately recognized British North America as a land of immense business opportunity not yet overexploited like other British overseas colonies. Commerce and trade had developed far later in Scotland than in England, and in the latter half of the eighteenth century Scottish businessmen were ready to "catch up". What they needed was a fresh marketplace as well as a dependable source of raw resources. The conquest of New France seemed to be the solution to all Scotland's commercial aspirations, and while the English were generally ambivalent about the new North American possessions, the Scots were vocal about not only retaining but embracing the new colonies. A 1760 editorial in the *Glasgow Journal* reflects how most Scots of the day viewed the upper half of British North America:

> Of all our acquisitions, the conquest of Quebec and consequently, of the country of Canada is the most important

> and most beneficial ... for such a source of trade and commerce will be opened to us here, as will be fully sufficient, had we no other, to employ all our trading and commercial people, and find a vent, or constant consumption, for all our goods, products, and manufactures. It is therefore above all things to be wished that the country of Canada may never be relinquished.

Another editorial that same year in the same newspaper again confirms the Scots' hopes for the new colony:

> The expense of this Conquest is the most thrifty disbursement ever made – an exclusive fishery! A boundless territory! The fur trade engrossed! and innumerable tribes ... contributing to the consumption of our staple! There are sources of exhaustless wealth! Ignorant and designing men have called this a quarrel for a few dirty acres of snow, but the public will soon have proof that Britain must sink or swim with her colonies.

In short, Scottish merchants enthusiastically embraced Canada and the Maritime colonies as a solution to their economic needs, while England was generally preoccupied with her other established overseas colonies and extensive trading network. This allowed Scottish businessmen to gain an early economic foothold in "Canada", which they never relinquished.

Between 1760 and 1800, hundreds of Scottish merchants poured into what is now Québec, seeking to get in on the ground level of what they felt would become an important hub of British trade. Finding themselves among thousands of French Canadiens, most Lowland businessmen asserted their clannish tendencies and created pockets of self-contained Scottish culture in their new home. Historian David Macmillan has written:

> [The Scots] tended to trade with their home ports and to congregate in their colonial settings with Scots from their own regions, if they were available. They also recruited clerks, craftsmen, and labourers from their own districts back in Scotland – and kinfolk wherever possible, often to the detriment of the colonial population seeking employment. It is not surprising that in Quebec and Montreal, the Scottish paramountcy in trade, commerce, and industry came to be bitterly resented by some of the local population.

The most prominent of the early Scottish merchants were the Finlay brothers, James based in Montréal and his brother Robert in Greenock, Scotland. By 1764, the brothers had established the first and most important regular shipping service between Britain and Québec, shipping out Scottish whiskey, woollens, ironware, guns, linens and tools and bringing back furs, lumber and potash. The brothers also exported hundreds of Scottish emigrants. On behalf of the many Scottish businessmen in Québec, the brothers advertised aggressively for "masons skilled in building, gardeners, quarries, and millers, fabricators of dry stone dykes, and good and sober men skilled in the management of flour and saw mills." Those who decided to make a new life in Québec were given free passage on a Finlay ship and guaranteed a well-paid job on arrival. In effect, the Finlays developed the first organized immigration service, which provided the new colony with a significant infusion of skilled Scottish craftsmen. These new immigrants were primarily responsible for the building boom that transformed Montréal during the 1760s, 1770s and 1790s.

The Finlay brothers were so successful that many other Scottish shipping firms emulated them. By 1800, thirty-five firms based in Greenock and Glasgow were trading regularly with Québec, Nova Scotia and New Brunswick. While English shipping magnates also got in on the trade, the Scots had managed to dominate the northern shipping routes early and continued to be responsible for the majority of transatlantic trade with what would later become Canada.

Among the many successful Scottish shipping tycoons that emerged in the northern colonies in the late 1700s and early 1800s, several stand out. Based in Halifax, William Forsyth, originally from Greenock, owned the largest fleet, some twenty ships, in the Maritimes and traded extensively not only with Scotland but also with the American colonies, England and British colonies in the West Indies. He contributed greatly to diversifying Maritime trade.

James Dunlop of Glasgow set up his base in Montréal and travelled extensively throughout what are now Ontario and Québec, securing contracts with producers of potash, timber, and grain. His strategy of actively seeking out raw materials and new markets helped greatly to stimulate the inland economy and create a reliable market for Scottish manufactured goods. Dunlop ploughed his profits into ship building, importing Scottish shipbuilders by the score. By 1810, he had the largest mercantile establishment in British North America, his ships moving up and down the St. Lawrence along a vast network of docks and warehouses and sailing to and from Europe and the West Indies. Dunlop helped establish Montréal as one of North America's busiest shipping ports.

Christopher Scott from Greenock came from a family of prominent Scottish shipbuilders. In 1797, he immigrated to New Brunswick in order to make use of the vast forests of shipbuilding timber. He recruited dozens of Scottish shipbuilders and within two years managed to send nineteen new ships laden with New Brunswick timber back to Scotland. Scott's venture not only kicked off New Brunswick's shipbuilding industry but also its timber industry. By 1807, for example, 156 primarily Scottish ships, with more than 20,000 tonnes of lumber, sailed for Britain.

The Scots' zeal for exploiting the potential of the northern colonies ensconced them very early as the country's dominant economic players, and their success helped galvanize further Scottish immigration, which continued at unprecedented levels during the 1820s, 1830s and 1840s. Of course, from the Conquest to the 1820s, the British northern colonies' most important industry by far was the fur trade, dominated by Highland Scots. In fact, it is reasonable to say that without the enormous profits generated by the fur trade, the economy would have lacked the critical mass to stimulate other industries. The vast majority of industrial activity, merchandising, shipping, and supplying, revolved around the fur trade to which most prominent businessmen, especially in Montréal, were connected. In essence, the fur trade was the economic springboard that launched industrial diversification in Canada's early history.

As we have already considered the fur trade rather extensively in a previous chapter, we need not do so in detail here. As already mentioned, fur trade barons such as Simon McTavish and other North West Company partners were, for two generations, some of Canada's most prominent and respected businessmen, their ostentatious houses towering imposingly in Montréal and Lachine, and their names appearing on the party list of every Montréal socialite. While the trade had yielded enormous profits, it was clear after the amalgamation of the two giant

THOMAS DAVIES / NATIONAL GALLERY OF CANADA / 6286

THE BURGEONING CITY OF MONTRÉAL, AS SEEN FROM THE SLOPES OF MOUNT ROYAL IN 1812.

fur trade companies in 1821 that the industry was falling into gradual decline. Many Scots who had profited so handsomely for so many years began to diversify their capital into other emerging industries.

James McGill is representative of the many self-made Scottish businessmen who used their fortunes not only to undertake new business ventures but also to build badly needed social institutions in their new country. McGill was born in Glasgow in 1744, the son of an ironsmith. Due to the unique egalitarian nature of the Scottish school and university systems of the day, McGill was able to attend a high quality parish school and then enter Glasgow University. At the age of twenty-one, he had a obtained a solid education with extensive knowledge in mathematics, merchant-style accounting and financial theory, in addition to Latin, English and French. In fact, McGill was able to speak French fluently before he moved to Montréal, which proved to be of great benefit in the Canadian fur trade.

Like many educated young Scots of that era, McGill believed that only from a position of economic advantage could a person effect constructive social change. In other words, without adequate financial resources, one was powerless. Unlike popular assumptions of today, which essentially hold that most businessmen have little or no social conscience and are only concerned with the bottom line, the Scottish merchant class of the late 1700s saw no contradiction between the goals of business and the overall social good. In fact, the Scots held quite an opposite view. Most felt that there was a hierarchy of needs and that it was incumbent on an individual who had a social conscience to first make a lot of money and then use part of his wealth to improve society. It was this line of thinking that resulted in such a high degree of philanthropy among self-made Scottish capitalists.

James McGill in later life

Dulongpre / National Archives of Canada / C-002873

In 1766, McGill set sail for Carolina to seek his fortune. Shortly after landing, however, he caught rumours of enormous profits being made in the Canadian fur trade, so he promptly packed up and moved to Montréal. Almost immediately, McGill became a *coureur de bois*, paddling his canoe to what is now Wisconsin and trading directly with Native trappers. Within six years, he had expanded his business to the point where he had twelve cargo canoes and seventy-five employees. Unlike many of the fur traders of the time who had little education, McGill had an excellent grasp of the economics behind the trade. This put him in a unique position and allowed him very quickly to become one of the most powerful merchants in Montréal. In 1773, he entered into a partnership with a powerful English fur trader, Isaac Todd, and the duo's company became enormously successful. By 1776, McGill quit his westward expeditions and settled permanently in Montréal, where he spent his time overseeing his business empire. In 1779, when the major fur traders of Montréal came together to form the North West Company, McGill was a major shareholder.

After 1779, McGill seems to have lost much of his interest in the fur trade. He was already wealthy and continued to receive huge dividends from his North West Company shares. Diversifying his fortune seemed the next logical step. Over the next twenty years, he bought enormous tracts of farmland throughout what is now Québec. He invested in Montréal shipping, bought a water lot at Sorel, engaged in private banking and set up a distillery. McGill is an example of how fur trade profits, reaped mostly by the Scots, filtered into other areas of Canada's early economy. Such investment of excess capital was critical to the development of the colonies.

Like so many Scottish capitalists of the eighteenth and nineteenth centuries, McGill threw himself with alacrity into public life, an impulse that stemmed from the Scottish notion of public duty, especially for those of means. The pattern of wealthy Scots entering the public domain repeated itself countless times throughout the eighteenth and nineteenth centuries.

Often declaring his "love" for Montréal, McGill was appointed a public magistrate in 1792, a position that made him responsible for the peace and general civic organization of the city. The same year, he was elected to Lower Canada's legislative assembly. In 1796, he was appointed Montréal's Justice of the Peace, and after his term had expired, he once again served in the legislature between 1800 and 1808. During the war of 1812, McGill was appointed a colonel responsible for leading three battalions of militiamen. During the American invasion of Montréal, McGill fought actively alongside his soldiers and helped repel the American forces. Over the span of his life, McGill's public duties took at least as much of his time and energy as his business duties. His desire to "give back" to the community that had allowed him to prosper to a large extent defined his life. As a final act of civic contribution in 1813, he willed upon his death his colossal Burnside estate on the southern slope of Mount Royal, along with £10,000 for the establishment of Canada's first institution of higher learning: McGill University in Montréal.

James McGill is a particularly interesting figure in Canadian history because he symbolizes how early fur trade profits were critical to furthering the economic development of the nation. But what is even more interesting is that McGill personifies eighteenth and nineteenth century Scottish views about the businessman's relationship to society. He was clearly a product of the Scottish

Enlightenment and the commercial culture in which he was raised. His property did in fact allow him to attach himself firmly to a community and express himself in public service as well as in business. Consistent with the assertions of eighteenth century Scottish philosophers, McGill clearly believed that his property allowed him to become a "whole and complete" human being.

By the beginning of the 1800s, immigrants from England, Ireland and Scotland were pouring into the colonies by the shipload. Ship operators would empty their hulls of Canadian raw materials onto British docks, and then needing some sort of ballast to stabilize the freighters, they would entice emigrants to pay a small fee and hop aboard for the return trip. The conditions on such ships were, for the most part, unspeakably horrid. Disease and hunger on the filthy, rat-infested hulks killed thousands.

Most immigrants during the early 1800s, especially after the War of 1812, chose to bypass Lower Canada (Québec) and head to English-speaking Upper Canada (Ontario). There they usually worked on farms during the summer, and many took up lumberjacking as a natural wintertime complement to agriculture. The timber industry was easy to enter and required little training, and Europe's appetite for wood was growing. In addition to sawn lumber, British North America exported huge amounts of potash, made from the ashes of burnt trees, a by-product of the massive land clearing that was taking place in the colonies. Potash was essential for Britain's burgeoning textile industry, and the market seemed insatiable. By 1821, when the North West Company was negotiated out of existence, lumber and potash accounted for a majority of Canadian exports.

The North West Company's demise hit Montréal hard. Many of the large shipping, warehousing, and supplying businesses that had revolved around the fur trade became casualties of the economic shift. Potent embodiments of fur trade prosperity, such as William McGillivray, declared bankruptcy. It was clear that the old economic order was changing.

In this economically turbulent period, it became clear to many Montréal merchants that a banking system was necessary to stabilize the colonies' wildly fluctuating currencies as well as to underwrite large capital projects. A new, diversified industrial economy would not be possible without sophisticated financing. In fact, the fur trade barons of Montréal, including Simon McTavish and James McGill, had tried twice to establish a bank, once in 1792 and again in 1808. Their efforts were unsuccessful, however, for very few people in British North America, especially French-Canadians, trusted the mostly Anglo-Scots business community and their new-fangled ideas, such as paper money. Furthermore, most historians contend that the colony's economy was too primitive and too dependent on a single industry – the fur trade – to support a bank. Soon, however, things would change.

The Birth of Banking

In the mid to late1700s, the great Scottish philosophers, Lord Kames, Adam Smith and David Hume, wrote and lectured extensively on the subject of property. In essence, they believed that man's very nature compelled him "to appropriate". Acquiring property, they believed, was man's greatest form of self-expression; an individual's possessions were a vital part of his identity.

GORDON TARTAN KILT COURTESY OF DUNCAN M. JESSIMAN / SPORRAN, SGIAN DHUB, KILT HOSE AND BELT COURTESY OF THE SCOTTISH CROFT, SYDNEY, BC

It was believed that owning property established a stake in a community. It was a critical psychological anchor as well as a commitment to society. Overall, property ownership allowed one to become a "whole and complete" human being.

Such ideas were not at all revolutionary in eighteenth century Scotland; rather, they reflected the widely held views of an emerging, empowered and dynamic commercial culture. For centuries, Scotland's economic development had lagged far behind England's and Europe's, but in the latter half of the eighteenth century, the Scottish Lowlands took off, rapidly becoming a commercial society and industrializing at an astonishing pace. It was in this climate that a great deal of pent-up entrepreneurial energy sought an outlet, and it was the new colony of Canada after the Conquest that provided it at precisely the right time in history.

Scottish entrepreneurs, usually without means but armed with unique mercantilist assumptions, excellent commercial training and a profound desire to acquire property, made an impact in Canada immediately after 1760. They rapidly took over the fur trade, establishing themselves very early as the new colony's most influential businessmen. They then used their wealth and influence to branch into other commercial ventures, such as shipping, banking, railroads, and manufacturing. The extent to which the Scots created Canada's economic infrastructure and influenced industrial development simply cannot be overemphasized. The modern, wealthy, industrialized nation we know today is due, to an amazing extent, to the boundless energy, gritty determination, and bold vision of eighteenth - and nineteenth-century Scottish businessmen.

After the War of 1812, as the English-speaking population continued to grow rapidly and people became used to spending paper money issued by the British military, the time was finally right for the creation of a bank in British North America. A new banking company was formed, and its stock was quickly snapped up by those who understood its potential. Half the investors were Scottish fur traders and merchants connected to the trade, while the other half consisted of English and American entrepreneurs.Interestingly, John Strachan, the Scottish *de facto* head of Upper Canada's Family Compact bought a large block of stock. Canada's first bank, the Bank of Montreal, opened its doors in Montréal in 1817.

From the day of its opening, the Bank of Montreal was successful. It immediately provided British North America with a stable and reliable medium of exchange in the form of bank notes, something that the Imperial Government of Britain had been either unwilling or unable to do. Prior to the creation of the bank, British North Americans relied on a strange mix of bartering, personal IOUs scrawled on paper, American, British and Spanish coins, and British military notes. No one really knew how to accurately compare the values of these disparate currencies, and the monetary system was anarchic and inefficient to say the least. The Bank of Montreal rapidly introduced stability to the colonies' systems of commerce.

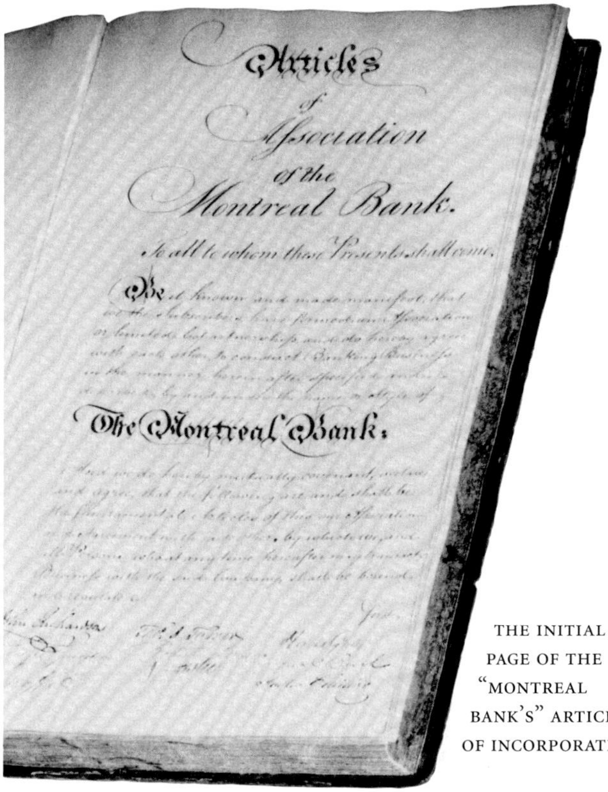
Articles of Association of the Montreal Bank.

To all to whom these Presents shall come.

The Montreal Bank.

COURTESY OF THE BMO FINANCIAL GROUP

THE INITIAL PAGE OF THE "MONTREAL BANK'S" ARTICLES OF INCORPORATION

John Richardson, the undisputed father of Canadian banking, was almost single-handedly responsible for creating the structure and operating principles of the Bank of Montreal. His methods were later widely emulated by other banks, which largely defined the character of Canadian banking. Yet despite his enormous impact on Canada's development, little has been written about Richardson.

Born in Edinburgh in 1755, Richardson studied banking and accounting as a young man before emigrating to New York to work at various banking houses. In 1790, he made his way to Montréal to take advantage of the free-wheeling commercial economy of the day and soon established several general stores. He then put his investment training to good use and bought into a myriad of commercial enterprises, rapidly becoming one of Montréal's most powerful merchants.

Richardson was a tough-minded, somewhat dour Scot with little use for frills or fanfare. He was a close friend of James McGill, and like McGill was elected to the legislative assembly in 1792, where he served for fifteen years. The canny entrepreneur became the leader of the English Commercial Party and vociferously advocated abolishing French as an official language, which won him the everlasting enmity of most French-Canadians. Such anti-French views, by the way, were not uncommon among Anglo-Scots merchants of the day. Despite his fluency in French, James McGill and almost all the British commercial elite of Lower Canada held similar opinions.

Richardson's personal hero was the renowned Scottish philosopher and economist Adam Smith, whom Richardson felt wrote "with an intelligence and profundity of observation beyond any other person." As a result, Richardson embraced the notion of laissez-faire economics and free trade, which heavily influenced his banking philosophy. Moreover, borrowing from Smith's theories, Richardson advocated the idea of a gold or silver standard as the ultimate security for a currency, stating, "Bank notes issued by people of undoubted credit, payable on demand, in gold and silver, without any condition … become in every respect as a circulating medium, equal to gold and silver." Overall, the philosophical framework behind Canada's early banking system stemmed from widely held Scottish theories of economics, instituted by John Richardson.

As far as the actual operating mechanics of the bank were concerned, Richardson borrowed heavily from his knowledge of Scottish banks, as is evidenced by the Bank of Montreal's constitution. Subsequent banks followed suit and adopted the Scottish model. In the early 1800s, the banks of Scotland were the most progressive and innovative in the world. England, Europe and North America looked to Scotland for modern and penetrating theories of economics and business. As historian David S. Macmillan writes: "… it was natural that [Banks in British North America] should follow the design of the 'new Scotch institutions' which revolutionized the whole concept of banking in Britain, if not in Europe. These were the Commercial Bank and the National Bank of Scotland, both founded in Edinburgh, with their novel system of 'cash-credits' and 'branch banking', and with the even more novel feature that they had large numbers of shareholders …" From early on, in both theory and practice, the Canadian banking system reflected that of Scotland but at the same time was cleverly adapted by Richardson to reflect the needs of the colonies. At a time when the American banking system was tied to land speculation and subject to wild experimentation and fluctuating economic cycles, the "Canadian" banking system, not tied to the vast tracts of semi-worthless British North-American land, was a model of stability.

Although Richardson chose not to become president or director of the Bank of Montreal (instead he became its biggest shareholder), he wielded enormous influence behind the scenes. He appointed as the bank's first president an independent English fur trader named John Gray. Gray had unique qualifications; he not only understood the fur trade, but was neutral and thus acceptable to both the North West Company and Hudson's Bay Company.

Half the Bank of Montreal's initial directors were Scottish merchants, including John Forsyth of the famous shipping family, who also happened to be John Richardson's first cousin. Over the next century, Scots dominated the bank's presidency and directorships, overseeing some of the most robust periods of industrial development in Canada's history. Their hegemony in the fur trade clearly put them in a position to become the nation's leading financiers and industrialists and, to some extent, prepared them for the decline of the North West Company.

When the Bank of Montreal opened for business in 1817, most of Upper Canada was a muddy, sleepy backwater, a forest frontier with 95,000 inhabitants spread thinly over the daunting terrain. Life there was relatively dull, and the stodgy Family Compact controlled most aspects of business. The Bank of Montreal soon set up a branch in the commercial centre of Kingston, then Upper Canada's biggest city, with 2,000 inhabitants. It wasn't long before this attracted the ire of the Family Compact, which did not like outsiders treading on Upper Canadian turf.

Members of the Family Compact, many of them Scots, knew that their colonial hinterland was starved for capital and that industrial development and large-scale economic infrastructure could not move forward without financing. In fact, they had been aware of this for some time. It was the Bank of Montreal's foray into their territory, however, that finally spurred them to action.

GEORGES DELFOSSE / COURTESY OF THE BMO FINANCIAL GROUP

THE BANK OF MONTREAL'S FIRST PERMANENT BUILDING IN OLD MONTRÉAL

In 1822, the Family Compact opened its own bank, the Bank of Upper Canada at "Muddy York", the dismal city of a thousand inhabitants that would later become Toronto. The Compact then barred the Bank of Montreal from doing business in Upper Canada and the new bank became the official agent for all government transactions. Despite this favoured position, the bank got off to a slow start. Historian Merril Denison writes, "The monopoly enjoyed by the Bank of Upper Canada and its affiliation with the reigning political oligarchy enabled its management to practice rank favouritism, discrimination against political opponents, and an investment policy which channeled funds into exchange transactions at the expense of discounts, to the detriment of commercial development." The Bank of Upper Canada was thus an obvious target of William Lyon Mackenzie's vitriolic rants.

William Allan, another self-made Scottish businessman, set up and ran the Bank of Upper Canada for the first dozen years of its operation. It will come as no surprise that Allan, born in Huntly, Scotland in 1770, had received a strong commercial education in the Scottish parish system before emigrating to Upper Canada and establishing himself as a successful land speculator, merchant, and insurance executive. Like most of his wealthy cronies, Allan also served in the Legislative Council of Upper Canada for fifteen years, as there were yet no such things as conflict of interest guidelines. Under the prodding of John Strachan, Allan drew up the articles necessary to form the Bank of Upper Canada and assumed its presidency. Patterned after the Bank of Montreal and the Bank of Scotland, the new bank was well run, and Allan, despite dubious tactics, has been acknowledged as an able president who effectively contributed to Upper Canada's early development.

While entrepreneurs (at least those with Tory leanings) were able to borrow money to expand their businesses, the fact remained that Upper Canadian businesses were stuck on the southern range of a coniferous forest and limited to producing fur, timber, potash, and wheat. The domestic market for goods was miniscule, and large-scale shipping was out of the question, thanks to the rapids that cut off the lakes of Upper Canada from Lower Canada and the St. Lawrence River. It was not until the construction of the canal system and later the railways that Upper Canada's full potential could be exploited.

As for banking in the Maritimes, many entrepreneurs followed the Bank of Montreal's lead and set up a plethora of banks in Nova Scotia, New Brunswick, and Prince Edward Island. And once again, Scots took the dominant roles. David S. Macmillan writes, "Of the twenty original board members of the Bank of New Brunswick, established in 1820 in St. John, no fewer than ten were Scots … including Christopher Scott, the shipbuilding entrepreneur. In the Charlotte County Bank, set up at St. Andrews in 1825, there were fourteen Scots in a total directorate of twenty-five." Such levels of active Scottish involvement were typical in the formation of early Canadian banks.

The Bank of Nova Scotia was formed in 1832. Again dominated by Scots, the bank rapidly swallowed up most of the small banks in the Maritimes before eventually moving westward in the 1880s and ultimately becoming a huge national bank with branches in every corner of the country.

Just as Scots dominated the presidencies and directorships of most early banks, they also made up a majority of managers and clerks. British North American banks began to recruit aggressively in Scotland in the 1820s, largely because young Lowland Scots were generally far better educated in finance and accounting than most of the colonial workforce. They also had an unmatched work ethic and were willing to accept paltry wages through a long period of apprenticeship, something most "Canadians" were reluctant to do. Such recruiting drives, which resulted in legions of clerks and managers swelling the ranks of the banks, only accelerated when Canadian banks began to branch out across the country in the 1840s. Overall, no group was more responsible for actually running early Canadian banks than the Scots.

When the North West Company died in 1821, the predominantly Scottish merchants of Montréal saw the writing on the wall. If British North American furs were going to be shipped out of Hudson's Bay and not Montréal, the city's economic future looked bleak. Almost immediately, a coalition of merchants came together and decided that action must be taken to preserve the commercial potential of the St. Lawrence and Montréal. The only way to do this was to construct a system of canals that would link inland industries with the St. Lawrence shipping route. That very year, 1821, with financing from the Bank of Montreal, the Lachine Canal was undertaken to bypass the treacherous Lachine rapids. It was the beginning of what would someday become the St. Lawrence Seaway system, linking the Great Lakes through a series of immense locks with the St. Lawrence River and the Atlantic Ocean.

Large-scale projects such as this drew considerable criticism from many French-Canadians, who believed the Anglo merchants of Lower Canada were attempting to tighten their economic stranglehold on the colony, and further disrupt French traditions and institutions. For their part, however, the mostly Scottish merchants saw themselves locked in a struggle against natural geographic obstacles that hindered the commercial development of their new country. While it was true that they generally viewed the French as backward, their main impetus was to push ahead in the name of "human progress", a popular idea of the Scottish enlightenment. The residue of these nineteenth-century tensions between the anglophone Montréal merchants and the francophone Canadiens can be felt in Québec even today.

While eastern waterways in Canada had been used for two centuries in the fur trade, such routes were of little value shipping bulky freight such as timber, potash and wheat. This began to change with the completion of the Lachine Canal in 1825. The new waterway was an immediate success, opening a shipping route farther inland than had ever been available before. It was followed by the construction of the Welland Canal in Upper Canada, completed in 1829. Forty locks, constructed of timber, linked Lake Ontario to Lake Erie, allowing ships to climb one hundred metres up the Niagara Escarpment. In 1832, the British government completed the Rideau Canal system; though designed to facilitate military movements in the colonies, in practice, the system was used almost entirely for commercial purposes. The Trent Canal, linking lake Ontario with Lake Huron, began in 1833 and continued in stages throughout most of the century.

Construction of the early canals marked a fundamental shift in Canadian history. The two Canadas began to forge important commercial ties with one another, a critical prerequisite of the process of confederation. Such economic interdependence was the first wobbly step away from furs and small-scale agriculture and towards a large-scale, industrialized continental economy.

Canada's economic infrastructure, of course, continued to grow rapidly throughout the rest of the nineteenth and twentieth centuries. Canal systems continued to expand, telegraph lines spread throughout the country, mines opened, steamboat traffic plied Canadian waterways, lumber mills popped up virtually everywhere, and railways bound disparate communities together with vast networks of steel track. Such symbols of industrial advancement in Canadian history are obvious, often cited, and easily understood. Behind the scenes, however, and perhaps the most vital and under-examined part of Canada's industrial development, was the Scottish-style system of banking, which made early economic progress possible.

When seriously studying Canada's economic development in the first half of the 1800s, one is confronted with just how difficult it was for early Canadians to overcome the formidable geography and severe climate of the north. The development of a modern nation from such inauspicious beginnings is truly awesome. In fact, this struggle is the essence of the Canadian story. Unlike the United States, which was endowed with a temperate climate, agricultural bounty, and relatively few natural barriers to settlement and industrialization, the thinly-spread Canadian population had to fight an almost unwinnable battle against the severe cold and the vast, pitiless Canadian terrain. Canadians also had to deal with punishing American tariffs, a miniscule internal market, and the exploitative mercantilist trade policies of Great Britain. Yet against overwhelming odds, they persevered and built one of the world's most enviable nations. If the average Canadian fully understood and appreciated this historical

JOHN LAMBERT / NATIONAL ARCHIVES OF CANADA / C-041075

background, there could never be a Canadian identity crisis.

During the 1830s, Upper Canada continued to grow rapidly, at a rate much greater than Lower Canada. "Muddy York" was no longer a dirty little eyesore of a frontier town; it had become Toronto, a thriving commercial hub with a population of more than 15,000. Still, Montréal was by far British North America's dominant industrial and cultural city with a population of more than 40,000. It would take another century before Toronto would be able to seriously challenge Montréal's financial primacy.

During the 1830s and '40s, a dynamic Montréal was brimming with entrepreneurial energy. The city had not only survived the decline of the North West Company, it had diversified and industrialized to become an increasingly powerful economic focal point in North America. A new generation of Scots was firmly in control of the vast majority of industry in the colonies, and most were headquartered in Montréal. The extent to which the Scots ruled during this period is nothing short of astonishing. Historian Gerald Tulchinsky comments on this phenomenon:

> The Scots comprised the dominant group in most forms of commerce ... Among brewers there was William Dow; among brokers John and Robert Esdaile; and Robert Anderson owned a glass and china company. All of these were leading firms in their fields. In the dry goods trade

> during the forties and early fifties the Scottish-dominated firms were those of the Gillespies, the Gilmours, J.G. Mackenzie, Joseph Mackay, William Stephen, Henry Morgan, and Dougald Stewart. John Young was prominent as a commission merchant. The Gilmours and the Allans owned the chief ocean shipping establishments, while the Redpaths, prominent contractors, became leading Montreal industrialists …

Tulchinsky goes on to expound on a dizzying number of prominent and wealthy Scots businessmen of the era: Campbell, Douglas, Fraser, Reid, Galbraith, MacFarlane, Gairbairn, Geddes, MacDougall, Dougall, Anderson, Bell, Auld, MacDonald, McKay, McNaught, Shaw, Macpherson, Young, and many more. Unfortunately, examining the business achievements of such men lies beyond the scope of this book. Suffice it to say that Scots, by and large, controlled British North America's economy through Montréal. Even in Upper Canada and the Maritimes, a large percentage of economic activity, industrial expansion, and capitalization was brought about by merchants acting as agents for large Scottish firms in Montreal. Some historians estimate that by the mid-1800s, as much as three-quarters of industrial capital was controlled directly by Scots.

Another important stimulus to Canada's early economic development, which historians have all but completely overlooked, has been Canada's life insurance industry. During the early 1800s, Scotland's dynamic commercial culture was producing some of the world's best-trained and most innovative accountants and statisticians. Groundbreaking theories of risk management and actuarial statistics soon followed, and thus the Scots became pioneers and leaders in the life insurance field. By the 1840s, most major life insurance companies in the Empire were headquartered in Scotland, including Standard Life Assurance Company, the North British Insurance Company of Edinburgh, the Scottish Widows Fund, the Edinburgh Life Assurance Company, and the Scottish Union Assurance Company.

In Canada, the relatively unsophisticated colonial population knew little about life insurance (or any other kind of insurance for that matter). The premature death of a breadwinner –an all-too-common occurrence in the harsh northern colonies – would often reduce a family to a lifetime of abject poverty. This began to change in 1844 when Scotland's Standard Life set up offices in Upper and Lower Canada.

A little-known historical fact is that Lord Elgin, Canada's governor general from 1847 to 1854 (see Shaping the Political Landscape), was named deputy governor of Standard Life in 1841, a position he held until his death in 1862. Elgin was, therefore, very interested in seeing his company take root and prosper in Canada, and he often took an active role in directing the company's Canadian affairs. Equally noteworthy is the fact is that Alexander Galt, one of Canada's most influential Fathers of Confederation, as well as the country's first finance minister, chaired the Canadian board of Standard Life for several years during the 1870s and was largely responsible for developing the company's aggressive marketing strategy.

While the Scottish firm, Standard Life, wrote more business than any other company from the 1840s to the early 1870s, American firms began to make inroads into the small Canadian market during this period. In general, however, the life insurance business was slow to take off, as the concept of spreading risk seemed too foreign for most colonists. In addition, some preachers even railed from their pulpits that life insurance was a wager against the will of God. The Scots, however, understood the concept of life insurance very well, since it had been part of their commercial culture for decades, and this explains in large part why they became by far the principal players in the Canadian life insurance industry.

Hugh Baker, a branch manager of the Bank of Montreal, launched the first Canadian company, the Canada Life Assurance Company, in Hamilton in 1847. The company's largest backers were Scottish merchants William McLaren, John Young and Archibald Kerr, but the best-known and biggest investor of all was Sir Allan MacNab (see the following chapter), the powerful Scottish industrialist and future prime minister of United Canada. From behind the scenes, MacNab played a large role in directing the company.

Canada Life recruited Scottish clerks and managers and grew slowly but steadily for the next three decades. In 1855, for example, in need of tighter accounting practices, the company hired from Scotland a stern Highlander, Thomas Macaulay, as chief accountant. Macaulay's stubbornly strict methods helped place the company on a firm financial footing and set a standard for future Canadian life insurance companies (Macaulay eventually joined Sun Life and became the company's longest-serving president, not to mention an icon in the industry). Canada Life also needed a higher degree of actuarial skill, so its principals travelled to Scotland in 1859 and enticed Alexander Gillespie, one of Scotland's best actuaries, to leave his job as secretary of the Scottish Amicable Assurance Society of Glasgow to join Canada Life as general manager. Such recruiting drives to Scotland became typical among almost all major Canadian life insurance companies for the next several decades.

Shortly after Confederation, the government passed a law stating that life insurance companies must place a $50,000 deposit with the government for the protection of policyholders. This caused outrage among the American companies operating in Canada, most of which packed up and left the country. The vacuum was quickly filled in the 1870s, '80s, and early '90s, however, by enthusiastic Canadian upstart companies backed and run principally by Scots, such as Sun Life, Mutual Life, Confederation Life, London Life, Manufacturers Life and Great West Life, all of which grew rapidly and eventually became highly respected multi-billion dollar companies.

Life insurance companies are important when considering Canada's economic history because, like banks, they were a constant source of investment capital for Canada's nascent industrial economy. Large pools of money from premiums had to be well invested, so Canadian insurance companies placed substantial amounts of capital in Canadian debentures, bonds, stocks, and mortgages and lent money to individuals as well as to secure businesses. Such large-scale investment was an enormous boost to Canada's industrial development.

As Scots were apt to do, Scots in the insurance industry tended to stick together in Canada and draw on talent from back home. They were also inclined to invest in one another's enterprises. This sort of clannishness, coupled with their unparalleled actuarial, accounting and managerial expertise, kept them in firm control of the Canadian life insurance industry well into the twentieth century. In fact, an unmistakable majority of Canadian insurance executives from the mid 1800s to now have born Scottish names. We'll leave this particular discussion with one last little-known fact: when the Manufacturers Life Insurance Company (Manulife) was created in 1887, its first elected president was none other than Canada's first prime minister, Sir John A. Macdonald.

A Revolution in Transportation

During the 1830s, steam locomotives had begun to revolutionize transportation in Britain. Within a few short years, the concept of distance came to mean something very different than it ever had before.

CAMPBELL TARTAN KILT COURTESY OF A. LORNE CAMPBELL 0C, QC / SPORRAN, SGIAN DHUB, KILT HOSE, SHOES AND BELT COURTESY OF THE SCOTTISH CROFT, SYDNEY, BC / LANTERN AND MAUL COURTESY OF KEN AND PAULA JONES

If railways could so radically "shrink" the United Kingdom – which was small to begin with – and at the same time stimulate massive industrialization, imagine what they could do for a sprawling British North America. In 1832, a group of Scots businessmen, led by George Moffat and Peter McGill, teamed up with Englishman John Molson, one of the most powerful members of Montréal's industrial elite. Together, they organized and financed Canada's first railroad: the Champlain and St. Lawrence Railroad Company. Completed in 1836, the railroad, designed to shorten the frustratingly indirect Richelieu River route to Montréal, was successful from its first day of operation. For the first time, massive loads of raw materials could be hauled directly and relatively cheaply from La Prairie to Saint-Jean-sur-Richelieu, which anglophones of the day called St. Johns.

The Champlain and St. Lawrence Railroad Company paid its investors well and set an auspicious precedent that spurred enthusiasm for railroads and attracted large pools of investment capital for the next half-century.

Peter McGill (a very distant relation of James McGill, who we met earlier in Chapter Five) was a highly successful and respected businessman of the era. His career is worth considering, as it illustrates many of the attitudes prevalent among the Scottish commercial elite of the day. McGill was born in 1789 in Wigtonshire, Scotland and emigrated to Montréal at the age of twenty in 1809. He served as a clerk with Parker, Gerrard and Ogilvy, a firm that held a significant number of shares in the North West Company and acted as one if its major suppliers. By 1820, McGill had learned enough to break out on his own, establishing a company that brokered and exported wheat and flour, operating very successfully for the next quarter-century.

In just a few years, Peter McGill was one of the most popular figures on the Montréal social circuit. By all accounts, he was handsome and charming and all who knew him were taken by his affability and ease of manner. He was also athletic and energetic, and stayed fit by walking briskly early in the morning and after dinner.

McGill could have rested on his laurels and spent the latter half of his life enjoying the fruits of his successful enterprise. Like many powerful Scots of the day, however, he felt impelled to push into new areas of commerce. This was a common pattern among many Scots capitalists. The challenge of seeking out and exploiting new business opportunities was often more interesting and enjoyable than the money success brought. Like many Montréal Scots, McGill began to invest in Upper Canada. He bought several sawmills in the Ottawa Valley and invested in steamboats and barges that ran between Bytown (now Ottawa) and Kingston. He also bought many large farms throughout Upper and Lower Canada, several mines and vast tracts of land containing large stands of timber to supply his sawmills. Finally, he owned a successful ironworks near Montréal. All these enterprises made McGill one of the richest and most influential men in the Canadas.

On top of all this, as if his own businesses were not enough to keep him busy, McGill served as director of the Bank of Montreal from 1819 to 1834 and then became its longest serving and arguably most successful president from 1834 until his death in 1860. During his tenure of more than a quarter-century, McGill was indefatigable to the point of being almost superhuman. He not only oversaw but also actively directed one of Canada's greatest periods of industrial development. He was chairman of the Champlain and St. Lawrence Railroad Company, president of the Ottawa Steamboat Company, and director of the Lachine Canal. Any one of these positions would have been a challenging full-time job. Moreover, as president of the country's most powerful financial institution, McGill was responsible, probably more than anyone else, for influencing the business climate in the Canadas during the mid 1800s.

NATIONAL ARCHIVES OF CANADA / 022784

INSET: PETER MCGILL, IN HIS PRIME.

NATIONAL ARCHIVES OF CANADA / C- 041255

THE THOUSAND ISLANDS, WHERE THE ST. LAWRENCE FLOWS INTO LAKE ONTARIO.

Like James McGill, Peter McGill had a profound love of his adopted home as well as an innate sense of civic responsibility. Again, this was a pattern that was common among Scots capitalists of the day. After establishing his vast wealth, he sought to serve the public good through an active life in public affairs. Adding to his astonishing work schedule, McGill became a member of the Legislative Council in Lower Canada in 1832 and a member of the Executive Council of the United Province of Canada in 1847. He was also Mayor of Montréal from 1840 to 1843 and president of the Montréal Board of Trade for many years, starting in 1848. In addition to all of the above, he was also president of many Montréal associations, including the St. Andrew's Society, the Lay Association of Montreal, the Montreal Auxiliary Bible Society, the British and Canadian School Society, and the Canadian branch of the Colonial Life Assurance Company. He was a trustee of Queen's College, McGill College and Montreal General Hospital. To top it all off, he was one of Canada's most generous philanthropists, seldom refusing money to anyone who asked for it.

Peter McGill's career is remarkable because it illustrates how interconnected the various financial enterprises of the day were. Scottish businessmen in Montréal controlled and directed much of the industrial capital of the time, even in Upper Canada (which became Canada West in 1841). Before the rise of corporate capitalism in Canada, men such as Peter McGill wielded enormous influence. Through energy, vision and force of personality, these men were able to exercise power to an extent that would be virtually impossible today.

McGill's career also reveals other interesting patterns among Scots capitalists. Influenced by the potent ideas of Scottish Enlightenment philosophers, men such as McGill directed their energies not only at building colossal fortunes but also at involving themselves deeply in public affairs. Scots culture placed an inordinate value on civic responsibility and community commitment. Clearly, one of the perks of financial prosperity was the leverage it afforded to bring about constructive change in society. This assumption among the Scots, personified by Peter McGill, is evident again and again when one examines their amazing levels of public involvement and philanthropy. To them, money was not the root of all evil, but rather the means by which one could have the leverage to do good.

By the mid-1800s, Montréal was, comparatively speaking, a metropolis with a population of over 80,000. While much of the francophone majority seemed to be stuck in a mean cycle of poverty, the power of the anglophone commercial elite continued to grow to almost unimaginable levels. The magnificent mansions of predominantly self-made Scots industrialists dominated the southern slope of Mount Royal. Colossal estates of men such as John Redpath (who had parlayed canal-building profits into a sugar refining empire), the Ogilvie family (Canada's largest flour millers and exporters), and Hugh Allan (one of the world's richest shipping magnates) constituted a Scottish enclave of wealth and power that stood in surreal contrast to the rest of the city. The mansions of "Scotch Row" – or "the Golden Mile" – as it was often called, were truly ostentatious, which undoubtedly contributed to the resentment many French-Canadiens felt towards the Anglos.

Many of the self-made Scots found themselves so fabulously wealthy that virtually any whim could be realized, no questions asked. This was often reflected in their grand homes, some of which were weird mixtures of architectural styles, created from odd nouveau riche notions. "Ravenscrag", for example, was Hugh Allan's gargantuan thirty-four-room mansion that towered condescendingly over the city. It was a peculiar fusion of Victorian, Roman, Neo-Gothic and Greek styles that spoke volumes about Allan's innate need to prove himself. Such estates were testament to the unbridled power of the Scottish merchant princes who controlled most of the country's wealth.

Hugh Allan was British North America's richest man and its closest approximation to an American robber baron. Like so many of his industrialist countrymen, he was self-educated and self-made. Born in 1810 in Saltcoats, Scotland, Allan had left school at thirteen to work as an office boy in a counting house in the shipping centre of Greenock. His father was a shipmaster who sailed regularly between Greenock and Québec, and from an early age, Allan was aware of the opportunities reported to exist in British North America. Young Allan was brought up primarily in the company of sailors, whom he pumped relentlessly for information about their travels. His first-hand knowledge of maritime culture, his romantic notions of British North America, and his keen desire for opportunity compelled him to emigrate to Montréal at the age of sixteen.

Initially, Allan worked for a dry goods company, while studying rapaciously until the early hours of the morning in an almost obsessive effort to make up for his lack of formal education. By the time he was twenty-one, he was fluent in French, well versed in the classics, and held a deep knowledge of the prevalent economic theories of the day. He also taught himself all aspects of accounting and business management. The same year, 1831, the already impressive and hard-driving Allan joined the major Miller shipbuilding firm, where he earned a partnership in only four years. By 1839, Allan felt he had acquired enough knowledge to start his own company. Just twenty-nine, he had lived so spartanly for the previous dozen years that he had already managed to save a large (though unknown) amount of capital, which he used, along with funds borrowed from his father and brother, to launch one of the most successful enterprises in Canadian history: the Montreal Ocean Steamship Company, popularly known as the Allan Line.

Allan's ravenous study of shipbuilding techniques was evident when his firm became the first in British North America to move away from sails and timbers toward steam and iron. His superior, fast-moving metal ships soon secured

MONTRÉAL'S STEAM BOAT WHARF IN 1837, TWO YEARS BEFORE HUGH ALLAN LAUNCHED THE ALLAN LINE.

JAMES D. DUNCAN / NATIONAL ARCHIVES OF CANADA / C-041069

contracts to carry mail and passengers between Montréal and Britain, to move British troops, and to transport vast tonnages of bulky cargo out of the colonies. Rigidly disciplined, Allan immediately sank his profits into enhancing the quality of his ships and building his fleet. Within ten years, the Allan Line was a truly monumental company, one of the largest fleets in the world and responsible for a majority of shipping activity in British North America.

Like so many Scots industrial potentates of his day, Allan continued to look for other commercial challenges. He realized that having his own bank would magnify his ability to raise and direct capital, so he started the Merchant's Bank of Canada in 1847, serving as its president. That same year, he also established and became president of the pioneering Montreal Telegraph Company, which connected such centres as Sackville (New Brunswick), Detroit, Montréal, Ottawa, Buffalo and Portland. The extent of Allan's financial interests was remarkable. He started fifteen corporations, acting as president, and owned interests in a myriad of other enterprises, in many cases acting as vice-president. His businesses included several coal mines in Nova Scotia, cattle ranches in Upper and Lower Canada, cotton and tobacco plantations in the United States, sawmills, railways, paper mills, grain elevators, grist mills, insurance companies, and construction companies. Starting with nothing, Allan had become the wealthiest and most powerful capitalist prince in British North America by the time he was fifty. His spectacular rise to the giddy stratosphere of unparalleled prosperity made him a revered celebrity in the colonies.

Yet, despite his stunning success, Allan does not emerge from the pages of Canadian history as a particularly sympathetic figure. Many of his actions seem to have been motivated by an underlying and unappeasable need to prove to the world that he was important. Allan's annual income in the mid-1800s was estimated to be a half-million dollars per year, a sum so staggering at the time that it was almost beyond the comprehension of the average person. An equivalent amount today might be somewhere close to fifty million dollars a year. But Allan was not particularly civic minded, and did not, like other many other Scots capitalists, assume many public responsibilities. True, he did serve as president of the Montréal Board of Trade from 1851 to 1854, but most historians agree that he did so only long enough to secure mail contracts for the Allan Line, after which he resigned. And one can only speculate on the significance of his curiously conspicuous home, with its ostentatious name. From the bell tower of Ravenscrag, Allan was able to view the Montréal harbour through a brass telescope. From this perch, he spent many an hour surveying his empire and watching his ships being loaded and unloaded.

Ravenscrag was also a luxury resort for influential men: politicians, royalty, journalists and fellow capitalists. In 1871, for example, Allan played host to Prince Arthur for several days and it seems his calculated charm and subtle pressure eventually paid off, for it earned him a knighthood. He was thereafter able to assuage some of his internal insecurities by placing a "Sir" in front of his name.

Hugh Allan's achievements are undeniable. He raised himself from an ill-educated, penniless youth to one of the world's most important men, circumventing an unpromising fate and catapulting himself into the upper echelons of power that few Canadians have rivaled. Yet, Sir Hugh's haughtiness, lack of humility and general egocentricity have tarnished his place in history. He was a man who seemed always to have ulterior motives and was well known to use people. He was a master briber, offering payoffs to newspapermen, politicians, government officials and members of Québec's clergy. Whatever it took to achieve his ends, Sir Hugh would do. Such questionable methods paint an unflattering portrait of Allan and offer an insight into his thinking. His most public faux pas came in 1873 when it was revealed that he had given enormous sums of money to Prime Minister John A. Macdonald, George-Étienne Cartier and several other members of the Conservative Government in an attempt to secure the gigantic Canadian Pacific Railway contract for himself and his American partners. The ensuing scandal brought down Macdonald's government and permanently stained Allan's credibility.

Despite these personality flaws, Allan remains, in many ways, an admirable character and symbolizes why Scottish capitalists in early Canada prospered to such an incredible extent. He was utterly strict in his daily habits, abstaining from liquor and tobacco, rising at 4 a.m. each day to study, and working every day until late at night. He was the quintessential disciplined Presbyterian, not inclined to philosophical reflection or ideological theorizing. He represented a certain breed of Scot who pursued concrete results rather than wasting time philosophizing. An incisive commentator of the day noted that Allan's only ideology was one of "steamboats and railroads". Nevertheless, one must admire, if only grudgingly, the single-minded focus that allowed Sir Hugh to rise to such rarified heights.

In 1850, British North America was still sparsely populated, with fewer than two million inhabitants. Despite the concentration of industrial activity occurring in and around Montréal, and to a lesser extent in Toronto and Kingston, only a small percentage of Canadians, fewer than one hundred thousand, made a living in industry. Almost everyone else was tied to the drudgery of the farm. After 1850, however, the pace of industrialization in other parts of Canada began to take off. Part of the reason was that railroads began to make large-scale staple industries feasible for the first time in geographically isolated locations. As usual, Scots entrepreneurs in various parts of the country provided the thrust behind the rapid industrialization that occurred in the latter half of the nineteenth century.

Allan MacNab, another public-minded Scots entrepreneur, had a significant impact on the industrial development of what is now Ontario. MacNab was born at Niagara-on-the-Lake in 1798 to Highland immigrant parents. His father, an army officer who had fought during the American Revolution, had settled in Upper Canada along with a wave of other Loyalists. MacNab *père* passed down strict Tory-Loyalist attitudes that would stick with MacNab *fils* for the remainder of his life. At just fourteen, Allan MacNab fought with distinction during the War of 1812, becoming an officer at sixteen. Perhaps it was his short childhood and heavy responsibility so early in life that contributed to his chronically grave manner.

MacNab started life with little except intrinsic intelligence and a deep desire for success. He had little formal education and no connections or financial support, so he worked at a number of menial jobs in York and during his free time studied like a man possessed; he is yet another example of the stiff Scots ethic that one can only count on oneself to better one's own condition. By 1826, he had saved a good deal of money and passed the bar exam, which allowed him to practice law in Upper Canada. It soon became clear, however, that without Family Compact connections, his practice would go nowhere. Thus, he decided to move to the fledgling community of Hamilton where the Compact's stranglehold was not quite so tight.

An opportunist by nature, MacNab speculated on and developed property in and around Hamilton; within a decade, he owned virtually all the city's real estate worth owning. As a monument to his success, he bought Dundurn Castle, a dark, seventy-two-room parody of a palace whence he reigned over his vast holdings.

Like other Scots capitalists of the day, MacNab realized that entering the big leagues of high finance would mean venturing into banks, railways and steamships. He therefore bought a controlling interest in the Upper Canadian upstart Gore Bank, which significantly increased his financial leverage. By 1837,

NATIONAL ARCHIVES OF CANADA / C-040111

DUNDURN CASTLE IN HAMILTON, WHERE ALLAN MACNAB PRESIDED OVER HIS MANY RAILWAY AND STEAMSHIP HOLDINGS.

MacNab operated a very profitable steamship line between Rochester, Oswego and Hamilton as well as an important wharf at Burlington Bay. He then financed and ran two small railway lines, the Hamilton and Port Dover Railways. Encouraged by the success of his small lines, MacNab organized financing, raised capital, and became director and major promoter for the Great Western Railway. He was the first industrialist in Canada to secure a government loan (to the tune of a million dollars) for a private enterprise. By 1853, the railway's main line ran profitably through Niagara Falls, Hamilton, London and Windsor, becoming a major step towards mobilizing trade in what is now Ontario; MacNab, meanwhile, made a fortune selling his land around Hamilton to the Great Western Railway.

Remarkably, while the stern, opportunistic MacNab was busy making large personal fortunes, he was also a very active politician, even serving as prime minister of the United Province of Canada from 1854-56. Obviously, there was no conflict of interest legislation at the time, and the clear psychological delineation between private and public sectors did not yet exist. In fact, there was an amazing consensus among those in power that what was good for business was good for the country. Before the advent of the welfare state, business was considered synonymous with social progress.

MacNab was elected to the Legislative Assembly of Upper Canada in 1830 and was active in politics for more than thirty years, all the while running his business empire. He was an archenemy of the rabble-rousing William Lyon Mackenzie and played a major part in getting Mackenzie ejected from the assembly. MacNab also led a column of Loyalist troops that put down Mackenzie's botched rebellion in 1837, earning MacNab a knighthood. Though he considered himself a Tory's Tory, he was, in fact, a relatively pragmatic, non-ideological businessman who took whatever action necessary to promote business in Canada. As prime minister, for example, MacNab entered into a coalition with the Reformers in order to pass legislation that broke up the last vestiges of Family Compact power, thus unlocking land in Canada West and paving the way for future railway expansion. MacNab's most famous remark, made in 1851, summed up his ideology: "All my politics are railroads."

Another pragmatic Scots businessman who brought his business outlook to government was Alexander Galt. Galt was a tough-minded entrepreneur who later became one of Canada's Fathers of Confederation as well as the country's first finance minister. Like MacNab, Galt strongly believed that what was good for business was good for the country.

Born in 1817, Alexander Galt was the son of the famous Scottish novelist John Galt of Irvine, Scotland. In 1825, the idealistic Galt Sr. moved his family to Upper Canada to found the Canada Company, an enterprise designed to sell partially developed homesteads to British citizens. John Galt's backers fired him in 1829, however, and the family moved back to Scotland. His short sojourn in the colonies had made an impact on young Alexander, and in 1835, as soon as he was legally able, he returned to Canada. Settling in Sherbrooke, Québec, he went to work as a clerk at the Canada Company his father had founded.

By 1844, Galt had climbed the company ladder to become chief commissioner, a position that impelled him to make an exhaustive study of various means by which British North America's vast raw resources could be tapped and exported. It soon became clear to him that only railways would allow Canada to reach its potential.

By this time Galt was a wealthy man, having invested his substantial wages and performance bonuses into his land company's stock and becoming a majority shareholder. His belief in the necessity of railroads, however, drove him to organize the ambitious St. Lawrence and Atlantic Railroad, the world's first international railway with construction beginning in 1846. The purpose of the line was to connect inland Québec towns, such as Sherbrooke and Montréal, with the ice-free port of Portland, Maine, thus promoting unobstructed year-round industry and shipping.

Galt mortgaged his land company to kick off the project. He also sold stock to the predominantly Scots merchants of Montréal, but when that was still not enough, he made a trip to England to raise even more capital to fund the project. From the outset, however, the company gobbled up alarming quantities of capital, so Galt applied pressure on his connections in government to help subsidize the project, persuasively invoking the powerful idea of "Canadian progress". The government responded with the Guarantee Act of 1849, establishing the principle of government assistance to railways, a pattern of part-private, part-government financing that thereafter characterized large-scale infrastructural development in Canada.

The St. Lawrence and Atlantic Railroad, completed in 1853, was immediately absorbed by the even more ambitious Grand Trunk Railroad, Canada's grandest and most extensive pre-confederation railway system, and Galt profited handsomely from the sale of his interests. From his experience bringing about the Guarantee Act, he realized that politics was the best way to put into effect his extensive theories on how to develop Canada and over the next twenty years, he became one of Canada's most influential politicians. He is best remembered as one of the most important architects of Confederation, having designed the framework of economic union. He also became Canada's first minister of finance, and helped to conceive and plan the great Canadian Pacific Railway project.

Men such as Allan MacNab and Alexander Galt are extremely important when considering Canada's early industrial and particularly railway development. Although both were financially very successful, their interests extended far beyond merely enriching themselves. Reflecting the values of their Scots heritage, each possessed a strong sense of civic responsibility as well as a vested and sincere desire to see Canada succeed. It is fascinating to consider how these two railway promoters/executives placed themselves at the very highest levels of government, bringing with them natural biases towards railways and set ideas on how Canada should proceed toward further industrialization. Their influence ultimately led to the Grand Trunk Railroad and the Canadian Pacific Railway, as well as the curious partnership between the public and private sectors, which is a hallmark of much Canadian industry to this day.

A major leap forward in Canadian economic history occurred in 1852 when the government of the United Province of Canada, dominated by wealthy businessmen, decided to open the interior. Their vehicle was a huge railway network, designed to extend "throughout the entire length of the Province of Canada, and from the eastern frontier thereof ... to the city and port of Halifax." Its main line was to run from Toronto to Montréal, providing the physical commercial link that many had dreamed of for a half-century. The problem was that there was neither the expertise nor nearly enough capital in all of Canada to mount such an immense project. Fortunately, there seemed to be no shortage of British investors willing to buy into the scheme. British railway companies had returned mighty profits to investors for a good decade, and the British were hungry for more. In retrospect, it was lucky for Canada that most of them had little conception of just how costly and difficult it would be to span rail lines over the forbidding, frost-heaved Canadian geography. The Grand Trunk Railway of Canada was incorporated, and though primarily promoted by the Government of Canada, it was built and financed almost entirely by the British and headquartered in London.

To make a long story short, the Grand Trunk Railway was critical to Canada's development. The company absorbed the smaller railways previously discussed in this chapter as well as several other small lines and ultimately spread across the most of what is now Eastern Canada, giving critical impetus to inland industrialization and settlements. The Grand Trunk, however, was never profitable; Canada's sparse population was incapable of producing enough rail traffic to make the company pay. Over the years, the government dumped vast sums of money into the ailing enterprise to keep it afloat until it finally went bankrupt in 1919. Most of its remains were eventually sold to the government-controlled Canadian National Railway system. Despite its financial problems, however, the Grand Trunk was a vital step on Canada's path to industrialization.

During the 1860s and 1870s, railways in Canada continued to generate excitement among entrepreneurs. As popular historian Pierre Berton puts it, "... it was impossible for any businessman of stature not to be connected with railways." Canada was still relatively undeveloped, and railways seemed to be the key to unlocking the hidden wealth of the country's vast land mass.

Railways were also a political necessity. In order for Confederation to work, the far-flung provinces had to be physically linked to Québec and Ontario; otherwise, all the grandiloquent talk of "nationhood" and a "continental destiny" would mean very little. Furthermore, in 1870, Hudson's Bay Company lands were turned over to the Canadian government, and Prime Minister John A. Macdonald knew that the prairies had to be settled by Canadians or risk being overrun by land-hungry "Yankees". Finally, British Columbia decided to join Canada in 1871, but only on the condition that the government would complete a transcontinental railway within ten years. In short, building a railway across Canada was audacious, even foolhardy, and it is truly amazing that a fledgling country of only 3.5 million people would take on one of the most awesome and expensive engineering feats ever attempted. The reality was, however, that political demands of the day outweighed common sense and sound economics. In order for a transcontinental Canada to exist, a railway to the Pacific had to be built.

After Confederation, the government commissioned the Intercolonial Railway, which eventually tied Nova Scotia and New Brunswick into the Grand Trunk system. The new 1,100-kilometre line posed many daunting technical problems and required the considerable talents of Canada's brightest engineer: Sandford Fleming.

Fleming, born in 1827 at Kirkcaldy, Scotland, had received a sound technical education before emigrating to what is now Ontario in 1845. He worked on several railway projects and by the late 1850s was considered among the most brilliant engineers of the empire. In 1858, he published his influential work, *A Railway to the Pacific through British Territory*, which offered for the first time persuasive speculation that a transcontinental railway could be built. The possibility of the elusive North West Passage finally being constructed overland generated much excitement in Canada and Britain. Fleming's publication tapped into the optimistic Victorian belief that virtually any natural obstacle could be overcome with British ingenuity, pluck, and modern technology.

In 1871, John A. Macdonald hired Fleming as chief engineer to carry out extensive preliminary surveys through the rocky forests of Ontario, over the immense muddy prairies, and into the frightening passes of the Rocky Mountains. Fleming worked at a phenomenal, punishing pace to complete the Intercolonial Railway while simultaneously conducting the arduous and painstaking surveys out west. He later confided to Charles Tupper, "I felt the weight of the responsibilities that were thrown upon me and I laboured day and night in a manner that will never be known." But, he also ruminated in typical Scots fashion, "... the sleeping fox catches no poultry ... there will be sleeping enough in the grave." By 1874, both tasks were finished. The Intercolonial was a reality, and though it would never be profitable, it was, nevertheless, an important symbol of nationhood. As well, Fleming's western surveys confirmed that a railway to the Pacific would be possible, although dreadfully expensive.

One interesting by-product of Fleming's western surveys was that he created standard time. He realized that railways, which allowed people to move rapidly over enormous distances, and through numerous lines of longitude, would render the old system of timekeeping obsolete. Instead of every major centre setting clocks independently, Fleming proposed a standard or mean time with corresponding and established time zones. He organized the International Prime Meridian Conference in Washington in 1884, where his system of international time was unanimously adopted. Since then, Fleming has often been referred to as "the father of standard time" and has been widely recognized as one of the chief pioneers of globalization.

Although Fleming's surveys provided the critical first step for the construction of the Pacific railway, politics and a lack of money got in the way until 1880. Hugh Allan's bribes of $350,000 (quite a sum in those days) to members of the Macdonald government, including Sir John A. himself, led to the Pacific Scandal. The Conservatives fell, and Mackenzie's Liberals half-heartedly authorized only small stages of the Pacific railway to be built. When Sir John A. rebounded in 1878, he pushed ahead full-throttle with his National Policy and searched for a private company to bid on what was obviously going to be the mother of all railway projects.

Unfortunately, no one in Canada, it seemed, had the experience or financing to make a plausible bid.

Finally, in 1880, a group of Scots, led by Donald Smith and his cousin George Stephen, formed a syndicate that was one of the most impressive assemblages of entrepreneurial talent in Canadian history. To understand Smith and Stephen is to understand not only a good portion of Canada's economic past but also to appreciate why the Scots prevailed to such an astonishing degree in Canadian industry.

Donald Smith was born in the Scottish town of Forres in 1820. His uncle, the well-known fur trader John Stuart, visited the Smith family in Scotland when Donald Smith was eighteen. Captivated by Stuart's stories of British North America's boreal wonderlands, Smith decided to seek employment with the Hudson's Bay Company. Armed with only a few pounds and a letter of introduction from his uncle, he sailed to Montréal, and on arrival, knocked on George Simpson's Lachine mansion door.

Simpson seems to have taken an immediate dislike to young Smith but hired him anyway, banishing him to HBC purgatory, the Tadoussac trading post in Labrador. There Smith spent the next thirty years, cut off from civilization, engaged in the dull task of trading manufactured items for smelly beaver pelts. Nevertheless, through diligence and an uncompromising work ethic that almost welcomed hardship, Smith rose steadily through the company's ranks, becoming a chief factor in 1862.

Most of the travails Donald Smith endured during these three decades can only be imagined, but on one occasion, he was afflicted with snow-blindness, an incredibly painful condition. Accompanied by Native guides, Smith snowshoed blindly more than eight hundred kilometres to Montréal to seek treatment. When George Simpson heard he had abandoned his post, he unleashed a torrent of verbal abuse, finally warning Smith, "If it's a question between your eyes and your service in the Hudson's Bay Company, you'll take my advice and return this instant." Smith headed dutifully back to Labrador, his eyes burning as if splashed with acid. On the way, the weather turned viciously cold, killing both guides. For days Smith groped towards home, exhausted, starving, freezing and full of fear. When asked to recount the story many years later, Smith replied, "No, no, I can't. It is too terrible to think about." Such stoicism and reticence characterized Smith throughout his life. Pierre Berton writes,"Wintry of temperament, courtly of manner, [Smith] wrapped himself in a screen of suavity which masked his inner fibres, bitter furies and the hard resolution of the soul."

Peter C. Newman also offers insights into Smith's character, and indeed into the characters of many Scots businessmen of that era: "The key to understanding Donald Alexander Smith is the Scottishness of the man – Scottish to the marrow of his soul, despite his English airs and Canadian domicile. Like all good Scots, he knew how to maximize the authority of pursed lips and disapproving glances, how to parlay endurance into salvation, and, above all, how to fight."

DONALD SMITH, FUR TRADER, AT NORTH WEST RIVER, NEW BRUNSWICK, ABOUT 1860.

WILLIAM G.R. HIND / NATIONAL ARCHIVES OF CANADA / C-033690

Serving as a company man, cataloging and shipping pelts for thirty years does not seem the most likely position from which to launch one of the most mighty and far-reaching financial empires in Canadian history. Yet that's exactly what Donald Smith did. After the age of fifty, when he finally emerged from the remote boondocks of Labrador, he pulled off a series of business *coups* so stunning that they seem, in retrospect, unbelievable.

During his years in Labrador, Donald Smith cultivated the reputation of someone to be trusted. He was also known as a wise money manager who knew a good deal about modern business. Like those of other Scots in this chapter, his day would often start at 4 a.m. with two hours of intense study. Smith read anything and everything he could get his hands on. Because he received mail only twice a year, he made sure to load up on enough old newspapers and books to keep his mind occupied for six months until the next batch of materials arrived. Fellow workers often noticed the light burning in Smith's cabin well after midnight, as he pored over the day's ledgers and studied.

Because Smith was believed to be astute with money, nearly fifty of his fellow HBC managers entrusted their paycheques to him to invest on their behalf. Smith offered them a generous return of three percent per annum, which he paid unfalteringly. Thus Smith became a one-man bank, with a huge pool of capital to work with. For many of his dreary years in Labrador, he quietly invested in HBC and Bank of Montreal stock, which, of course, grew at a much more rapid rate than three percent. By the time Smith emerged from the unforgiving Labrador bush in 1869, he was no country bumpkin; he was a powerful force – a disciplined, tough, self-educated man whose many years of isolation had only enhanced his sense of self-reliance and focused his powers of self-determination. His years of patiently and regularly investing had made him one of the largest holders of HBC and Bank of Montreal stock. In short, at the age of fifty, Donald Smith was poised to take on the world.

Meanwhile, Donald Smith's cousin, George Stephen, had become one of the most powerful businessmen in Montréal. The owner of a hugely profitable textiles firm and head of the Montreal Board of Trade, Stephen was a polished, well-groomed gentleman, with an impressive mansion on "Scotch Row" and a bevy of servants at his beck and call. Remarkably, despite being cousins, Smith and Stephen did not know one another until they met in 1866, three years before Smith left Labrador.

When the two finally did meet, the contrast could not have been more striking. Smith showed up at Stephen's door looking every bit the fur trader he was, with his shaggy Labrador beard, weathered skin, and rumpled, outdated clothes. Stephen greeted him coolly, wondering what the Labrador bushwhacker wanted. It didn't take long, however, before Stephen realized that there was much more to Smith than met the eye. The two, in fact, had a great deal in common. Like Smith, for many years Stephen had been quietly and systematically investing in Bank of Montreal stock. The two soon discovered that together they held enough stock to virtually control the bank.

Historians have hailed Stephen as "the greatest genius in the whole history of Canadian finance," and many see him as the man most responsible for the development of Western Canada. There is no doubt that he possessed one of the keenest financial minds of his age, and like so many Scots businessmen, he was completely self-made.

George Stephen was born in Dufftown, Scotland in 1829. At his parish grammar school in Banffshire (after which Banff National Park was named), Stephen distinguished himself as one of the finest mathematicians the school had ever known. After receiving a solid education, the lad moved to Montréal in 1850 to work as an employee at the textile firm of a distant relatives. It wasn't long before young Stephen employed his genius to restructure the company, making it radically more profitable, while investing his wages in company shares. Within several years, he owned a controlling interest and he continued to expand until the company became Montréal's largest textiles firm.

Stephen's success, refinement and gentle civility made him a sought-after guest on the Montréal social circuit, but while he was able to mingle easily with the city's elite, he preferred a life of diligent work and quiet study. He used most of his spare time to teach himself advanced banking and financial theory, knowledge that would pay off enormously when Donald Smith approached him with a bold scheme to take over an ailing Minnesota railroad. Stephen had realized relatively early that those who controlled finance and transport controlled the economy. He thus turned his energies increasingly away from manufacturing and towards banking and railroads. In 1873, Stephen became an influential director of the Bank of Montreal and was elected president in 1876, serving for five years. Ultimately, he became Canada's most powerful banker and financier, but he is probably best remembered as one of the nation's most successful railroad magnates.

Donald Smith left Labrador in 1869 (the year George Simpson died) to become head of the HBC's Montréal department at the company's headquarters in Lachine. As indicated in Chapter Two, 1869 was also the year that Louis Riel created his provisional government at Red River and Prime Minister John A. Macdonald's government asked Smith, as a high-ranking HBC official who understood the Métis people, to act as special commissioner and negotiate with Riel. And as indicated earlier, Macdonald also gave Smith the resources to buy off as many of Riel's supporters as possible, thus weakening Riel's authority. Working thus behind the scenes, Smith paved the way for the negotiations that resulted in the creation of Manitoba.

Smith's work in Manitoba on behalf of the federal government contributed greatly to his visibility and stature. He also became a member of Manitoba's Legislative Assembly between 1870 and '74 and, during much of the same time, a member of the House of Commons in Macdonald's government between 1871 and '78.

Travelling back and forth between Ottawa, Montréal and Red River, Smith often chose the southern route via steamboat and railway through Minnesota. He realized that the rapidly growing Red River region needed a railroad to connect it to the outside world, and he began to examine the bankrupt St. Paul and Pacific Railway, an unfinished, rusting line owned by Dutch owners anxious to unload it. Smith's travels brought him in contact with J.J. Hill, a wealthy Canadian-born coal producer living in Minnesota, who also saw the possibilities of buying the defunct railroad and building a line north to Red River. Smith and Hill convinced George Stephen to put his financial talents to work, and Stephen managed to secure Bank of Montreal financing (he was president at the time) and negotiate a shrewd deal with the Amsterdam owners. Those who have studied Stephen's innovative financing scheme, with its elaborate and creative utilization of bond rollovers, options, and stock transfers, conclude that it was nothing short of a stroke of sheer genius. The trio soon had clear title to the railway and renamed it the St. Paul, Minneapolis and Manitoba Railway. Stephen became the company's president, organizing its finances and managing risk. Hill began to build a line north to the Manitoba border, and Smith used his political influence to convince the Mackenzie government to build a railway from Red River south to meet Hill. By 1878, all the work paid off, and the railway was an immediate and resounding success. Within a decade, each of the partners had earned a cool $20 million, a mind-boggling sum for the time. Over the next thirty years, they pocketed a collective $500 million in interest-bearing securities, not including dividends. This was one of the most stupefying financial conquests in Canadian history, but it was not enough for Smith.

In 1880, Donald Smith quietly let it be known that he could form a syndicate capable of constructing a railway to the Pacific. On hearing this, Agriculture Minister John Henry Pope rushed to Macdonald's office to inform the prime minister that finally a group of reputable, experienced railway magnates had emerged who could get the job done. "Catch them," Pope exhorted, "before they invest their profits."

When Smith approached Stephen with the scheme, Stephen was hesitant. He was busy with his other enterprises in addition to his duties as president of the Bank of Montreal. Nevertheless, he studied the financial aspects of the Canadian Pacific Railway project for several days, finally pronouncing that the new venture would be, "the ruin of us all." And it nearly was.

Despite his fears, Stephen decided to take on the massive challenge, becoming president of the Canadian Pacific Railway Company in 1881. To increase the financial power of the syndicate, Stephen and Smith recruited their former partner J.J. Hill, as well as three high-profile Scots financiers, Duncan McIntyre, J.S. Kennedy and Richard Angus.

Construction of the CPR was far more difficult and costly than even the cautious realist George Stephen had ever imagined. Though the partners pledged their considerable assets to the CPR, and George Stephen worked miracles to keep a huge cash flow funneling into the project, laying down track over the muskeg of the Canadian Shield and through the Rocky Mountains gobbled up alarming amounts of capital. The federal government kicked in massive subsidies of cash and land, but it was nowhere near enough. Several times, the company teetered on the brink of bankruptcy, but a nervous Stephen somehow managed to keep the cash coming so that workers could be paid. At the beginning of 1885, however, the end of the rope was finally reached. The partners' fortunes had been spent, and the government was not willing to bleed taxpayers any further. It appeared as though the dream of a railway from sea to sea was going to die.

At this critical point, Louis Riel inadvertently saved the CPR by staging his last rebellion. The Macdonald government, seeing the military necessity of the railway, agreed to secure the CPR's loans while troops were loaded on a train and rushed to crush Riel and his followers. Construction of the line again forged ahead.

By late 1885, only five years after the Scots had formed their syndicate, the trans-Canada railway was completed. At Craigellachie, B.C. (named after the ancestral homeland of Smith and Stephen's clan) Donald Smith, as senior member of the syndicate, drove the last spike. The photo of his ceremonial act became one of the most famous images in Canadian history, the precise moment frozen on film when the theory of Canada as a transcontinental nation became a reality.

The construction of the CPR certainly ranks as one of the great defining periods in the creation of modern Canada, the impact of which cannot be exaggerated. Hudson's Bay Company lands, jealously sealed off for two centuries, were busted wide open. Settlers seeking a new life poured on to the prairies. British Columbia, splendidly isolated for so long, became linked to the great Canadian experiment. The forbidding geography that had stood in the way of a continental destiny had finally been conquered. The North West Passage, which had eluded so many for so long, now existed in a different form, blasted through rock and

NATIONAL LIBRARY OF CANADA / 22648

DONALD SMITH AND THE LAST SPIKE: THE RAILWAY AT LAST LINKED CANADA SEA TO SEA.

hammered down over the vast plains. The CPR was undoubtedly the boldest affirmation of Canadian resolve, aspiration and identity in the nation's history.

The CPR went on to become one of the biggest and most important corporate conglomerates in Canada. The company set up telegraph lines alongside its railways and became a leader in communications. It diversified into locomotive and steamship building, mining, pulp and paper, gas and oil, hotels, and stockyards. It set up a system of national parks and became a leader in the Canadian tourist trade. Eventually, the CPR would dominate trucking and western airline routes. Overall, the CPR laid the foundation for western industrialization.

The CPR partners, particularly Smith and Stephen, ultimately made a killing. The government's cash and land subsidies alone were pegged at well over $100 million, a sum dwarfed by CPR stock values and impressive dividends.

The indefatigable Smith went on to other equally impressive feats. He became a long-serving president of the Bank of Montreal as well as president of Royal Trust. He became CEO of the still-powerful Hudson's Bay Company, overseeing the company's transition from fur seller to merchandising giant. He was appointed Canadian high commissioner in London, where he hobnobbed with the Royal Family and was frequently toasted as the Empire's most prominent figure. From a lowly HBC fur clerk, Smith had catapulted himself to the very pinnacle of British society, ultimately receiving the title, Lord Strathcona, named for his colossal Scottish estate (one of seven opulent homes he purchased). Over a thirty-year period, until his death at ninety-four, Smith gave away millions to a wide assortment of groups.

LORD STRATHCONA, CANADIAN HIGH COMMISSIONER

After his CPR triumph, an exhausted George Stephen had had enough. He resigned from his many presidencies and directorates and retired quietly to England. Like Smith, Stephen also became a peer, Lord Mount Stephen, and also spent the rest of his life giving away a good portion of his money.

At a public address, when he received the freedom of the City of Aberdeen, Stephen made revealing comments that offer valuable insight into why Scots businessmen were so successful:

> Any success I may have had in life is due in great measure to the somewhat Spartan training I received during my Aberdeen apprenticeship, in which I entered as a boy of 15. To that training, coupled with the fact that I seem to have been born utterly without the faculty of doing more than one thing at a time … I had but few wants and no distractions to draw me away from the work I had in hand. It was impressed upon me from my earliest years by one of the best mothers that ever lived that I must aim at being a thorough master of my work, whatever that might be, to the exclusion of every other thing. I soon discovered that if I ever accomplished anything in life it would be by pursuing my object with a persistent determination to attain it. I had neither the training nor the talents to accomplish anything without hard work, and fortunately I knew it.

In Western Canada, patterns of Scottish industrial domination paralleled those of the East. In British Columbia, for example, the first and most powerful multi-millionaire industrialist, a man who virtually ran the province's economy, was Robert Dunsmuir. Born in Ayrshire, Scotland in 1825, Dunsmuir accepted employment in British Columbia in 1851 as a mining engineer when the HBC chief factor, James Douglas, recruited hundreds of Scottish miners to exploit British Columbia coalfields. Dunsmuir was not, however, a company man for very long.

On a Vancouver Island fishing trip, he discovered an outcropping of coal. After testing it extensively, he determined that he had stumbled onto an extremely rich vein. He set up a mine and established his own town, the island hamlet of Wellington. Over the next thirty years, Dunsmuir ran his operations with an iron hand, busting unions, exploiting Asian labour, and disregarding his workers' safety. Hundreds of miners died due to unscrupulous, cutthroat mining practices and Dunsmuir's empire grew at an astonishing rate, eventually including ships, iron works, and real estate. His biggest plunder came in 1883 when the Canadian government asked him to build a railway from Nanaimo to Victoria. Dunsmuir agreed on the condition that he receive $750,000 and a land grant amounting to one-quarter of Vancouver Island. The government acquiesced, giving Dunsmuir not only an enormous chunk of some of the world's best real estate but also the rights to all the coal, oil, minerals, slates, clay, and ores that lay beneath the surface. Dunsmuir celebrated by building a fantastic mansion in Victoria, Craigdarroch Castle, which operates today as a tourist destination.

When Robert Dunsmuir died in 1889, his son James continued to bust unions, oppress workers and increase the family's financial empire, streamlining operations and employing bold new technologies. James Dunsmuir not only controlled much of British Columbia's industry, but was also a leading member of the legislature for many years, as well as provincial premier from 1900 to 1902. Though he disliked politics, he served more from a feeling of public duty than from any desire for political power. In 1906, he agreed, albeit hesitantly, to become the province's lieutenant governor. But by 1909, James Dunsmuir had dropped from public view, glad finally to enjoy his vast wealth in peace.

The transfer of wealth and influence from father to son, as exemplified in the case of the Dunsmuirs, is a common occurrence in the business world, and this phenomenon has been particularly true among Scots well into the twentieth century. Enterprising Scottish immigrants had virtually controlled Canada's early industrialization, and their sons and grandsons came to play a leading role in the Canadian economy in the twentieth century. Alexander Ross once noted in *Canadian Business*, "Canada is widely assumed to be an egalitarian society, but the extent to which rich men's sons dominated the financial news [until] the 1970s was absolutely astonishing. It was almost as though control of major portions of the Canadian economy were being passed on, like family memberships in the Granite Club."

The examination of modern business elites in Canada lies well beyond the scope of this book. Suffice it to say that when one peruses a list of Canada's financial movers and shakers, one is immediately struck by the preponderance of Scottish names. This phenomenon stands to reason, since the Scots firmly established themselves early as the dominant players in virtually every industry in Canada, including furs, shipping, banks, communications, railroads, lumber, agriculture, mining, manufacturing, and so on. When Canada's population burgeoned in the early 1900s, and a new form of corporate capitalism took root, commercial families, already positioned as the country's leading financial players, were the ones with the capital and experience to control the economy of the twentieth century.

This and the preceding chapters have offered only a brief survey of a broad and complicated topic. In fact, for every Scottish entrepreneur cited, there are perhaps hundreds who deserve recognition as important builders of Canada's economy. Yet it remains clear at any level of examination that the Scots were without a doubt the predominant builders of Canada's economic infrastructure.

An examination of Scottish economic influence in Canada's history reveals certain factors that allowed the Scots to dominate to such a remarkable degree. The conquest of Québec in 1760 coincided with not only the Highland Clearances but also with the growing commercial aspirations of Scottish Lowlanders to establish their own colonies. Unlike most English businessmen, Scottish entrepreneurs embraced British North America as a land of fresh opportunity as

THE DOMINION ILLUSTRATED / NATIONAL ARCHIVES OF CANADA / C-007905

SECURELY ENSCONCED AT THE PINNACLE OF MONTRÉAL'S SOCIAL HIERARCHY, THE CITY'S SCOTS CELEBRATED AT THE ANNUAL ST. ANDREW'S BALL IN DECEMBER 1890.

well as the key to unlocking Scotland's economic potential. In short, it was Scots merchants who rushed to establish themselves in a vast, cold corner of the British Empire when few others seemed to be interested. Canada has thus often been characterized as Scotland's "informal colony", and the Scots themselves have called it "Scotland's revenge on England".

The Scots also arrived in Canada with attitudes and skills that placed them in society's most powerful financial echelons. The Scottish Enlightenment had a profound influence on the Scotland's commercial culture of the 1700s and 1800s. Acquiring property was considered to be an admirable act of self-expression as well as a valuable component of one's identity. Ownership was an affirmation of and a commitment to a community and allowed a person to exercise his or her potential. This was a radical concept in most of Europe, particularly in Protestant countries, where it was widely believed that earthly wealth was a barrier to heaven. Not so with the Scots. On the contrary, the predominant view among the emerging Scottish commercial classes was that wealth was a requisite to self-actualization.

Property allowed one the leverage to affect society for the good. And with wealth and power came social responsibility, a strong sense of *noblesse oblige.* In short, wealth was good. Without it, one had little to offer anyone else. Such views were fused with a stiff, uncompromising, Presbyterian ethic, which held that God would help those who helped themselves, hard work was the path to salvation, and discipline and stoicism were next to Godliness. These secular and religious ideas combined to produce a merchant culture of merchants that was spectacularly successful yet socially conscious, particularly in the wide-open, developing Canada of the late eighteenth and nineteenth centuries.

When discussing the creation of Canada, it is important to realize that economic integration was a vital precursor to Confederation. Without economic union, the disparate regions of Canada would never have been able form a viable political union. Thus, the economic infrastructure that allowed interprovincial trade from sea to sea was arguably the greatest achievement in Canada's development. And the main builders of this infrastructure were invariably Scots enterprisers. In industries such as shipping, banking, canals, telegraphs, and railways, Scottish businessmen were undisputedly the leaders who physically laid down the economic foundation of Canada. Thus, in a very literal sense, the Scots built the country.

UNIVERSITIES

Through the latter half of the 1700s and for most of the 1800s, Scottish universities were considered to be the best and most progressive in the world. Unlike their English counterparts, they were not "ivory towers," accessible only to young Anglican aristocrats. Instead, Scottish universities reflected the democratic ideals of the Scottish Enlightenment and were open to virtually all qualified students, regardless of social class.

MACKAY TARTAN KILT COURTESY OF JAMES W. BURNS / SPORRAN, KILT HOSE, BELT AND SHOES COURTESY OF THE SCOTTISH CROFT, SYDNEY, BC / ACADEMIC GOWN COURTESY OF PROFESSOR PETER ST. JOHN

THEY WERE ALSO INTERNATIONALLY RECOGNIZED as centres of lively debate and inquiry as well as intellectual hubs that promoted a free exchange of groundbreaking ideas. While English universities perpetuated a rigid class system, Scottish universities reflected the values of a dynamic commercial culture, one that celebrated self-determination and self-edification. For this reason, members of England's exploding bourgeoisie increasingly sent their sons to study in Scotland.

Because commerce-minded Scots who had been educated "back home" controlled much of Canada, it is little wonder that Canadian universities came to bear such a close resemblance to those of Scotland. While there was a good deal of competition among various churches to control education in early Canada, the system that eventually dominated was a uniquely Canadian one that shared many of the fundamental characteristics of Scottish universities, such as Scottish teaching methods, a focus on "practical" education, accessibility to all qualified students, and a non-sectarian, increasingly secular view of the world. Four Canadian universities, Dalhousie, McGill, Queen's, and the University of Toronto, strongly reflected Scottish values and were thus best suited to serve the needs of a relatively classless, frontier, commerce-oriented Canada. These four universities eventually became the vital nucleus of the Canadian university system as well as the template used to establish subsequent universities. In brief, the Scots grafted their system of higher education, which took very well, onto the wilds of Canada and the system became an important building block of the nation's overall social structure.

Education had long been a crucial national priority in Scotland. A network of Presbyterian parish schools spanned the Scottish landscape, and throughout the 1700s and 1800s, Scotland was Europe's most literate nation. In fact, the little country had been the world's first modern literate society, where a majority of the population could read well and thus participate in civic matters. Most sociologists and political theorists would agree that literacy is a vital requisite for developing a democratic society. Perhaps it was Scotland's impressive literacy rates, estimated by 1750 to be around seventy-five per cent, that gave the country such a head start in developing egalitarian values. It would take until the 1880s before the average Englishman could read as well as the average Scot.

Reading and self-education was a way of life for the Scots. Historian Arthur Herman writes:

> An official national survey in 1795 showed that out of a population of 1.5 million, nearly twenty thousand Scots depended for their livelihood on writing and publishing – and 10,500 on teaching. All this meant that despite its relative poverty and small population, Scottish culture had a built-in bias toward reading, learning, and education in general. In no other European country did education count for so much, or enjoy so broad a base.

In addition to democratic notions fostered by high levels of literacy, the Scots were moving away from traditional, Calvinistic, "fire and brimstone" interpretations of the Bible. Many Enlightenment theologians began to put forward theories that life was meant to be enjoyed and the human condition need not be one of suffering. Perhaps God was not wrathful after all, but benevolent. Maybe God

CHARLES WILLIAM JEFFREYS / NATIONAL ARCHIVES OF CANADA / C-069650

desired to see man flourish and reach his earthly potential instead of enduring unrelenting hardship to pay for his sins. Such ideas were radical for the time and illustrate the Scots' progress towards a view of a more self-determined and empowered man.

Scottish Enlightenment philosophers and educators also saw no fundamental contradiction between science and religion. They held the novel belief that the study of man should be scientific, rational and non-mystical. Thus, they created the social sciences: economics, sociology, history, psychology, etc. to explain human behaviour. They also believed that scientific methodology would reveal God's grand design, not lead to questioning his existence. Instead of condemning and suppressing scientific inquiry as a threat to Christian doctrine, the Scots welcomed it. This was a bold and innovative way of viewing the world, one that caused nervousness, if not outright agitation, among many traditional Calvinists throughout Europe. Progressive thinkers everywhere, on the other hand, marvelled at Scottish openness and open-mindedness. An awed Voltaire once exclaimed, "It is to Scotland that we look for our ideas of civilization."

One of the most amazing aspects of Scottish higher education in the late 1700s and early 1800s was its pervasiveness. A majority of Scottish businessmen had attended university for a year or two and could read Latin and Greek as well as account and market. There was no perceived inconsistency between the lofty ideals of moral philosophy and the mundane self-interest of commerce. In fact, both higher education and property were needed to become a cultivated gentleman. The study of business and economics was considered honourable and valuable. By the late 1700s, fully one-half of Scottish university students were sons of businessmen, compared with only eight per cent of English students. The idea of elitist institutions serving only exclusive landed gentry simply did not exist in Scotland.

Scottish universities were also relatively cheap. To attend, one only needed a good knowledge of Latin, something taught at all parish schools, and a paltry five pounds per year, one-tenth the tuition cost at Oxford or Cambridge. The result was that Scotland had three times the level of public participation in the university system compared to England, and that was only from tuition-paying students. A favourite activity among many Scottish townsfolk, men and women alike, was to audit university lectures. University "community outreach" programs became very popular in Scottish university towns.

In British North America, universities were slow to develop, since the cold upper half of North America had only a small, thinly-spread, relatively uneducated population. The British government established the three King's Colleges at Windsor, Nova Scotia in 1789, York (Toronto) in 1827, and Frederiction, New Brunswick in 1828. These colleges were virtual replicas of English universities, designed to promote Anglicanism in Canada. They were residential, and the primary method of teaching was through tutorials, generally conducted by teaching assistants; professors usually had little to do with students. In 1843, the Anglican Church also set up Bishop's College (now Bishop's University) in Lennoxville, Québec.

Other religious groups also established their own colleges. For example, the Methodists established Mount Allison University in Sackville, New Brunswick in 1839. The Baptists set up Acadia University in Wolfville, Nova Scotia in 1838. English Catholics built St. Francis Xavier University in Antigonish, Nova Scotia in 1855, and French Catholics established Laval University in Québec City in 1852. Scottish Presbyterians also launched several colleges of their own in the first half of the 1800s: Pictou Academy in Nova Scotia, Queen's college in Kingston, Morin College in Québec City, and Manitoba College in Winnipeg.

Most church-affiliated colleges and universities were small, each with fewer than a hundred resident students, and their primary purpose was to prepare men for the ministry. Churches generally saw universities as a means of furnishing the colonies with a constant supply of missionaries and members of the church hierarchy.

An interesting aspect of Scottish Presbyterianism of the late 1700s and early 1800s was that its governing structure was not completely hierarchical, as was the case with many other European churches. In fact, there was a unique mix of democratic and hierarchical elements, resulting in an innovative balance of power between the congregation and the clergy. The unusual corporate structure of Scotland's Presbyterian churches was such that individual leadership was not much of a factor in church life. It is interesting to consider that even within the confines of a rigid Calvinistic ideology, the Scots' propensity for democratic ideals was evident. Perhaps it was the church's relatively democratic structure that allowed the staunch Presbyterian Lowlanders to think more freely and eventually develop fresh ideas about man's relationship to God and society.

By the late eighteenth and early nineteenth centuries, Scotland's universities (St. Andrew's, Glasgow, Aberdeen, and Edinburgh) had developed a "system". They had already moved away from exclusively preaching church doctrine and were focusing increasingly on social sciences. As for teaching methods, the universities had done away with teaching assistants (who had always acted as a buffer between students and professors) and insisted that distinguished scholars actually do some teaching. Thus, most Scottish professors gave several lectures per week directly to students, usually in large lecture halls.

One of the men most responsible for transplanting the Scottish "system" of higher education onto Canadian soil was Thomas McCulloch, who set up the first of the Presbyterian colleges, Pictou Academy, in 1816. Although a stern Presbyterian, McCulloch was a new sort of scholar with wide interests in many fields. Born in Renfrewshire, Scotland, McCulloch had studied at Glasgow University before emigrating to Nova Scotia in 1803. He was a driven man with a large ego, and he pumped out a prodigious number of publications on topics as diverse as scientific methodology, the physiology of birds, the Hebrew language, and the sociology of the colonies. He also wrote several well-known novels.

McCulloch became widely known in the Maritimes as the expert on higher education, writing about how universities in the colonies should be laid out and exerting a powerful influence on most educators of the day. McCulloch applied to the colonial government to help fund his academy, but the government refused, stating it would fund only Anglican institutions. This enraged McCulloch, who founded a reformist newspaper with which to lambaste the government's narrow-mindedness. Eventually, the frustrated McCulloch made an agreement with Glasgow University to grant degrees to graduates of Pictou Academy. Because of this, some of Canada's first university graduates were granted not Canadian degrees but Scottish ones. Overall, McCulloch is widely credited with establishing the Scottish system of higher education in the Maritimes.

Another big name among educators of early Canada was John Strachan, the stubborn hanger-on of tradition who eventually became head of the exclusive Family Compact in Upper Canada. Strachan was born in Aberdeen in 1778 and attended the local university, graduating as a teacher in 1797. He had been a strict Presbyterian until he moved to Upper Canada to escape the fierce competition for teaching jobs in Scotland. In Upper Canada, he soon noticed that he would receive far more offers for employment were he Anglican, so he quickly converted and was even ordained as a priest. Strachan's strategy immediately paid off in spades; he became the rector of Cornwall and also ran a church school. From there, he worked his way up to become rector of York, where his influence among Loyalist conservatives continued to grow. In 1818, he was appointed to the Executive Council of the province, where he wielded enormous power until William Lyon Mackenzie's rebellion of '37.

Just before King's College (later renamed the University of Toronto) was established in 1827, William Lyon Mackenzie voiced some of the concerns of non-Anglicans towards the new institution: "If it is to be an arm of our hierarchy; if students are to be tied down by tests and oaths, to support particular dogmas, as in the case of Oxford, the institution will answer here no good purpose ..."

John Strachan paid little attention to the strident Mackenzie and exerted strict control over the three King's Colleges according to what he thought were traditional Anglican, aristocratic principles. Strachan, however, was a Scot who had been educated in Scotland. He was, therefore, most familiar with the Scottish system of higher education, and when it fell to him to hire scholars and manage the King's Colleges, he turned to what he knew.

Strachan wrote to London that he preferred the Scottish university system to the English one because "much more may be done at one fourth of the expense. In the English universities, the public professors seldom lecture more than once a week – many of them not at all – the whole system of teaching is conducted by tutor." It wasn't that Strachan was philosophically opposed to the elitism of English universities; rather, he wanted to make his funds stretch as far as he could, and it was well known that Scottish professors would work harder for much less money than their English counterparts. They also would be far more likely to endure the relatively primitive living conditions in Canada. Strachan wrote to London: "The great opulence of Cambridge and Oxford is far beyond our reach, and although I should be sorry ever to see them lose a shilling for I think them wisely adapted to so rich and populous and learned a country as England, I think them unfit for this country. Learning they may have in abundance, but the industry, the labour (I may say drudgery) and accommodation to circumstances cannot be expected from them."

In an effort to optimize his limited resources, Strachan thought it shrewd to adopt a Scottish-style system of delivering higher education and to recruit predominantly Scottish professors. Ironically, the fresh young scholars from Scotland brought Enlightenment ideas with them to Canada, which ultimately led to more openness and equality and displaced Strachan and his traditionalist stranglehold on Canada's system of higher education.

Meanwhile in the Maritimes, important events were taking place that would ultimately have a far-reaching impact on Canada's university system. One of the key players was George Ramsay, the 9th Earl of Dalhousie, a Scottish nobleman from a proud aristocratic family. Dalhousie Castle, the dark gothic structure still standing near Edinburgh, was the family home that Lord Dalhousie inherited, along with his title, at the age of seventeen.

Dalhousie was born in 1770, and like many young bluebloods of the day, he pursued a military career. In the late 1700s and early 1800s, Great Britain was at almost constant war with France, and Dalhousie served with distinction throughout the Empire as a reliable and

Lord Dalhousie, lieutenant governor of Nova Scotia and later governor general of British North America.

able officer. In 1815, he played a major part in defeating Napoleon at Waterloo. In those days, successful army officers who were past their fighting prime could expect lucrative assignments to govern one of the colonies. Dalhousie was offered the position of lieutenant governor of Nova Scotia in 1816, which he enthusiastically accepted.

For the next four years, Dalhousie ran the colony of Nova Scotia with great diligence and interest. By all accounts, he was hard working, honest, and fair. Despite his powerful position, he did not derive much satisfaction from pomp and ceremony. Instead, he crisscrossed the colony, talking with anyone and everyone, regardless of social class, and made a genuine effort to understand the needs of the people. "Dalhousie is very much a Scot," writes historian Marjory Whitelaw. "He is a friendly man; in unofficial relationships he altogether lacks the kind of hauteur which at that time might have characterized an Englishman of equal rank."

In terms of his attitude towards his king and country, Dalhousie was an exemplary company man. He was a rigid monarchist who felt that democracy was dangerous. In light of his growing up during the French Revolution, his views are understandable. Dalhousie was also, of course, a diehard British loyalist who had spent a lifetime defending the integrity of the Empire. Despite all of this, however, his Scottishness asserted itself when it came to higher education in Nova Scotia. As lieutenant governor, Dalhousie was supposed to support the state church and thus King's College in Windsor, Nova Scotia. This he refused to do.

Dalhousie was dismayed that in Nova Scotia, where only one-fifth the

W.H. COVERDALE COLLECTION / NATIONAL ARCHIVES OF CANADA / C-041950

DALHOUSIE, NEW BRUNSWICK, CIRCA 1866.

population was Anglican, King's College was accessible only to a small minority. Like most educated Scottish Presbyterians, Dalhousie believed firmly that a solid, non-sectarian education should be the right of every man. He was therefore adamant that the exclusive King's College was completely unsuitable for the needs of the colony. In 1817, he began to correspond extensively with the University of Edinburgh, seeking advice on how best to set up a new, more open system of higher education.

Dalhousie submitted a proposal for a new Scottish-style college, but the British Government refused to fund it. Dalhousie got around this obstacle by collecting customs duties from American traders in Maine and diverting the funds into his college. In 1818, Dalhousie began to build Dalhousie College in Halifax.

In 1820, at a ceremony during which Dalhousie laid his college's cornerstone, he gave a speech that would resonate for many years:

> Before I proceed in this ceremony, I think it necessary to state to you, gentlemen, the object of and intention of this important work ... This College of Halifax is founded for the instruction of youth in the higher classics and in all philosophic studies; it is formed in imitation of the University of Edinburgh; its doors will be open to all who profess the Christian religion; to the youth of His Majesty's North American Colonies, to strangers residing here, to gentlemen of the military as well as learned professions, to all, in short, who may be disposed to devote a small part of their time to study ... It is founded upon the principles of religious toleration secured to you by the laws, and upon that paternal protection which the King of England extends to all his subjects.

The speech was very liberal, reflecting the values of the Scottish Enlightenment that had shaped Lord Dalhousie. The creation of Dalhousie College marked a radical break from the sectarian, exclusive English model of higher education.

In 1820, Lord Dalhousie left his bucolic life in Nova Scotia for Montréal to become governor general for all of British North America. For the next eight years, he wrangled with French Canadians in Lower Canada as well as with disaffected Anglo settlers in Upper Canada. The morass of Canadian politics during this period would have frustrated any administrator. Dalhousie attempted to maintain the King's grip on power in the colonies, but the popular tide for legislative reform proved formidable, resulting in an exasperating and somewhat unhappy term for Dalhousie. Many considered him to be an intransigent authoritarian, which was not a fair characterization. Dalhousie's resistance to legislative reform was simply an attempt to hold the colonies together and effectively perform his principal duty: namely, to preserve the integrity of the empire. In 1828, the discouraged Dalhousie returned to England and accepted the posting of commander-in-chief for British forces in India.

Without Dalhousie's firm support, and with the opposition of the British government and of King's College, Dalhousie College languished for twenty years. A lack of strong leadership and meager funding were serious problems for the upstart college. Only in 1838 did it receive the energy and direction it needed, when Thomas McCulloch, the founder and head of Pictou Academy, took over Dalhousie College, bringing with him his expertise and impressive reputation. Until his death in 1843, McCulloch put Dalhousie College on a firm footing, hiring Scottish professors and modelling the College's curriculum after the Scottish universities. At the outset of his tenure, he insisted that Dalhousie College focus on studies that were practical, not esoteric. McCulloch maintained that if students could "direct attention to the real business of life they will not have just cause to complain that they have spent their youth on studies foreign to their success." He went on to say, "If Dalhousie College acquires usefulness and eminence it will be not by an imitation of Oxford, but as an institution of science and practical intelligence." Thus, in addition to the classics, Dalhousie placed a special emphasis on modern scientific studies as well as on business studies.

Over the next twenty years, Dalhousie College took faltering steps forward. Its Scottish-style, practical, accessible and secular brand of education was widely criticized by those affiliated with the various religious colleges. Nevertheless, Dalhousie proved popular and eventually most Maritime colleges either closely emulated it or were forced to close down. In effect, Dalhousie had set the standard for higher education in the eastern colonies. In 1863, Lord Dalhousie's college became the first full university in the Maritimes, growing continuously since then to become the region's dominant post-secondary institution.

In the early 1800s in Lower Canada, the Catholic Church firmly controlled all aspects of education. This fact irritated James McGill, the prominent fur trader, merchant, administrator, politician, soldier, and philanthropist (see Chapter Five, Scottish Enterprise). McGill, though married, did not have any children, and in 1811, at the age of sixty-seven, he began to realize his days were numbered. It was a conversation with John Strachan that convinced McGill that Montreal needed a college that would serve the needs of young anglophones. Ironically, James McGill's creation, McGill College, evolved into virtually the last kind of institution that the dogmatic Strachan would have wanted.

McGill knew that the Montréal he had known throughout his life was on the verge of rapid change. The fur trade was showing the first signs of decline, and the primary stages of industrialization were already evident. McGill believed that in order to thrive in this new, more civilized environment, young men would require a much higher level of education than ever before. The late eminent Canadian writer, Hugh MacLennan, wrote, "James McGill had always been a reader [interpreter], and perhaps he guessed from the signs that the pioneering days were over in the Montreal district and that if history were any guide, the future would require a different type of man from the great adventurers with whom he had passed his own life. He was a realist, and about Montreal he had few illusions."

CHARLES WILLIAM JEFFREYS / NATIONAL ARCHIVES OF CANADA / C-069595

THE HOME AND STORE OF JAMES MCGILL IN OLD MONTRÉAL. IT WAS MCGILL'S COUNTRY ESTATE, BURNSIDE, THAT THE SCOTTISH ENTREPRENEUR DONATED TO THE CITY.

In 1813, at the age of sixty-nine, McGill died suddenly of a heart attack. In his will, he donated his beloved Burnside estate, a picturesque eighteen-hectare farm on the slope of Mount Royal above Montréal, as well as £10,000, for the establishment of a non-denominational, anglophone college. For several years following McGill's death, his wife's relatives contested his will, concocting weird legal arguments in an attempt to lay their hands on every last shilling of his estate. Eventually, the courts upheld McGill's will, and finally, in 1821, the necessary cash was unfrozen and McGill College was finally chartered. Buildings, however, were not erected until 1829.

Of course Great Britain wanted nothing to do with the non-denominational college and refused to fund it; thus, McGill College was completely private until

1960. During its first half-century of operation, the college would not have been able to operate, expand, and thrive were it not for the colossal donations of several Scottish magnates: Peter Redpath (the sugar baron), William MacDonald (the Montréal tobacco king), and Donald Smith (the one-man corporate conglomerate). Englishman John Molson also poured vast sums of money into McGill College.

Like Dalhousie, McGill College hired predominantly Scottish scholars and adopted a curriculum that closely resembled that of the University of Edinburgh. And like Dalhousie, the non-sectarian, practical education offered at McGill seemed well suited to the colony's needs. By the 1850s, McGill College had become a university, the largest and most influential in British North America.

In 1852, John William Dawson, a Canadian-born Scot, became principal of McGill University. Dawson had been trained at Thomas McCulloch's Pictou Academy and at the University of Edinburgh. Under his thirty-eight-year direction, McGill University became an internationally-recognized research university. But Dawson's influence reached far beyond Montréal. McGill University's reputation, not to mention Dawson's own fame, allowed him to set up a scheme which permitted affiliated colleges across Canada to teach the Scottish-style McGill curriculum, one that placed special emphasis on scientific research and professional disciplines, as opposed to the Oxford curriculum of "natural philosophy".

Thus, the Scottish model of higher education spread throughout Canada, from the University of Toronto and Queen's to the far west. Since British Columbia had not yet build a college of its own, McGill University established a satellite campus in 1906 named McGill University College of British Columbia, which offered McGill degrees. The college eventually formed the backbone of the new University of British Columbia, established in 1915. UBC grew to become one of Canada's big research universities, but always maintained its Scottish curriculum and character.

Unlike in the Maritimes and Lower Canada, no visionaries took the initiative to establish a non-sectarian college in Upper Canada. This may be due partly to the fact that the Family Compact held such an iron grip on power. Church groups, however, were allowed to set up colleges, and one of Canada's most prestigious universities, Queen's University in Kingston, started out in 1841 as a Presbyterian college associated with the Church of Scotland. Its purpose was to train young men for the ministry. To this day, the University's Scottish roots are evident; tams and tartans adorn the halls, and the Gaelic battle cry, "Cha Gheill", can be heard in the school song.

In its early days, Queen's College (named after Queen Victoria who granted the college's charter) was a modest little school with only five Scottish teachers and a handful of students. While the teachers, including principal John Machar, were devout Presbyterians, they were also moderate Scots who had studied either at the University of Edinburgh or at St. Andrews. It is not surprising, then, that from the outset, Queen's College adopted, lock, stock and barrel, the curriculum of the University of Edinburgh and all the Enlightenment ideas that came with it. As the college began to grow, more non-Presbyterians were admitted, and more non-theological courses were offered. Thus, the College's denominational ties progressively diminished.

By the early 1870s, Queen's University had grown, and had, for all intents and purposes, become a non-denominational school, teaching a wide variety of subjects to a diverse group of students. Although the university still employed almost exclusively Scottish Presbyterian teachers, the curriculum was decidedly rational and scientific. In essence, it was these Scottish scholars who led the way towards the secularization of higher education. In 1872, Canada's foremost early philosopher, John Watson of Glasgow, was granted the chair of philosophy at Queen's. In a speech, he summed up the Scottish attitude towards doctrinaire religion:

> The older men, and especially the older clergymen, who found their favourite formulas quietly set aside might grumble and prophesy disaster, but the younger men, more alive to the advance of scientific discovery and of an aggressive enlightenment, which threatened to destroy all faith in higher things, felt that the new philosophy enabled them to preserve the essence of religion while giving it a more rational form.

This was quite a statement. The Scots' belief that the Bible should not necessarily be taken literally, but rather metaphorically, and that the principles of religion were not inconsistent with the cold rationality of science marked a fundamental break from the old paradigm of higher education. In Canada, as they had done in Great Britain, the Scots helped free universities from the orbit of Christian orthodoxy. This was especially true in the case of Queen's University, which exercised such an important liberalizing influence on higher education in Upper Canada.

Another of Upper Canada's important colleges was King's College in York, which became what is now Canada's largest university, the University of Toronto. The college was chartered in 1827 and was originally open only to young Anglicans. From the start, however, the college was a lightning rod for criticism. Reformers such as William Lyon Mackenzie saw the exclusive college as a rotten appendage of the establishment designed to promote the elitist status quo. In fact, many Baptists, Roman Catholics, Presbyterians, Methodists, etc. resented the exclusivity of King's College and railed bitterly against it. It was clear that an Anglican college in a multi-sectarian colony was a bad idea. This sort of criticism was the main reason that it got off to a slow start and actually had very few students until the late 1830s. By this time, Mackenzie's rebellion had taken place, and there was intense pressure on the government to reform the colony's institutions.

Pressure for reforming King's College was not only external but internal as well. Strachan had hired a mainly Scottish teaching staff, and these young scholars were naturally a product of the Scottish education system, one that encouraged a practical curriculum and high levels of public participation regardless of faith. Ultimately, the pressure from without and within reached critical mass, and in 1850, the liberal Scottish governor general, Lord Elgin, secularized King's College, renaming it the University of Toronto.

Lord Elgin was a quintessential moderate Scot who knew the key to the colony's success was plurality and cooperation among its diverse citizenry. He stated to Earl Grey, the colonial secretary, "... it must be remembered that the object of our recent legislation on the University question has been to set up one great institution in the province where a high educational standard might be maintained and which should give degrees which shall be worth having." Lord Elgin strongly championed the Scottish, "practical", secular model of education, which is what the University of Toronto adopted fully after 1850.

John Strachan was becoming an anachronism in Upper Canada. Things were changing; major reforms were being implemented and Strachan's power was waning. But the stubborn Scot did not submit quietly. In 1851, he set out for England, seeking a charter and money for a new Anglican school in Toronto, Trinity College, which he claimed, "fed by the heavenly stream of pure religion, may fuel to the lamp of genius and enable it to burn with a brighter and purer flame." Strachan got his charter, and Trinity College became precisely the kind of institution that King's College was supposed to have been all along.

The new University of Toronto, full of young Scottish teachers, immediately began to move away from a curriculum that took traditional Christian orthodoxy seriously. This is not to say, however, that most professors did not believe in God. Indeed, almost all of them did. But the Scottish-style system of education promoted open, scientific inquiry, and most educated Scottish Christians did not feel threatened by the challenging new scientific theories of the day. Daniel Wilson, recruited from the University of Edinburgh as professor of History and Literature at the new University of Toronto summed up this attitude: "Truth has nothing to fear in the long run from the researches of men such as Darwin and Huxley. I think it suffers far more from the shackles with which orthodox zeal would hamper inquiry with the most honest intentions. … Truth has everything to gain from the most absolute freedom of inquiry." Such became the educational tone at the University of Toronto from the 1850s on.

The four Canadian Scottish-style universities had become the accepted mould used to cast the many universities that sprang up in Canada after Confederation and into the early 1900s. As educational historian, Robin S. Harris notes, "[The Scots] were particularly influential in the nineteenth-century development of Dalhousie, McGill, Queen's and Toronto, the four institutions which above all others set the pattern for Canadian education in the first fifty years of the twentieth century."

Despite Canada's immensity and regionalism, the country's universities constitute a "system", sharing practically uniform standards in terms of curriculum, teaching methods, and openness to qualified students. This system can be firmly traced to the values of the Scottish Enlightenment of the late 1700s, which were transmitted to Canada through transplanted Scots who brought with them their Scottish educational culture.

Inspired by Scottish notions of egalitarianism and open access to all qualified students, Canada has developed a non-elitist university model that differs greatly from the two-tier university systems of the United States and England. In Canada, there is neither an "Ivy League" nor an Oxford or a Cambridge. Rather, all non-theological Canadian universities are publicly funded, and all seek to offer a comprehensive range of subjects in the arts, sciences, and business. Moreover, all Canadian universities offer research-based graduate programs to qualified students. The effect has been that public participation in university courses is higher in Canada, not only among eighteen to twenty-four-year olds but also among "mature" students, than in any other country.

As far as "practicality" is concerned, Canadian university students study career-related subjects more than in any other country except the U.S., where statistics closely resemble Canada's. This fact, of course, causes many educators (including me) to lament that the ideal of education for education's sake has all but vanished and that the economic value attached to university degrees has been over-emphasized. A compelling counter-argument is that the egalitarian Canadian university system was designed for non-aristocratic students and thus fulfills the very practical social need of training self-made professionals.

Overall, the Scottish influence on several of Canada's early key universities created the prototype for the Canadian university system. Thus, the current Canadian model (consisting of a secular, research-oriented, egalitarian form of education delivered by expert professor-researchers to large groups of students) was very much derived from the Scottish system. In a very real sense, the Scots invented and laid the foundation for higher education in Canada.

LITERATURE

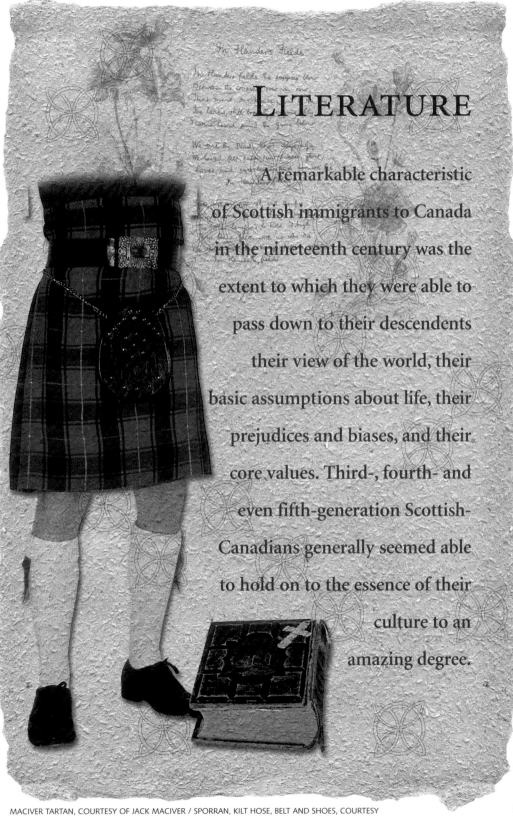

A remarkable characteristic of Scottish immigrants to Canada in the nineteenth century was the extent to which they were able to pass down to their descendents their view of the world, their basic assumptions about life, their prejudices and biases, and their core values. Third-, fourth- and even fifth-generation Scottish-Canadians generally seemed able to hold on to the essence of their culture to an amazing degree.

MACIVER TARTAN, COURTESY OF JACK MACIVER / SPORRAN, KILT HOSE, BELT AND SHOES, COURTESY OF THE SCOTTISH CROFT, SYDNEY, BC. / FAMILY BIBLE COURTESY OF PAT CORMIE

Nowhere was this phenomenon more clearly expressed than among writers. Because the Scots were among Canada's earliest active immigrant groups, and because they were relatively well educated, they were in a unique position to create and shape the literary ethos of English-speaking Canada. Through writing, Scottish culture spread throughout the country, from one generation to the next, profoundly affecting Canadian sensibilities as well as national identity. In essence, Scottish writers established many of the fundamental literary themes and antecedents from which subsequent English-Canadian literature evolved.

When one really thinks about them, the parallels between Scotland and Canada are truly amazing. Both countries share the same northern latitudes (though Scottish winters are nothing compared to ours), both countries have had to deal with two co-existing cultures, languages and religions, and both have always stood in the shadow of a giant commercial superpower and cultural juggernaut to the south. Such historical similarities have led to an almost instinctive understanding between Scots and Canadians. Because we have had to face similar obstacles and fight comparable battles, we are able to identify easily with one another. It is little wonder, then, that in the 1800s, the major modes and themes of Scottish literature transplanted so effortlessly and so completely to Canada.

Scottish-born travel writers, novelists, poets, essayists, reporters, and editors dominated Canadian literature throughout the 1800s. This was largely because they were trained and equipped to do so. In the late 1700s and throughout most of the 1800s, Scottish society was the most literate in the world and consumed, per capita, more written material, including newspapers, magazines and books, than any other nation. Publishing accounted for a significant percentage of the Scottish economy (see Universities chapter). Practically every hamlet in Scotland had a local newspaper run by a skilled editor. Not surprisingly, Scottish immigrants brought with them their publishing expertise as well as their insatiable appetite for all varieties of literature.

It is also important to understand that in the early 1800s, many of the most celebrated writers in the English-speaking world were Scots. Robert Burns was considered among critics to be the best lyrical poet of modern times if not ever. Sir Walter Scott and Robert Louis Stevenson each wrote a stack of best-selling novels and enjoyed celebrity status all over the English-speaking world. Thomas Macaulay and Thomas Carlyle were heralded as the greatest popular historians ever. James Matthew Barrie's dramatic plays were wildly successful throughout the British Empire. Therefore, when the Scottish immigrants came to Canada, they had very strong models in mind of what literature was, what issues it should address, and how it should be conveyed. Such powerful Scottish literary models did much to define the parameters of Canadian literature for many years to come.

Exactly why Scottish-style literature so readily took off in Canada is a subject for endless academic speculation and debate. Was it because the Scots controlled publishing and were generally the most educated group in Canada, so they naturally shaped the literature of the country to suit their tastes? Or were the conditions in Canada such that Scottish-style literature immediately struck a chord with readers of all ethnic origins? The answer is undoubtedly both. The Scots were definitely in control of the majority of publishing enterprises in early Canada, so their biases influenced what got published and what did not. But as already mentioned, the similarities between Scotland and Canada ran very deep, so Scottish-style literature naturally addressed issues that resonated strongly for Canadians of all backgrounds.

What was the Scottish-style literature? There were several basic recurring themes that seemed particularly relevant to the life of a Scotsman, ones that were obviously just as relevant to Canadians: (1) The simple life of the past has been lost. The old ways revolving around community, tradition and honour are disappearing. "Progress" has made us lose something valuable. (2) Though the weather is cold and the land harsh, the warmth of the family hearth will see a man through. (3) While nature is beautiful, it can also be fickle and deadly (this theme really rang true with Canadians). (4) A working man may be simple and of limited means, but his forthright character and purity of heart can give him the dignity of a king. (5) We are a small, underdog nation on the periphery of a great empire, but we are proud and independent, and we love our homeland. (6) We are outsiders with an autonomous perspective on the world; therefore, we are objective and see things the way they truly are. We view the world with irony, humour and sometimes melancholy.

Scottish-style literature was pithy, written for unpretentious folk to enjoy. It also was often laced with wistfulness or sadness, reflecting the Scots' suffering throughout their history. Most fiction was set in small towns and almost never in urban centres. It was a rural literature that analyzed the human condition within the microcosm of country communities. Moreover, unlike English literature, which tended in the late 1700s and early 1800s to focus on the emotional plights of the landed gentry, Scottish literature dealt with communities that were non-hierarchical and more egalitarian. Main characters were usually decent, hard-working people trying their best to make a way in the world. For this reason, Scottish-style literature spoke to the average Canadian far more than English literature ever could.

In the early 1800s, a majority of Canadian literature in English was straightforward exploration and travel literature, most of it written with very little literary pretense. As fur traders, explorers, and adventurers fanned out across the mysterious geography of British North America, they often recorded their encounters with a cool, almost scientific precision. Such literature proved extremely important because it served as a foundation upon which much subsequent Canadian literature was built. Notions of exotic and sometimes fierce Natives as well as perilous winters and daunting, unforgiving geography took root in the Canadian imagination. The idea that a lone man could face and overcome such physical challenges (and in the process face and overcome himself) became the premise of a good deal of Canadian literature for many years.

While the stereotypical American frontiersman, with his coonskin cap and squirrel rifle, was illiterate and inarticulate, the predominantly Scottish fur traders and explorers were relatively well educated and had the ability to turn clever phrases in their journals. Their "practical" educations were reflected in their often detached, matter-of-fact observations along their incredible journeys. Alexander Mackenzie's *Voyages*, published in 1801, became a best seller all over the English-speaking world. Another Scottish fur trader, Alexander Henry, published *Travels and Adventure in Canada and the Indian Territories* in 1809, which became a classic of Canadian travel literature. The journals of other Scottish traders such as Simon Fraser and John Rae (who traversed much of the Canadian Arctic and discovered the remains of the Franklin expedition) were posthumously published; both accounts had a significant effect in promoting the view of British North America as a strikingly beautiful but rugged and often hostile land.

Other writers were more romantic and less reserved about Canada's spectacular geography. George Heriot, a Scot who had served in the British Army and then settled in Upper Canada, published his classic *Travels Through the Canadas* in 1807. His purpose was to convey "an idea of some of the picturesque scenery of the St. Lawrence, at once the largest and most wonderful body of fresh waters on this globe." Heriot's effervescent prose sparkles with unrestrained enthusiasm for his new land. He writes, for example, "The falls of Niagara surpass in sublimity every description which the powers of language can afford of that celebrated scene, the most wonderful which the habitable world presents."

Travel and exploration literature accounted for a majority of Canadian writing in the early 1800s, but by mid-century, Scottish Canadian poets began to produce sophisticated satirical work. One of the most famous of the era was Alexander McLachlan who had emigrated from Glasgow as a penniless youth in 1840. An enthusiastic fan of Robert Burns, McLachlan emulated Burns' rollicking, ironic style. The titles of many of his poems offer insight into why McLachlin's verse found such a receptive audience in Canada: "Acres of His Own", "Up and be a Hero", "Young Canada", "Jack's as Good as his Master", and "The Man Who Rose from Nothing". McLachlan was often heralded as "the Burns of Canada", the ultimate compliment, as Burns was almost a deity among Scots.

To the delight of many of his readers, McLachlan lambasted many aspects of Canada's pioneer culture. In the spirit of Burns, he satirized settlers who were overly pious:

> Ye clog the soil of nature
> With your wretched little creeds,
> Then hold up your hands in wonder
> At the dearth of noble deeds.

He also warned sardonically against the invasion of American values in Canada:

> Talk not of old cathedral woods,
> Their gothic arches throwing,
> John only sees in all those trees
> So mony saw-logs growing.
>
> He laughs at all our ecstasies
> And he keeps still repeating
> You say 'tis fair, but will it wear?
> And is it good for eating?

McLachlan successfully emulated Burns' style and adapted Burns' themes to address the realities of the immigrant culture of Canada. His work spoke so clearly, not only to Scots but also to all immigrants, and proved so popular, that it set a standard for other Canadian poets to follow for decades.

Scottish-Canadian novelists were also very popular in Canada and abroad and established the literary tone for subsequent Canadian novels. One of the most well known was John Richardson, born in Upper Canada in 1796, the son of a Scottish military surgeon stationed in British North America.

At the age of sixteen, Richardson followed family tradition and signed on as a cadet in the British army. The War of 1812 broke out shortly after, and Richardson soon found himself fighting alongside the great warrior chief, Tecumseh. After the war, Richardson decided to quit the army and devote his life to writing. He spent the next twenty years living a bohemian life, primarily in the cafés and pubs of Paris and London.

Richardson's first poem, "Tecumseh", failed to attract much attention, but the work contained the seeds of what would later germinate into greater works. For inspiration and subject matter, Richardson drew on his youthful experiences in Canada, as that had been the defining period of his life. In 1832, he produced his masterpiece, the historical novel, *Wacousta*, also titled *The Prophecy: A Tale of the Canadas*, which dealt with Chief Pontiac's rebellion in the 1760s.

Richardson's literary idol had been Walter Scott, the literary giant and best-selling creator of the historical novel. Scott's settings were, in large part, the romantic Scotland and Britain of the past. Largely spun from his imagination, this was an idealized, semi-mythical time where men were more honourable, stronger, and nobler than their modern counterparts. This, of course, was a typically Scottish theme: generations of yore possessed something valuable that has been lost.

Although adopting Canadian settings, Richardson's work was a virtual facsimile of Walter Scott's. Since *Wacousta* had sold well, an encouraged Richardson published *The Canadian Brothers* in 1840, a novel set during the War of 1812. The book's sales were disappointing, however, so Richardson turned to writing non-fiction, albeit with a highly romantic slant. In 1842, he published *The War of 1812* and in 1847 his autobiography, *Eight Years in Canada*.

Richardson's historical importance is that he portrayed Canada for the first time as thrilling and romantic, worthy on its own terms of international attention. This was a significant break from traditional travel and exploration literature. He also assumed Walter Scott's style, establishing a strong precedent for historical fiction in Canada.

Another central Scottish-Canadian writer of the same era was John Galt (see Chapter Four, Scottish Settlements). Galt had already been a relatively successful novelist in Scotland before he emigrated to Québec in 1825 to run the Canada Company. In fact, he had been heralded by British critics as an up-and-coming young writer very likely to succeed Walter Scott as the champion of historical fiction. Unfortunately, Galt never enjoyed fame and acclaim on such a grand scale.

In 1829, Galt returned to Scotland and began to write his "Canadian" novels, *Lawrie Todd* (1830) and *Bogle Corbit* (1831), both realistically portraying the lives of immigrants. Galt had a penetrating, sociological approach that accurately exposed the struggles of ordinary people. Had he stayed with the proven, public-pleasing style of Walter Scott, his work would have undoubtedly fared much better. Instead, his "Canadian" novels, although admired by critics, never sold well in Britain. They did, however, become all the rage in the miniscule Canadian market.

PUBLISHED IN MAY 1822, *THE PROVOST* SOLD OUT IN A FORTNIGHT.

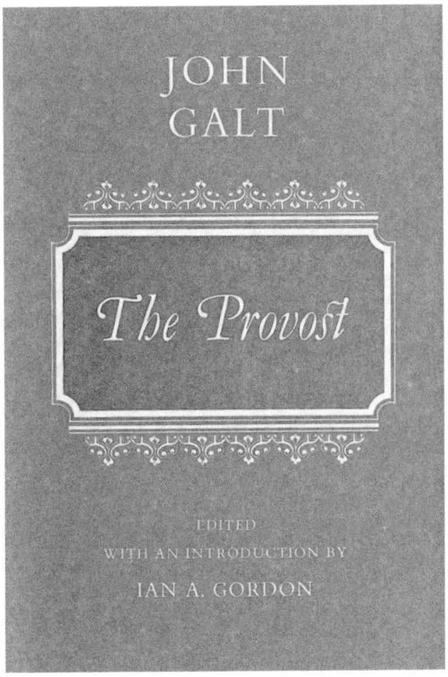

COVER FROM 1973 OXFORD UNIVERSITY PRESS EDITION

Canadian literary critic Elizabeth Waterston writes, "Galt democratized Canadian fiction twenty years before Uncle Tom's Cabin did this job for American best sellers. He democratized it in a way distinct from Dickens' way – in a way divested of caricature or exaggeration." Galt's "Canadian" works marked a fundamental step towards a more sophisticated form of novel, one that explored the human condition in the context of rugged Canadian life. Long before working-class characters in literature became in vogue in the rest of the English-speaking world, Galt had transplanted the Scottish-style, egalitarian workingman's literature in Canada.

Thomas McCulloch, in addition to being one of Canada's gurus of higher education (see Chapter Eight, Universities), was also a literary pioneer and Canada's first notable satirist. Though a relatively conservative Presbyterian minister and serious-minded academic, McCulloch had a sharp wit and sardonic eye. As a way to exhort his fellow Nova Scotians to be more productive and educated citizens, he gently (and sometimes not so gently) goaded them with satire. His most famous fictional work, *Letters of Mephibosheth Stepsure*, began appearing in serial form in the *Acadian Recorder* in 1822. In it, McCulloch poked gentle fun at the hayseed nature of Nova Scotians, chiding them to improve themselves. He also extolled the cherished Scottish values of thrift and hard work as a means for overcoming almost any of life's obstacles.

Letters of Mephibosheth Stepsure found a wide and responsive readership, illustrating that Canadians were hungry for cheeky satire. This fact inspired one of Canada's best-known writers ever, the Nova Scotia-born Thomas Haliburton, to pen the spectacularly successful *Clockmaker* in 1835, which featured the memorable character Sam Slick.

Haliburton's fictional Sam Slick was an uncouth, enterprising Yankee who exhibited virtually every stereotypically unsavory American trait. At the same time, Slick was a straight talker who had a flair for folksy wisdom. His observations invariably contained a mordant ring of truth. Through Slick, Haliburton lampooned the all-talk-no-action nature of Nova Scotians, the materialism of Americans, the pretentiousness of Englishmen, and the too-conservative character of Upper Canadians. For example, Slick makes the following biting observations about Canadian farmers: "If a man don't hoe his corn, and he don't get a crop, he says it is all owing to the bank; and if he runs into debt and is sued, why he says the lawyers are a curse to the country."

Haliburton became Canada's first homegrown international literary celebrity, popular everywhere in the English-speaking world. He also produced sequel after sequel and became one of the highest paid authors of his generation.

Thomas McCulloch, through wit and satire, had held a mirror up to Nova Scotian society and found it wanting. Haliburton emulated McCulloch and was able to export his sarcastic observations all over the world. These two men kick-started a new trend in Canadian literature that popularized satirical self-scrutiny and self-analysis.

Until Confederation in 1867, the predominant themes in Canadian literature revolved around the immigrant experience. Many books dealing with the lives of newcomers were somber and painted a relatively bleak picture of life in rural Canada. Susanna Moodie, for example, was an English gentlewoman who had immigrated with her husband to Upper Canada and attempted to carve a new home out of the virgin woods. This experience proved miserable, and as a reaction, Moodie wrote the popular book *Roughing it in the Bush*, a Canadian classic. In it, Moodie basically warns would-be immigrants to stay away from Canada. For example, she comments that immigrants' homes are "dens of dirt and misery, which would in many instances be shamed by an English pig-sty."

William "Tiger" Dunlop, one of the most celebrated and influential literary figures in Canada, decided to counter-balance such grave "immigrant" literature with a fresher, more humorous look at life in the northern colonies. Employing his razor-sharp wit, he began to parody books such as Susanna Moodie's.

Tiger Dunlop was born in Greenock, Scotland in 1792 and studied medicine at the University of Edinburgh. He became a military surgeon and came to Canada during the War of 1812. Although very fond of British North America, he returned with his regiment to Britain after the war but soon quit to become editor of the *Times* in Calcutta, India. It was there that he earned his nickname "Tiger" for eagerly tracking and killing large roaming tigers that were threatening settlers and livestock.

After a near fatal bout of malaria, Dunlop moved back to Edinburgh, where his droll essays began to attract considerable attention. His literary notoriety in Scotland brought him to the notice of John Galt, who immediately took a liking to Dunlop and offered him a job in Canada at the Canada Company. Dunlop gladly packed his bags and made Upper Canada his home for the rest of his life.

Tiger Dunlop was an eccentric, colourful fellow, with a raucous sense of humor and a character that radiated good-natured bluff and bluster. His personality, accentuated by his dramatic bushy sideburns and penetrating eyes, could fill any room. He would laugh heartily and was prepared to drink anyone under the table during night after night of rambunctious intellectual banter at one of the local the pubs.

Tiger Dunlop adapted well to the freewheeling life of Canada. He worked for the Canada Company for a decade and became a member of the legislature of the United Province of Canada in 1841. He also became superintendent of the Lachine Canal in 1846. In addition to his work, the Tiger established himself as Canada's most influential literary voice, writing many humorous, satirical articles on virtually every subject and editing the *Literary Garland* of Montreal and the *Canadian Literary Magazine* of Toronto. He also founded the Toronto Literary Club in 1836. His popularity and influence set a tone that was very different from all the sober immigrant literature being written at the time.

In 1836, Dunlop published *Statistical Sketches of Upper Canada, for the Use of Immigrants,* employing his pen name, "A Backwoodsman". While the book's title appears extremely dull, the content was anything but. It was a funny, genial look at immigrant life in Canada, with generous helpings of burlesque buffoonery and general silliness. Dunlop's prose was peppered with witticisms guaranteed to make readers chortle. He wrote, for example, "If there were in nature (which is doubtful) such a being as a sober blacksmith, he might make a fortune"; or, "It would be perhaps too much to expect people to practice as well as to preach Christian charity."

Dunlop's style contrasted sharply with other writers of "immigrant" literature and paved the way for a lighter, more humourous form of Canadian writing. Stephen Leacock, a later Canadian writer who was in his day (the early 1900s) the most popular humourist in the English-speaking world, was greatly influenced by the Tiger. Moreover, Dunlop's control of Canada's two top literary journals made him a pivotal figure in determining the course and tone of Canadian literature.

Of course, Tiger Dunlop was not the only powerful Scot to influence Canadian publishing. Throughout the 1800s, Scots controlled the vast majority of magazines, newspapers, journals and book publishing companies. Journal editors, for example, included Alex Spark (*Quebec Gazette,* 1792), John Strachan (*Christian Examiner,* 1819) David Chisholme (*Canadian Magazine and Literary Repository,* and *Canadian Review and Magazine,* 1824). A.J. Christie (*Canadian Magazine and Literary Repository,* 1824), George Stewart (*Literary Magazine,* 1836), and Hugh Thompson (*Upper Canada Herald,* 1872). Successful book publishers, established in the first half of the 1800s included A. and W. Mackinlay (Halifax), John McMillan (Saint John), Hew Ramsay (Montréal), Andrew Armour (Montréal), Robert

Middleton (Québec), John Neilson (Québec), G. Mercer Adam (Montréal and Toronto), Thomas Maclear (Toronto), Thomas Hunter (Toronto), G.M. Rose (Toronto), James Campbell (Toronto) and James Lessie (Toronto and Kingston). Naturally, all these Scots had a strong bias toward Scottish-style literature.

No less important to Canada's literary development during the mid-1800s were the legions of Scottish newspapermen who churned out the majority of the country's reviews, essays and editorials. Editors with names such as Hunter, Rose, Anderson, Dougall, Brown, Christie and Stewart dominated Canada's pre-Confederation newspapers.

After Confederation, Scots continued to control not only the big city newspapers, (such as George Brown's *Globe* and John Roberston's *Telegram* in Toronto as well as A.J. Roberston's *Gazette* in Montréal); they also ran a large majority of small newspapers: Thomas McQueen was editor of the Goderich *Huron Signal*; James Innis, the Guelph *Mercury*; James Somerville, the Ayr *Observer*; Robert Sellar, the Huntington *Gleaner*, to name but a few. Indeed, the sheer number of Scots in newspaper publishing was extraordinary. Many historians have remarked that throughout the later nineteenth century, virtually every English-speaking Canadian village contained three prominent community pillars: the pastor, the Scottish-trained schoolmaster, and the Scottish-trained journalist-printer. With so many Scots running Canada's presses, it is no mystery why Scottish-style literature was so widely published and read.

As the nineteenth century reached its midpoint, Canadian literature was becoming increasingly sophisticated. Yet the literary stereotype of Canada as an icy and unforgiving land full of ferocious beasts and deadly Natives would, unfortunately, endure for a long time to come. The annoyingly persistent image abroad of Canada as an uncivilized country was due in large part to the efforts of Robert Michael Ballantyne. The Edinburgh-born Hudson's Bay Company employee had emigrated to Canada as a young man and served at a number of fur trading outposts between 1841 and 1846. From 1848 to his death in 1894, Ballantyne drew on his experiences (albeit with considerable artistic license) to churn out more than a hundred boys' adventure novels, mainly set in the wilds of Canada. His works included *Hudson's Bay* (1848) and *The Young Fur Traders* (1856). In his day, Ballantyne was a big-name writer, and his books sold well all over the British Empire and United States. His style had a major influence on Robert Louis Stevenson, who often referred affectionately to his fellow Edinburgher as "Ballantyne the brave". Although Ballantyne's novels had limited artistic merit, they were immensely popular and became what most people abroad thought of as Canadian literature.

In the latter half of the 1800s, immigrant writers began increasingly to give way to Canadian-born writers. Yet the Scottish flavour of Canadian literature carried on, as Scottish literary themes that had been so firmly established in the first half of the century continued to be as relevant as ever to the growing Canadian nation.

At the same time, the winds of change were blowing through Canada; everyone in the country could feel them. Prior to Confederation, a growing sense of nationhood took root, a feeling that the colonies could share a common destiny. After Confederation, a majority of Canadian writers preoccupied themselves with attempting to define and even create a cultural identity for the new country of Canada. Given the social and political forces at work at the time, it is not surprising that Scottish immigrants and first generation Scots played a leading role in producing some of the best and most pertinent literature of the era. After all, the Scots had been experts at describing and preserving their distinctive culture for several hundred years. Leading Scottish-Canadian writers included William Murdock (*Song of the Emigrant,* 1860), Lachlan MacGoun ("Tramp Tramp Tramp", an anti-Fenian song, 1866), Alexander Muir ("The Maple Leaf Forever", 1867), Charles Mair, (*Dreamland and Other Poems,* 1868), Alex Rae Garvie (*Thistletown,* 1875), W.W. Smith (*Poems,* 1880), G.F. Cameron (*Lyrics on Freedom,* 1887), W.D. Lighthall (*Songs of the Great Dominion,* 1889), D. Anderson (*Lays of Canada,* 1890), Elizabeth MacLeod (*Carols of Canada,* 1893), J.D. Edgar (*This Canada of Ours,* 1893), and Agnes Machar (*Lays of the True North,* 1899). These writers, all very popular in Canada, contributed greatly to shaping a Canadian identity and fostering a sense of patriotism.

The most famous and arguably most gifted Canadian writers of the late 1800s were five men known as the "Confederation Poets," a curious label, since none of them was more than eight years old in 1867. Douglas Campbell Scott, William Campbell, Charles G.D. Roberts, Bliss Carman and Archibald Lampman did for Canadian literature what the "Group of Seven" painters did for Canadian art. Each had an uncanny ability to portray the human condition in a uniquely Canadian context, comment on important Canadian social trends, and somehow plumb the depths of the collective Canadian psyche in ways that were extremely compelling and sometimes intellectually very provocative. These five writers were poetic virtuosos, and each deserves to be studied in depth separately. Indeed, it is somewhat unfortunate that they should be so readily clumped together by modern readers. Yet since they were all Canadian born within a year or two of 1860, and since they all knew and influenced one another, addressing similar issues and exploring similar themes, their group identity is perhaps unavoidable.

Scott and Campbell were of Scottish descent, while Roberts, Carman, and Lampman came from an English-Loyalist background. Nevertheless, the three non-Scots were serious students of Scottish and Scottish-Canadian literature, and each acknowledged the deep influence Robert Burns and Alexander McLachlan had on their poetry. Carman had even studied Scottish literature at the University of Edinburgh for two years. Together, the five represent a remarkable transmission and adaptation of Scottish sensibilities and themes to the rapidly changing society of post-confederation Canada.

Duncan Campbell Scott's work, "The Happy Fatalist", portrays the ultimate human issue, man's awareness of his own mortality, in the context of the life of a hard-working immigrant. There is a paradoxical duality in the actions of the immigrant who is attempting to build a better future, all the while knowing his life is going to be full of suffering and eventual death:

We plough the field,
And harrow the clod,
And hurl the seed.
The germ yields,
The wheat brairds,
We gather the sheaf,
Deed for deed:
The stubble moulds,
The chaff is cast,
Dust for dust:
The man is worn,
His days are bound,
But his labor returns,
The child learns
Round for round:
The god is astir,
Firm and free,
Weaving his plan,
Swelling the tree,
Bracing the man:
All is for good,
Sweet or acerb,
Laughter or pain,
Freedom or curb:
Follow your bent,
Cry life is joy,
Cry life is woe,
The god is content,
Impartial in power,
Tranquil – and lo!
Like the kernels in quern,
Each in turn,
Comes to his hour,
Nor fast nor slow:
It is well: even so.

In "Winter Thought", Archibald Lampman captures the dichotomous nature of life in the northern climes, a popular theme in both Scottish and Canadian literature. Summer is pure joy, while winter is a time for somber reflection, longing and brooding.

The wind-swayed daisies, that on every side
Throng the wide fields in whispering companies,
Serene and gently smiling like the eyes
Of tender children long beatified,
The delicate thought-wrapped buttercups that glide
Like sparks of fire above the wavering grass,

And swing and toss with all the airs that pass,
Yet seem so peaceful, so preoccupied;
These are the emblems of pure pleasures flown,
I scarce can think of pleasure without these.
Even to dream of them is to disown
The cold forlorn midwinter reveries,
Lulled with the perfume of old hopes new-blown,
No longer dreams, but dear realities.

In his poem "Canada," Charles G. D. Roberts captures the nascent sense of nationalism in early Canada as well as the Canadian desire to assert independence from the English. This theme, of course, had a long tradition in Scottish literature as well.

O child of Nations, giant-limbed,
Who stand'st among the nations now
Unheeded, unadorned, unhymned,
With unanointed brow,
How long the ignoble sloth, in greatness not thine own?
Surely the lion's brood is strong
To front the world alone!

The "Confederation Poets" addressed issues important to a growing Canadian population that was generally more reflective and introspective due to increased levels of education and leisure time. They were able to adapt traditional Scottish literary currents, such as fatalness, wistfulness and proud independence, to create stirring portraits of life in Canada. Building on the antecedents of Scottish-Canadian literature, they fashioned a pan-Canadian literary ethos that has resonated with Canadians ever since. They also set a literary standard that has been hard to match.

Scottish-style literature, so firmly established in Canada during the 1800s, carried through into the 1900s with its essence largely intact. This is logical, as urbanization, a daunting geography and punishing climate, and proximity to one of the world's foremost cultural superpowers continued to be major factors in the lives of Canadians. And while Canadian writers of all ethnic backgrounds built on and added to the Scottish literary tradition of the previous century to create a distinctive "Canadian" body of work, Canadian-born sons and daughters of Scots continued to exert a disproportionately strong influence on the nation's literature.

The most popular Canadian writer of the early 1900s was a Presbyterian minister by the name of Charles Gordon, better known by his pen name, Ralph

Connor. Gordon was born in 1860 into a strict Scottish Presbyterian family living in Glengarry in what is now Ontario. He studied theology at the Universities of Toronto and Edinburgh and was ordained a minister in 1890, after which he served a mission in Banff for several years before settling permanently in Winnipeg.

Gordon's books, most notably his run-away best sellers, *The Man from Glengarry* (1901) and *Glengarry School Days* (1902) were shockingly simplistic and appear to modern readers somewhat inane and overly didactic. Nevertheless, until World War I, they were among the most popular books in the English-speaking world.

Gordon's novels were set in the idealized, rural Glengarry County of the late 1800s, a time and place where men were generally more morally upright and virtuous. The hero of each of Gordon's books was invariably forced to employ his unflagging moral confidence and physical prowess to beat (literally) his opponents into submission. Thus, the conflict was always overcome. Gordon's novels seemed to give new meaning to the term "muscular Christianity".

Ever since, literary critics have loved to trash Ralph Connor. For example, Canadian critic W.J. Keith asserts that Connor's works are "cliché-ridden, predictable stuff, demonstrating all too clearly that Connor's devotees (in Britain and the United States as well as in Canada) were ill-equipped to respond to the challenges of complex, probing fiction."

Yet Ralph Connor novels remain very important in the story of Canadian literature, if only because so many people worldwide read them with such passion. Despite their hackneyed plots and shallow characters, the novels carried easily-identifiable Scottish-Canadian themes to new generations of readers, such as a deep longing nostalgia for a pre-commercial, pre-industrial past, where moral certainty was easier, as well as the idea that a man's forthrightness and moral rectitude were great sources of personal dignity, which would see him through any of life's hindrances. On the whole, "Ralph Connor" exercised a very dramatic influence on subsequent Canadian writers.

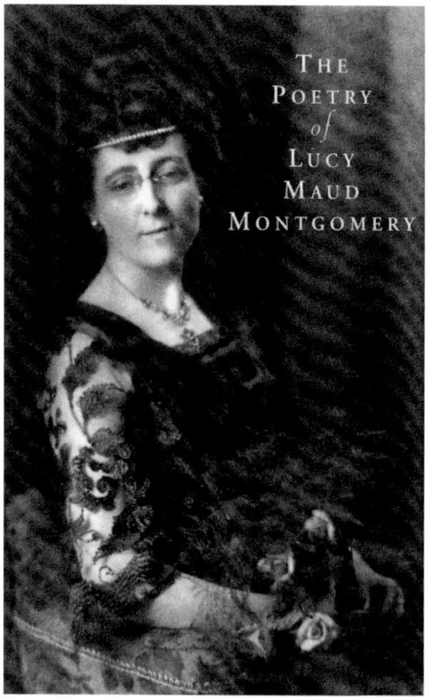

BOOKS BY AND ABOUT LUCY MAUD MONTGOMERY ARE STILL WIDELY AVAILABLE.

COVER FROM FITZHENRY & WHITESIDE, 1987 EDITION

Another icon of Canadian literature is Lucy Maud Montgomery, a Scots-descended Canadian who wrote during the same period as Charles Gordon. Although not as famous as "Ralph Connor" during her lifetime, Montgomery's renown has continued to grow to the point where she is now nothing short of a world phenomenon, not to mention one of Canada's best-known cultural exports.

Montgomery wrote many things, but her most widely acclaimed work by far is *Anne of Green Gables*. First published in 1908, it immediately became an international best seller and led to seven sequels. *Anne of Green Gables* is set in the bucolic, uncomplicated Prince Edward Island of Montgomery's childhood. It is essentially the story of a precocious young orphan who finds in her adoptive pastoral village the belonging and nurturing required to flower into a bright and beautiful young woman.

Montgomery's novels are quaint, sweet and highly sentimental and have been a favourite among children and adults alike for a century. One can only marvel at their enduring popularity. Obviously, the nostalgic yearning for a simpler, more wholesome life of a pre-industrial past has struck a deep chord with many millions of readers worldwide. Like Charles Gordon, Lucy Maud Montgomery has had a deep effect on Canadian literature, casting it in the minds of many as a genre close to nature, hearty, rustic and innocent. Although Montgomery's view of Canadian life lacks many of the realistic hard edges of previous Canadian literature, her Scottish-style nostalgia shines through and has inspired scores of emulators.

As the 1900s advanced, Canadian literary figures of Scottish descent managed to preserve and promote their Scottish way of thinking to a remarkable degree. But to mention even a fraction of them would require a several volume set. For the purposes of this book, we must confine ourselves to touching on a few superlatives to make our point. One of the best-known poems in the English language, "In Flanders Fields", was written in 1915 by John McCrae, a Canadian medical officer serving in World War I.

JOHN MCCRAE & UNKNOWN ARTIST / NATIONAL ARCHIVES OF CANADA / C-009038

IN THREE SHORT VERSES WRITTEN IN 1915, JOHN MCCRAE CAPTURED THE HORROR OF WAR AND INSPIRED A CALL TO ARMS. TODAY, ALMOST 100 YEARS LATER, "IN FLANDERS FIELDS"IS AS MUCH A PART OF CANADA'S REMEMBRANCE DAY CEREMONIES AS POPPIES ARE.

The most widely and most successfully translated Canadian novelist to date has been Hugh MacLennan whose writings from the 1940s to the '80s were devoted principally to analyzing Canada's national character. The Canadian writer Marshal McLuhan became the world's most famous communications theorist ever. His bold writings in the '60s on the nature of mass media forever altered the way modern societies examine themselves. And speaking of media, the largest and most influential magazine in Canada is *Maclean's,* established in 1905 by John Maclean. George Brown's *Globe* grew into the *Globe and Mail* and for many years has been the most powerful national newspaper in the land. McClelland & Stewart, established in 1914 by a pair of Scots, is the largest Canadian book publisher in the country. Farley Mowat is Canada's most widely read author, his books printed in over forty countries. In short, Canadian literary figures of Scottish descent have played a gargantuan role in the shaping and maturation of Canada's twentieth and twenty-first century literature.

Over the last century, Canadian literature has become increasingly sophisticated and varied, as Canadians from of all ethnic backgrounds as well as international influences have added to Canada's impressive and colourful literary tapestry. Yet there remains a general flavour in Canadian writing that has remained constant – essential qualities very distinct from other strains of literature. And this is due principally to the fact that Canadian literature written in English was derived largely from a Scottish foundation rather than an English one. The thematic structure of Canadian literature, characterized by a wistful nostalgia, a reverence for nature, small-town or rural settings, proud working-class characters, the ironic, often humourous views of an outsider, and a deep desire to preserve cultural distinctiveness and independence, can all be easily traced to the literary tradition laid down by nineteenth-century Scottish writers.

Because of Canada's fundamental similarities to Scotland, Scottish-style literature transplanted effortlessly to the new country. And since Scottish-style writing best addressed the concerns of a largely immigrant society, it became the Canada's preferred literary mode for self-analysis and self-expression. This was combined with the fact that the Scots in the 1800s were generally Canada's best educated citizens and were uniquely positioned, through writing, publishing, printing and bookselling, to disseminate their values, ideals, and biases. Thus, Scottish culture spread throughout the country, from one generation to the next, profoundly affecting Canadian sensibilities as well as national identity. Overall, the Scots created a literary foundation from which subsequent Canadian literature has evolved while maintaining its vital and distinctive Scottish flavour.

Conclusion

HIGHLAND BAGPIPES AND DRUM, COURTESY OF THE LYNNE GRIFFITHS
STUDIO OF HIGHLAND DANCE, VICTORIA, BC.

When asked about the Scots' contribution to Canada, the average Canadian almost invariably scratches his or her head, reflects for a moment, and then points to obvious Scottish symbols that lie on the very surface of Canadian culture. To many, the word "Scottish" conjures up mental images of kilts, tartans, bagpipes, fiddles, Highland dancers, curling, and golf – quaint, stereotypical notions that belie just how momentous and profound the overall Scottish influence on Canada has been. Yet such symbols are worth considering.

Most Canadians are very familiar with the Highland Games, held every year at almost every major city throughout Canada. The Games originated in the Highlands of Scotland hundreds of years ago and were an important inter-community cultural event that Highlanders of all ages anticipated for months in advance. In the early 1800s, Scottish fur traders transplanted the Games to Canada, which have grown steadily to become an important Canadian tradition in every region of the country. Events that celebrate physical prowess, such as caber tossing, putting the stone, wrestling, and tug-o'-war, are complemented by Highland dancing, bagpiping and marching in full Highland regalia.

Since their introduction to Canada, many prominent Scots have been passionate participants in the Games. Wealthy Nor'Wester partners in Montréal, such as the McGillivray brothers, were instrumental in establishing and dispersing the Games throughout Eastern Canada. Lord Dalhousie, George Brown and John A. Macdonald also loved the games and participated enthusiastically year after year. John Diefenbaker (whose mother was born in the Highlands) often attended the games wearing a kilt. Given the remarkable power of the Scots in Canadian history, it is perhaps not surprising that the Highland Games are the only major trans-Canadian event that celebrates a specific ethnicity.

Most Canadians are also aware that Scottish dance and music are extremely popular in Canada, and indeed are a major staple of Canadian culture. Throughout the country, Highland dancing is among the most popular children's activities.

Yet many thousands of adults also enjoy participating as well. Almost every Canadian town of any size has a club where children can train for competition. In fact, so popular is Highland dancing that in 1987 ScotDance Canada was established, rapidly becoming one of the largest and most important governing dance organizations in the world, overseeing inter-provincial and international competitions and establishing rigid standards for dancers. Interestingly, Highland dancing has become more popular and widespread in Canada than even in Scotland itself.

The Scottish musical tradition in Canada has also been nothing short of extraordinary. Some of the country's most successful and respected musicians, such as Loreena McKennit, Ashley MacIsaac, Natalie McMaster, Rita MacNeil, and the Rankins, compose and perform music that reflects Canada's deep Scottish roots. Moreover, almost every major Canadian town has a "Celtic club," where traditional Scottish music is enjoyed and transmitted from one generation to the next. In fact, nowhere in the world is Scottish-Celtic music more widespread and well loved than in Canada.

As for the bagpipes, Canada has far more bagpipers than Scotland itself. At virtually every public function – military gatherings, convocations, funerals, curling bonspiels, sporting events, parliamentary ceremonies, etc. – the unique wailing of the old Highland war-pipes can be heard. For two centuries in Canada, the kilt-clad piper has been a vital symbol of pride, honour and tradition.

And speaking of tradition, it is fascinating to note just how potent Highland symbols are to Canadians. Years ago, when I was an undergrad student at Simon Fraser University, near Vancouver, British Columbia, I was intrigued by the university's Highland Scottish motif. Kilted young musicians would often roam the halls, tartans adorned the walls, and while listening to lectures, I could frequently hear the faint martial tunes of bagpipe bands practicing in the parking lot.

Universities are nothing if not heavily symbolic. They need to project an aura of honour, respectability, and deep, almost sacrosanct tradition. Simon Fraser University was constructed practically overnight in 1965 to meet the demands of a demographic glut of baby boomers. Since it had no tradition, its founders searched for one to tap into, ultimately deciding to name the university after the famous Scottish-Canadian fur trader/adventurer/explorer. Their decision also recognized that Fraser was instrumental in opening up British Columbia to European settlement. The university even went as far as adopting the Fraser clan's coat of arms as its official crest, which it proudly displays on all university degrees and literature.

The founders of Simon Fraser University were not necessarily trying to immortalize Fraser as much as they were using him to personify the Scottish values of earnestness, hard work, duty, honour, and tradition. By garbing itself in such symbolism, the university was able to tap into Canadians' innate reverence for the proud Highlanders. Indeed, very few symbols in Canadian culture carry as much emotional weight as a Highlander decked out in full ceremonial dress; it is the very archetype in Canada of solemn dignity and honour. The symbolism deliberately employed by Simon Fraser University to project an aura of respect and tradition is a fascinating example of just how powerful Scottish Highland imagery is in the collective Canadian consciousness.

Most Canadians also know that the Scots were responsible for importing curling, a game that has become so popular that Canada is now the undisputed home of the sport. Scottish soldiers brought the game to Canada during the Seven Years' War (1756-63), and it grew in popularity as Canada grew. Many members of Montréal's Beaver Club, mostly well-off partners in the North West Company, were fanatical about the game and started the Montreal Curling Club in 1807. Within twenty years, many more clubs had sprung up throughout what are now Québec, Ontario and the Maritimes. Interestingly, Canada's climate gave curling a special impetus. Dependably frigid weather and a limitless number of lakes and rivers guaranteed plentiful safe ice. This meant that the conditions in Canada were even better than they were in Scotland, a rare occurrence for a transplanted sport. Because the weather often got too cold to play outside, many clubs decided to construct indoor curling rinks, and by the early 1900s, almost every town, no matter how small, had a rink. To this day, far more Canadians curl, both in absolute numbers and per capita, than in any other country including Scotland.

Another well-known Scottish import is golf, a game millions of Canadians take pleasure in every year during six or seven snowless months. Scottish immigrants started the first golf club in Montréal in 1873. In 1874, more Scots set up the Québec City golf club on a field adjacent to the Plains of Abraham. In 1876, Toronto too had its own club. The game grew exponentially so that by 1900, almost every Canadian municipality of any size boasted a golf club. During the late 1800s and early 1900s, it was common to recruit golf pros from Scotland in order to teach Canadians the finer points of the game. Golf has a relatively democratic

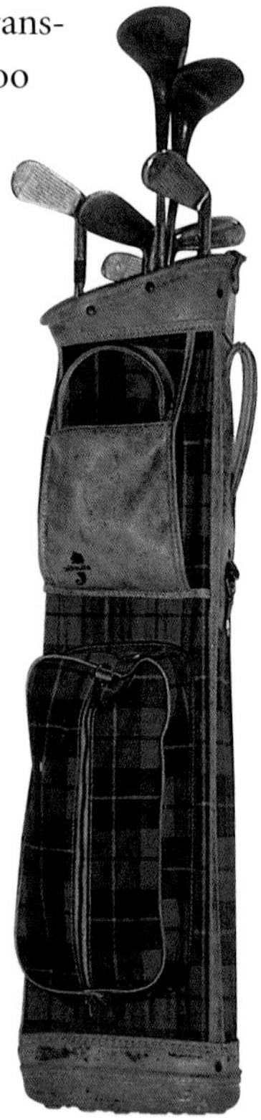

Antique and modern curling rocks courtesy of the Victoria Curling Club / Golf bag and clubs courtesy of Annette Moman

tradition in Canada; it has never been a game reserved for society's elites as is often case in other countries. Indeed, in Canada more people per capita participate in golf than in any other nation.

Unfortunately, most Canadians, particularly younger generations, are aware of only the most obvious symbols of Scottish influence in Canada, as outlined above. And while these symbols are valuable in their own right, they only hint at just how critically important the Scots have been to shaping the Canadian nation. The deeper story is truly extraordinary. The Scots' ubiquity in every field of endeavor, the surprising extent of their power and influence, and their lasting impact on Canadian society and culture are truly one of the great and largely unexplored chapters in the story of Canada.

Social and economic forces in Scotland, such as the Highland Clearances and Lowland economic stagnation, particularly in agriculture, coincided roughly with the opening up of British North America. Thus, over the course of several decades, many thousands of Scots sailed away from their sad, beloved homeland in search of a better life in the new world. Once transplanted in what would later become Canada, it soon became evident that the Scots possessed valuable advantages, such as habituation to physical hardship and a cold climate, amazing powers of cultural adaptation, an indomitable work ethic, strong educations, an independent, sometimes stubborn nature, and an egalitarian social tradition that encouraged public participation. All these factors combined to make the Scots natural leaders in their rugged new land.

The incredible yet true story of the Scots in Canada is that they were largely responsible for laying the foundation upon which the modern Canadian nation was built. Scottish fur traders controlled Canada's first large-scale commercial enterprise, which set the stage for modern commercial society. They also kept would-be American settlers out of Hudson's Bay territory, inadvertently preserving the West and North for the day when Canada was ready to become a transcontinental nation. Moreover, fur trade explorers mapped out the savage wilderness and waterways, essentially drawing the blueprints for future settlement.

Scottish politicians, including prime ministers, Fathers of Confederation, and governors, literally drew up and forged the transcontinental political entity called Canada. The federation of provinces, constitutional recognition of two founding peoples, bilingualism, the basic machinery of government, and the nation's unique political culture all came about largely through the efforts of Scottish political architects.

Scottish soldiers played a vital role in establishing British rule in the upper half of North America. They were also instrumental in repelling American invaders and preserving Canadian territorial integrity. In many bloody conflicts, they fought and won battles that shaped the nation, and they bore the burden, more than any other ethnic group, of horrific casualties. Their skill and sacrifice is responsible, in no small measure, for the Canada that exists today.

Scottish immigrants, more than any other group, got in on the ground floor of British North America and established themselves as titled landholders very early on. This gave them a vital foothold in Canada as well as a vested interest in shaping their new society. The result was that Scots in general wielded subsequent power and influence far beyond their numbers. Their patterns of settlement, which laid much of the country's cultural and social foundation, became a major determinant of the diligent and conservative Canadian national character.

Scottish entrepreneurs were astoundingly successful in early Canada, constructing the fundamental commercial infrastructure without which Confederation would have been impossible. In industries such as shipping, banking, canals, telegraphs, and railways, the Scots were the undisputed innovators, risk-takers, and leaders who physically overcame seemingly insurmountable obstacles to physically lay down much of Canada's economic foundation.

The Scots not only conceived and built some of Canada's earliest and most important universities, they imported their egalitarian system of higher education to create the template for the modern Canadian university system. Canadian educational values, such as secularization, access, equality of opportunity, and practicality, were all derived from the Scottish system of higher education.

Scottish writers best addressed the concerns of a largely immigrant society, and therefore, Scottish-style literature became the preferred literary mode for Canadian self-analysis and self-expression. Moreover, the Scots controlled, to a large extent, Canadian publishing, printing, and bookselling in the 1800s, resulting in a wide diffusion and transmission of their ideas. To this day, most Canadian literature in English reflects its distinctive Scottish roots.

The real story of the Scots in Canada is nothing short of astonishing. And explaining the historical paradox associated with them is a challenge. Indeed, it may never be possible to clarify fully how a minority of relatively poor immigrants to Canada became so powerful and influential, controlling almost every facet of early Canadian society. One thing, however, is certain. After all they have done to create Canada, the Scots deserve to be regarded not in terms of popular, quaintly anachronistic symbols but rather with the fullest appreciation and admiration of their remarkable achievements.

Bibliography

Baker, Ray Palmer. *A History of English-Canadian Literature to the Confederation: Its Relation to the Literature of Great Britain and the United States.* Cambridge: Harvard University Press, 1920.

Barclay, James A. *Golf in Canada: A History.* Toronto: McClelland & Stewart, 1992.

Baskerville, Peter, ed. *The Bank of Upper Canada: A Collection of Documents.* Toronto: The Champlain Society in Cooperation with the Ontario Heritage Foundation, 1987.

Berton, Pierre. *The Great Railway Illustrated.* Toronto: McClelland & Stewart, 1972.

---. *The National Dream: The Great Railway 1871-1881.* Toronto: McClelland & Stewart, 1972.

---. *The Last Spike: The Great Railway 1881-1885.* Toronto: McClelland & Stewart, 1977.

Bliss, Michael. *A Living Profit: Studies in the Social History of Canadian Business, 1883-1911.* Toronto: McClelland & Stewart, 1974.

Bourinot, Sir John G. *Canada Under British Rule 1760-1900.* Toronto: Copp Clark Pitman, 1901.

Bowering, George. *Bowering's B.C.: A Swashbuckling History.* Toronto: Penguin, 1996.

---. *Egotists and Autocrats: The Prime Ministers of Canada.* Toronto: Penguin, 1999.

Brown, Craig, ed. *The Illustrated History of Canada.* Toronto: Key Porter, 2000.

Bryce, George. *The Scotsman in Canada: Western Canada. Including Manitoba, Saskatchewan, Alberta, British Columbia, and portions of old Rupert's Land and the Indian Territories.* Volume II. Toronto: Musson, 1911.

Bumstead, J.M. *Fur Trading Wars: The Founding of Western Canada.* Winnipeg: Great Plains, 1999.

---. *The Peoples of Canada: A Post-Confederation History.* Toronto: Oxford University Press, 1992.

---. *The People's Clearance: Highland Emigration to British North America: 1770-1815.* Edinburgh: Edinburgh University Press, 1982.

---. *The Scots in Canada.* Ottawa: Canadian Historical Association, 1982.

Burpee, Lawrence J. *Sandford Fleming: Empire Builder.* London: Humphrey Milford, Oxford University Press, 1915.

Campbell, Marjorie Wilkins. *The North West Company.* Toronto: MacMillan, 1957.

---. *The Nor'Westers: The Fight for the Fur Trade.* Calgary: Fifth House, 2002.

Campbell, Wilfred. *The Scotsman In Canada.* Vol. 1. Toronto: Musson, 1911.

Careless, J.M.S. and R. Craig Brown, eds. *The Canadians 1867-1967.* Toronto: MacMillan, 1967.

Chodos, Robert. *The CPR: A Century of Corporate Welfare.* Toronto: Lorimer, 1973.

Collins, J.E. *Life and Times of The Right Honourable Sir John A. MacDonald.* Toronto: Rose, 1883.

Colquhoun, A.H.U. *Fathers of Confederation: A Chronicle of the Birth of the Dominion. Chronicles of Canada: Volume 28.* Toronto: University of Toronto Press, 1964.

Councill, Irma. *Canada's Prime Ministers, Governors General and Fathers of Confederation.* Markham, ON: Pembrook, 1999.

Cruxton, J. Bradley and W. Douglas Wilson. *Oxford Canadian History: Flashback Canada.* 4th ed. Ontario: Oxford University Press, 2000.

Davies, K.G. *Letters From Hudson Bay 1703-40.* Toronto: The Hudson's Bay Record Society, 1965

Denison, Merrill. *Canada's First Bank: A History of the Bank of Montreal.* 2 vols. Toronto: McClelland & Stewart, 1966.

Duncan, K.J. "Patterns of Settlement in the East." *The Scottish Tradition in Canada.* Ed. W. Stanford Reid. Toronto: McClelland & Stewart & the Minister of Supply Services, 1976. 49-75.

Dunn, Charles. *Highland Settler: A Portrait of the Scottish Gael in Nova Scotia.* Toronto: University of Toronto Press, 1953.

Evans, A. Margaret MacLaren. "The Scot as Politician." *The Scottish Tradition in Canada.* Ed. W. Stanford Reid. Toronto: McClelland & Stewart & the Minister of Supply Services, 1976. 273-301.

Francis, R. Douglas, Richard Jones and Donald B. Smith. *Destinies: Canadian History Since Confederation.* 4th ed. Toronto: Harcourt, 2000.

---. *Origins: Canadian History to Confederation.* 4th ed. Toronto: Harcourt, 2000.

Frost, Stanley Brice. *James McGill of Montreal.* Montreal: McGill-Queen's University Press, 1995.

Fryer, Mary Beacock. *Battlefields of Canada.* Toronto: Dundurn, 1986.

Galbraith, John Kenneth. *The Scotch.* Toronto: MacMillan, 1964.

Gibbon, J. Murray. *Scots In Canada.* Toronto: Musson, 1911.

Gillmor, Don, and Pierre Turgeon. *Canada: A People's History.* Vol. 1. Toronto: McClelland & Stewart, 2000.

Gillmor, Don, Achille Michaud, and Pierre Turgeon. *Canada: A People's History.* Vol. 2. Toronto: McClelland & Stewart, 2002.

Goodacre, Richard. *Dunsmuir's Dream. Ladysmith, the First Fifty Years.* Victoria: Porcepic, 1991.

Grant, Agnes. *James McKay: Métis Builder of Canada.* Winnipeg: Pemmican, 1994.

Gray, John Morgan. *Lord Selkirk of Red River.* Toronto: MacMillan, 1963.

Hanna, Charles A. *The Scotch-Irish or The Scot in North Britain, North Ireland, and North America.* Vol. 1. Baltimore: Genealogical Publishing Company, 1968.

Harris, Robin S. *A History of Higher Education in Canada 1663-1960.* Toronto: University of Toronto Press, 1976.

Hayes, Derek. *First Crossing: Alexander Mackenzie, His Expedition Across North America, and the Opening of the Continent.* Vancouver: Douglas & McIntyre, 2001.

Herman, Arthur. *How the Scots Invented the Modern World: The True Story of How Western Europe's Poorest Nation Created Our World & Everything in It.* New York: Three Rivers, 2001.

Herstein, H.H., L.J. Hughes, and R.C. Kirbyson. *Challenge & Survival: The History of Canada.* Scarborough, ON: Prentice-Hall, 1970.

Huck, Barbara, et al. *Exploring the Fur Trade Routes of North America: Discover the Highways that Opened a Continent.* Winnipeg: Heartland Associates, 2002.

Hunter, James. *A Dance Called America: The Scottish Highlands, the United States and Canada.* Edinburgh: Mainstream, 1994.

Hutchinson, Bruce. *The Incredible Canadian: A candid portrait of Mackenzie King: his works, his times, and his nation.* Toronto: Longmans, Green and Company, 1952.

Jenkins, Kathleen. *Montreal: Island City of the St. Lawrence.* New York: Doubleday, 1996.

Johnson, F. Henry. *A Brief History of Canadian Education.* Toronto: McGraw-Hill, 1968.

Keith, W. J. *Canadian Literature in English.* London: Longman, 1985.

Klink, Carl F. et al., eds. *Literary History of Canada: Canadian Literature in English.* 2nd ed. 3 vols. Toronto: University of Toronto Press, 1976.

Lamb, W. Kaye. *The Letters and Journals of Simon Fraser: 1806–1808.* Toronto: MacMillan, 1960.

Laut, Agnes C. *The Cariboo Trail: A Chronicle of the Gold-fields of British Columbia.* Chronicles of Canada: Volume 23. Toronto: University of Toronto Press, 1964.

MacKay, Donald. Scotland Farwell: *The People of the Hector.* Toronto: McGraw-Hill Ryerson, 1980.

MacKenzie, Cecil W. *Donald MacKenzie "King of the NorthWest" The story of an International hero of the Oregon County and the Red River Settlement at Lower Fort Garry (Winnipeg).* Los Angeles: Ivan Deach Jr., Publisher, 1937.

MacMillan, David S. *Canadian Business History: Selected Studies, 1497-1971.* Toronto: McClelland and Stewart, 1972.

---. "The Scot as Businessman." *The Scottish Tradition in Canada.* Ed. W. Stanford Reid. Toronto: McClelland & Stewart & the Minister of Supply Services, 1976. 179-202.

MacNeil, Neil. *The Highland Heart in Nova Scotia.* Wreck Cove, NS : Breton Books, 1998.

Malcolm, Andrew H. *The Canadians: A Probing Yet Affectionate Look at the Land and the People.* Markham, ON: Fitzhenry & Whiteside, 1985.

Masters, D. C. "The Scottish Tradition in Higher Education." *The Scottish Tradition in Canada.* Ed. W. Stanford Reid. Toronto: McClelland & Stewart & the Minister of Supply Services, 1976. 248-272.

Martin, Ged. Canada's Heritage In Scotland. Toronto: Dundurn, 1989.

Marr, William L., and Donald G. Paterson. *Canada: An Economic History.* Toronto: MacMillan, 1980.

Canada

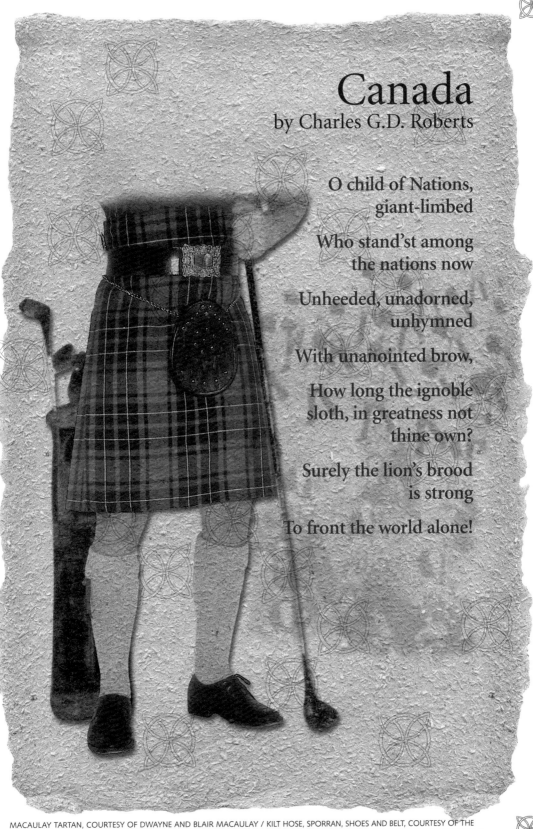

by Charles G.D. Roberts

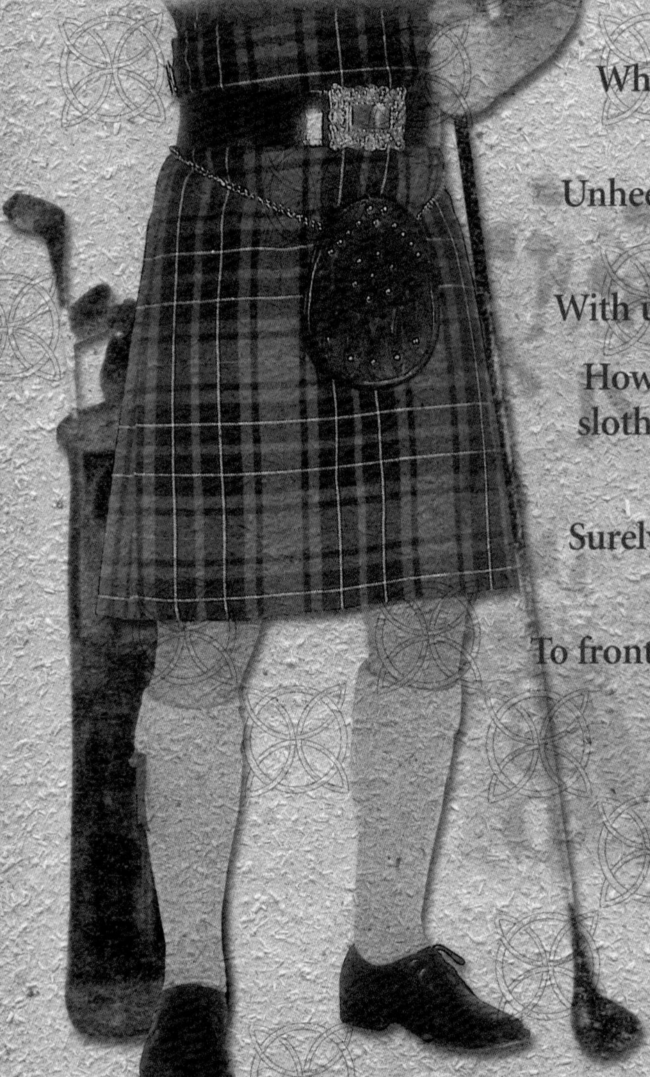

O child of Nations,
giant-limbed
Who stand'st among
the nations now
Unheeded, unadorned,
unhymned
With unanointed brow,
How long the ignoble
sloth, in greatness not
thine own?
Surely the lion's brood
is strong
To front the world alone!

MACAULAY TARTAN, COURTESY OF DWAYNE AND BLAIR MACAULAY / KILT HOSE, SPORRAN, SHOES AND BELT, COURTESY OF THE SCOTTISH CROFT, SYDNEY, BC. / GOLF CLUB AND BAG COURTESY OF ANNETTE MOMAN / BACKGROUND POSTER BY SOPHIE BAKER / THE BAND OF COLDSTREAM GUARDS, ROYAL SCOTS DRAGOON GUARDS, 1981 / NATIONAL ARCHIVES OF CANADA / C–118757.

Mathews, Hazel, C. *The Mark of Honour.* Toronto: University of Toronto Press, 1965.

McCalla, Douglas, ed. *Perspectives on Canadian Economic History.* Toronto: Copp Clark Pitman, 1987.

McCague, James. *Moguls and Iron Men.* New York: Harper & Row, 1964.

McInnis, Edgar, and Michiel Horn. *Canada: A Political & Social History.* 4th ed. Toronto: Holt, Rinehart and Winston, 1982.

McLean, Marianne. *The People of Glengarry: Highlanders in Transition, 1745-1820.* Montreal, Kingston: McGill-Queen's University Press, 1991.

McLeod, Jack, ed. The Oxford Book of Canadian Political Anecdotes. Toronto: Oxford University Press, 1988.

McLeod, Thomas H. and Ian McLeod. *Tommy Douglas: The Road to Jerusalem.* Edmonton: Hurtig, 1987.

Milner, Marc. *Canadian Military History: Selected Readings.* Toronto: Copp Clark Pitman, 1993.

Mitchell, Elaine Allan. "The Scot in the Fur Trade." *The Scottish Tradition in Canada.* Ed. W. Stanford Reid. Toronto: McClelland & Stewart & the Minister of Supply Services, 1976. 27-48.

Molyneux, Geoffrey. *British Columbia: An Illustrated History.* Vancouver: Raincoast, 2002.

Morrison, Dorothy Nafus. *The Eagle & The Fort: The Story of John McLoughlin.* 2nd ed. Oregon: Western Imprints, 1984.

Morton, Desmond. *A Military History of Canada.* Edmonton: Hurtig, 1985.

Mowat, Farley. *The Farfarers: Before the Norse.* Toronto: Seal, 1998.

Naylor, Tom. *The History of Canadian Business 1867–1914.* Volume I: The Banks and Finance Capital. Toronto: Lorimer, 1975.

---. *The History of Canadian Business 1867–1914.* Volume II: Industrial Development. Toronto: Lorimer, 1975.

New, W.H. *A History of Canadian Literature.* New York: New Amsterdam, 1989.

Newman, Peter C. *The Aquisitors. The Canadian Establishment.* Vol. 2. Toronto: McClelland & Stewart, 1981.

---. *Caesars of the Wilderness: Company of Adventurers.* Vol. 2. Toronto: (Viking) Penguin, 1987.

---. *The Canadian Establishment.* Vol. 1. Toronto: McClelland and Stewart, 1975.

---. Company of Adventurers. Vol. 1. Toronto: (Viking) Penguin, 1985.

---. *Empire of the Bay: The Company of Adventurers that Seized a Continent.* Toronto: Penguin, 1998.

---. *Merchant Princes: Company of Adventurers.* Vol. 3. Toronto: (Viking) Penguin, 1991.

--- *Titans. The Canadian Establishment.* Vol. 3. Toronto: McClelland and Stewart, 1981.

Norton, Wayne. *Help us to a Better Land: Crofter Colonies in the Prairie West.* Regina: Canadian Plains Research Centre, University of Regina, 1994.

O'Brien, *J.W. Canadian Money & Banking.* Toronto: McGraw Hill, 1964.

Ondaatje, Christopher, and Donald Swanson. *The Prime Ministers of Canada: 1867-1968.* Toronto: Pagurian, 1968.

Ormsby, Margaret A. *British Columbia: A History.* Vancouver: MacMillan, 1958.

Pope, Sir Joseph, (Made by his Literary Executor) *Correspondence of Sir John MacDonald: Selections from the Correspondence of the Right Honorable Sir John Alexander MacDonald, G.C.B. First Prime Minister of the Dominion of Canada.* Toronto: Oxford University Press, Canadian Branch, 1921.

---. *The Day of Sir John Macdonald: A Chronicle of the First Prime Minister of the Dominion. Chronicles of Canada: Volume 29.* Toronto: University of Toronto Press, 1964.

Porter, Glenn, and Robert Cluff, eds. *Enterprise and National Development: Essays in Canadian Business and Economic History.* Toronto: Hakkert, 1973.

Rawlinson, H. Graham, and J.L. Granatstein. *The Canadian 100: The 100 Most Influential Canadians of the 20th Century.* Toronto: Little, Brown, 1997.

Reid, W. Stanford. "The Scottish Background." *The Scottish Tradition In Canada.* Ed. W. Stanford Reid. Toronto: McClelland & Stewart & the Minister of Supply Services, 1976. 1-14.

Rich, E.E. *The Fur Trade and the Northwest to 1857.* Toronto: McClelland & Stewart, 1967.

Riddell, R.G., ed. *Canadian Portraits, CBC Broadcasts.* Toronto: Oxford University Press, 1940.

Riddell, William Renwick. *Upper Canada Sketches: Incidents in the Early Times of the Provinces.* Toronto: Carswell, 1922.

Roy, James A. *The Scot and Canada.* Toronto: McClelland & Stewart, 1947.

Rybczynski, Witold, et al. *McGill, A Celebration: A Portrait in Words and Photographs of a Great University.* Montreal: McGill-Queen's University Press, 1991.

Sellar, Robert. *A Scotsman In Upper Canada.* Toronto: Clarke, Irwin, 1969.

Sewell, John. *Mackenzie: A Political biography of William Lyon Mackenzie.* Toronto: Lorimer, 2002.

Shortt, Adam. *Adam Shortt's History of Canadian Currency and Banking 1600–1880.* Toronto: Canadian Banker's Association, 1986.

Skelton, Oscar D. *The Railway Builders: A Chronicle of Overland Highways. Chronicles of Canada: Volume 32.* George M. Wrong and H.H. Langton, eds. Toronto: University of Toronto Press, 1964.

Smith, William. *Political Leaders of Upper Canada.* Toronto: Nelson, 1931.

Stanley, George M. "The Scottish Military Tradition." The Scottish Tradition in Canada. Ed. W. Stanford Reid. Toronto: McClelland & Stewart & the Minister of Supply Services, 1976. 137-160.

Stevens, G.R *Canadian National Railways: Volume I: Sixty years of Trail and Error (1836-1896).* Toronto: Clarke, Irwin, 1960.

---. *History of the Canadian National Railways.* New York: The MacMillan, 1973.

Stouck, David. *Major Canadian Authors: A Critical Introduction to Canadian Literature in English.* 2nd ed. Lincoln: University of Nebraska Press, 1988.

Suthren, Victor. ed. *The Oxford Book of Canadian Military Anecdotes.* Toronto: Oxford University Press, 1989.

Thorner, Thomas. ed. "A Few Acres of Snow": *Documents in Canadian History, 1577-1867.* Peterborough, ON: Broadview, 1997.

Town, Florida. *The Northwest Company: Frontier Merchants.* Toronto: North West, 1999.

Tulchinsky, Gerald J.J. *The River Barons: Montreal Businessmen and the Growth of Industry and Transportation 1837–53.* Toronto: University of Toronto Press, 1977.

Turner, Alan R. "Scottish Settlement of the West." *The Scottish Tradition in Canada.* Ed. W. Stanford Reid. Toronto: McClelland & Stewart & the Minister of Supply Services, 1976. 76-91.

Tyre, Robert. *Douglas in Saskatchewan: The Story of a Socialist Experiment.* Vancouver: Mitchell, 1962.

Waite, P.B. *Macdonald: His Life and World.* Toronto: McGraw-Hill Ryerson, 1975.

Wallace, W. Stewart. *The Family Compact: A Chronicle of the Rebellion in Upper Canada. Chronicles of Canada: Volume 24.* H.H. Langton and George M. Wrong, eds. Toronto: University of Toronto Press, 1964.

Waterston, Elizabeth. "The Lowland Tradition in Canadian Literature." *The Scottish Tradition in Canada.* Ed. W. Stanford Reid. Toronto: McClelland & Stewart & the Minister of Supply Services, 1976. 203-231.

---. *Survey: A Short History of Canadian Literature.* Toronto: Methuen, 1973.

Watts, George S. *The Bank of Canada: Origins & Early History.* Ottawa: Carleton University Press, 1993.

Whitelaw, Marjory. ed. *The Dalhousie Journals.* Canada: Oberon, 1978.

---. *The Dalhousie Journals.* Vol. 2. Canada: Oberon, 1981.

Woodcock, George. *100 Great Canadians.* Edmonton: Hurtig, 1980.

---. *Faces From History: Canadian Profiles & Portraits.* Edmonton: Hurtig, 1978.

Matthew Shaw

Matthew Shaw was born in Montana but has lived most of his life in B.C. He spent several years as a sawmill labourer and as a financial consultant. He eventually went to school and graduated from the Université d'Aix-Marseille and Simon Fraser University and later received an MA from California State University. His eclectic background and education have led him inexorably to writing.

For the last thirteen years, Matthew and his wife have been Humanities teachers at an Adult Education school in Prince George, B.C. Their interests include travelling, canoeing and hiking. They have a four-year-old son.

Matthew's writing interests are varied. His first book, *To Live Deliberately*, was published in 2001. His essays have appeared frequently in the national media, including in *Maclean's* magazine and on CBC Radio. One of his enduring interests is the complex and seemingly indefinable nature of Canadian identity.